Advance Praise

'In *Nastik: Why I am not an Atheist*, Kushal traverses the transformative journey of an irate neo-atheist whose quest for truth uproots him from the strident battlegrounds of modern scepticism and plants him in the fertile soil of Dharmic Nirīśvaravāda. This compelling narrative reveals a man's struggle with the dogmatic fervour of neo-Abrahamic atheism only to find solace in the ancient wisdom of Hindu philosophy. The book masterfully contrasts the confrontational nature of Western atheism with its roots in Abrahamic traditions against the introspective and inclusive scepticism of Hindu Nāstik thought. It lays bare the key differences: one seeks to negate while the other seeks to understand; one is combative while the other is contemplative. As our protagonist delves into the teachings of Hindu Nāstik traditions, he discovers that scepticism does not preclude spirituality nor does disbelief sever one from the dharmic way of life. Through his eyes, we learn that Hinduism's embrace of Nirīśvaravāda—a nuanced scepticism that acknowledges the limits of human understanding— welcomes disbelievers as an integral thread in the vast tapestry of Hinduism. This book is a revelation, a testament to the idea that seeking is the essence of Hinduism, and that sceptics and disbelievers are as Hindu as the most devout believers. Join the journey and witness a profound transformation that challenges and redefines the very notion of belief and identity within the world's oldest living tradition.'

Anand Ranganathan, author and scientist

'Kushal has taken an intellectually sharp knife to cut through the kitsch that surrounds any social, religious, philosophical and political discussion, especially in India, the world's largest democracy and oldest extant civilization and also a very young nation-state. His attitude is thoroughly dharmic: he tries to approach truth ever closer with every iteration no matter where it may lead or even if its full realisation remains elusive. His work represents the coming of age of the Indian writer—the Hindu thought leader—who can confidently take on the world on his or her own terms, not by creating hermeneutically sealed enclaves and accentuating the anxiety of difference but by accepting the only true universalism, the one embedded in non-relativistic pluralism.'

Harsh Madhusudhan Gupta, author and economist

'Just as the changing nature of Hindu religious identity is being hotly debated, here is an important and timely book on what shapes Indian atheism. Kushal Mehra's book looks at the complex entanglement between Indian atheism and dharmic intellectual traditions. They are not binaries. Western atheism is constricted by a disbelief in the existence of God and an angry rejection of divinity. But concepts of Nāstika and Nirīśvaravāda in Indic histories are part of philosophical and spiritual enquiry of Hinduism. There is no mutual disdain between the believers and sceptics in India. Atheists here don't have to necessarily dissociate from religious festivals and rituals as a precondition, unlike the neo-atheists of the West. The latter's cultural rootlessness and religion's decline in the West has created a void that wokeism is filling today, he writes.'

Shekhar Gupta, founder and editor-in-chief, ThePrint

'Kushal Mehra's *Nastik: Why I am Not an Atheist* could not have come out at a more opportune time. Even as societies and nations grapple with organized religions—some dogmatic, others less so—this book lays bare a very significant aspect of the Bharatiya mind and philosophy. And that is of godlessness or Nirīśvaravāda. Agnosticism and constant questioning have been fundamental to us right from the oldest text of this civilization, the *Rig Veda*, which has in its 10th mandala and 129th a hymn called the "Nasadiya Sukta" that deals with aspects of cosmology and the origin of the universe. While all other organized religions believe in a most definitive manner about a certain dualistic and anthropomorphic being called "God", who sat in some high skies and commanded the universe to be formed at his (it is never a 'her', unlike here!) will in a certain prescribed timetable, this sukta is the exemplar of how a true questioning mind and a seeker ought to be. In a series of questions over seven shlokas, it gets to the heart of the matter and wonders if that high and mighty God indeed existed, or even if he/she did, did they indeed know the real truth! In the Bharatiya tradition, there was no blasphemy or heresy, and this foundational hymn is in itself agnostic about the existence of an all-powerful, supreme, reigning God that created the universe. That one could belong to the broad Sanatana umbrella and still have varied interpretations of divinity and its relationship with the mortal, as characterized by the six theistic and three atheistic schools of philosophy, has been the strength of this civilization. And it is this fundamental difference between Bharatiya Nirīśvaravāda and Western atheism, which blindly demonized religion, that Kushal skilfully navigates and exposes in this extremely readable and well-written book. His work is hence as dharmic as it can get, as questioning or scepticism has never been looked down upon or punished brutally in this country. Kushal takes the readers through several aspects of Nirīśvaravāda or Nāstika in the Indian paradigm, contrasting it constantly with the Abrahamic world view of monotheistic superiority and non-inclusiveness. Coming from his own deeply personal space and poignant experiences, Kushal has made a delightful interpolation of the personal and the philosophical. Through Kushal's work, we now have a language, hermeneutics and lexicon for the subject without having to depend on the crutches and alibis of its Western counterparts, which are in any case a bad fit that is forcibly superimposed on Bharat. Richly nuanced, referenced and anecdotal, the book makes for a delightful reading for the believer, non-believer, agnostic and everyone else who lies in between the broad, fuzzy ranges of this faith spectrum.'

Vikram Sampath, author and historian

Nastik

Why I Am Not an Atheist

Kushal Mehra

ISBN: 978-93-92209-67-3

First published in India 2024
This edition published 2024

BluOne Ink Pvt. Ltd
A-76, 2nd Floor, Sector 136, Noida
Uttar Pradesh 201301
www.bluone.ink
publisher@bluone.ink

Printed and bound in India at Thomson Press India Ltd.

यावज्जीवेत्सुखं जीवेत् ऋणं कृत्वा घृतं पिबेत् ।

भस्मीभूतस्य देहस्य पुनरागमनं कुतः ।

To my family and friends, who have stood by me and encouraged me throughout my life.
Without their support, I would not have written this book or become a podcaster.

Contents

Introduction

In today's fast-paced, interconnected world, we are constantly bombarded with information from every corner of the globe. Social media platforms have become breeding grounds for sensationalism, with users vying for attention through shock and awe tactics. The more outrageous and provocative the content, the more likely it is to go viral, eliciting emotions ranging from awe to disgust. This constant barrage of shocking content has left many of us tired and our senses numbed to life's ordinary and mundane aspects.

I was acutely aware of the expectations this culture of recreational outrage created as I set out to narrate my journey into disbelief. Any story worth telling had to be filled with bombastic revelations, dramatic confrontations, and life-altering epiphanies. Yet, my journey was not marked by any of these elements. I had no harrowing tales of persecution, no bitter arguments with religious zealots, and no moment of transcendent realisation that led me to abandon my faith. I remember the first time I started having doubts about a creator God. I remember telling my mother about my lack of faith, and all I got in return was, 'Fine, now eat your breakfast'. My story is shared by many sceptics in India—a slow, gradual process of questioning and introspection, taking place against the backdrop of a society that largely accepts diverse viewpoints and beliefs regarding the question of belief in divine claims.

While my story may not be the stuff of Hollywood blockbusters or viral social media posts, it is worth telling.

In a world where we are constantly bombarded with extremes and hyperboles, there is something to be said about the quiet, unassuming journeys that shape our lives in more subtle ways. These stories frequently go untold because of sensationalism's deafening clamour. But in their simplicity and authenticity, they offer a glimpse into the human experience that is both relatable and profound.

As it does for many, my journey into disbelief began with questions. I was raised in a religious, but not very ritualistic, household. My father is a *murti pujak* (icon worshipper), and my mother comes from a staunch Arya Samaji family. I wish I could say how, like many atheists from the Western world, I was taught about the importance of faith and the power of prayer. However, as I grew older, I grappled with doubts and uncertainties. How, I wondered, did a benevolent and all-powerful deity allow for so much suffering and injustice in the world? How could I reconcile the teachings of my faith with the ever-expanding body of scientific knowledge that seemed to contradict so much of what I had been taught? But the fact is that nothing like that happened to me. My exposure to Hinduism was Diwali puja, especially Navratri puja, where we become strictly vegetarian for nine days every year and a Ramayana recitation (रामायण पाठ) that would happen at my uncle's house. We would go to temples to pray on and off, but I would not pray daily in our temple inside our house.

Growing up, God was like an outsourcing agent to me. I would outsource my 'problems' to God, like 'Please ensure that I get good grades', 'Sachin Tendulkar scores a hundred', or 'Mike Tyson wins a fight'. I was not scared of God or in awe of God. I did not read religious texts as a child. The only religious mantras I knew were the ones my mother taught me as my daily prayers. I would chant the Gayatri mantra every morning and night before sleeping. I do not even remember why I lost my faith in the divine. One day, I thought this did not make sense, and as there was no resistance from my parents, I did not bother to explore further.

My first encounter with Abrahamic religions was on a flight from London (England) to Detroit (USA), where I was sitting beside a young man who was a drummer. I started playing the drums when I turned 18, thanks to a gift from my elder brother, who bought me my first-ever drum kit. The conversation went well until this young man threw a googly at me. He told me he became a drummer because of Jesus. He then told me he was a Christian missionary who had gone to Morocco to 'save' Muslims from going to hell. It then led to him trying to 'save' me, and the next five hours were exciting and entertaining. He introduced me to his entire group of sixteen young Americans travelling on Christian missions to different parts of the world.

I had not recovered from this experience when I was subjected to the world of *dawah*. My brother, who was studying in the USA, had a roommate from Pakistan. As I was hanging out with this young Muslim male from Pakistan on campus, he invited me to embrace Islam. I had never experienced anyone trying to 'convert' me to another faith in the last eighteen years. This experience of two individuals from two different religions trying to convert me out of my so-called demonic faith left me in shock. I had already begun to lose confidence in God. Still, I wanted to know what this religion business was about.

That was the moment I decided to read religious texts. I had not read any religious texts before that. The Bible and the Quran were the first religious texts I encountered in my journey of disbelief. As sacred scriptures are revered by billions of people worldwide, I was eager to delve into their pages and explore the wisdom, guidance, and moral teachings they purported to offer. However, as I began to immerse myself in these texts, I was left in shock and bewilderment, struggling to reconcile the image of a benevolent, loving deity with the wrathful, jealous God that emerged from the pages.

The numerous instances of God displaying rage, jealousy, and even vengeance as I read the Bible struck me. From the story of the Great Flood, where God wiped out almost all of humanity due to their wickedness, to the tale of Sodom and Gomorrah, where He destroyed entire cities for their sinful ways, I questioned the nature of this divine being. How could a loving, compassionate God be so prone to anger and jealousy, and what does this say about the nature of the divine?

My experience with the Quran was similarly jarring. While the text contained passages extolling the virtues of compassion, mercy, and forgiveness, it also depicted a God quick to punish those who strayed from His path. The concept of hell, a place of eternal torment for unbelievers and wrongdoers, was difficult to reconcile with my understanding of a benevolent deity.

These experiences left me in a state of confusion and deep introspection. I grappled with the contradictions and inconsistencies I encountered in these religious texts. I struggled to make sense of the divine as it was portrayed in their pages. In many ways, this shock catalysed my journey into disbelief, prompting me to become a very angry young atheist for a while.

As I continued to explore and question, I sought out alternative interpretations and perspectives on these texts, hoping to find a way to reconcile the conflicting images of God they presented. I read or heard lectures from religious leaders, scholars, and other believers, each offering unique insights and understandings. While some of these discussions were enlightening and thought-provoking, none could fully assuage my doubts and concerns.

Growing up as a Hindu child, I was raised with a different understanding of the divine. Hinduism, with its vast pantheon of gods (*devatas*) and goddesses (*devis*) and its emphasis on the interconnectedness of all things, presented a far more inclusive and tolerant worldview than I encountered in the Bible and the Quran. In my native faith, there was no overarching concept of an angry, vengeful God, nor was there a disdain for atheists or non-believers. Instead, there was an understanding that individuals would follow their unique spiritual paths, each seeking truth and meaning.

This background made my encounter with the Bible and the Quran all the more disorienting. The stark contrast between the deities of my Hindu upbringing and the wrathful, jealous God depicted in these texts was challenging to comprehend. I struggled to reconcile the hostility and divisiveness that seemed to underpin these faiths with the more inclusive and accepting approach of my native religion.

In many ways, my experience as a Hindu encountering the Bible and the Quran highlights the importance of context and cultural background in shaping our understanding of spirituality and belief. The confusion I experienced stemmed from the content of these texts and the stark contrast between their worldview and that of my native faith. This dissonance forced me to confront the complexities and contradictions of religious belief, ultimately leading me on a journey of self-discovery and growth. While my story may not be marked by the dramatic confrontations and life-altering epiphanies of a daily soap, it is nonetheless a testament to the transformative power of questioning, introspection, and the search for meaning.

In many ways, my experience with monotheism made me understand my own dharma. On my exploration and self-discovery path, I sought answers from various sources — religious texts, philosophical treatises, and conversations with friends and family. Surprisingly, I was not met with resistance or hostility from my community. Instead, I found a space where my doubts and questions were welcomed and engaged, allowing me to delve deeper into my native faith's beliefs and assumptions.

As I progressed down this path, I met more sceptics and non-believers in India and overseas. I recall participating in several online atheist forums. But two in particular have left an unforgettable impression on me. One was called Nirmukta, while the other was an online forum on the website of the famous British author and scientist Richard Dawkins. I am one of the few people who have been banned from atheist forums for not being sufficiently angry at religions. I thought atheists were my people, but they didn't like my lack of rage towards religions. Strangely, I had similar experiences when I read the Bible and the Quran while engaging with other atheists in these forums. These atheists were as enraged as the Bible's God. These atheists were equally hostile to ideas that differed from their core beliefs. At the same time, I was astounded by the variety of experiences and viewpoints represented in these online forums, with each person's journey having its own distinct set of difficulties and victories.

But, for me, the quieter, more unassuming stories resonated the most. These were the stories of individuals who, like me, had embarked on a journey of questioning and introspection in a society that allowed them the space to do so. They were not met with persecution or ostracism but with understanding and acceptance. Additionally, their journeys might not have been filled with the same dramatic twists and turns that frequently capture our attention. Still, they were nonetheless potent in their sincerity and relatability.

This book is about these folks, that includes both Āstikas and Nāstikas. The best analogy I could come up with is a line from Russell Peters' comedy special *Outsourced*. There's a part called 'beat your kids', in which Peters discusses how white kids feel left out in multicultural schools because black and brown kids get an 'ass-whupping' at home. In contrast, white kids are sent to their rooms when their parents are upset with them. Regarding atheists, Eastern disbelievers are those white youths who don't get shamed by believers and feel left out in these heated atheist forums dominated by Abrahamic atheists who are frequently assaulted.

It is these stories—the stories of everyday sceptics and non-believers in India—that this book seeks to bring to the forefront. In doing so, I hope we can challenge the culture of negativity that so often dominates our conversations about faith and disbelief and instead focus on the quieter, more nuanced journeys that get overshadowed by their more sensational counterparts.

Through these stories, we can better understand the complex interplay between culture, religion, and identity in India and explore how individuals navigate these often-conflicting forces in their search for truth and meaning. We can also gain valuable insights into the nature of scepticism and disbelief in a society characterised by its diversity and pluralism and how this context shapes the experiences of non-believers. This diversity has given rise to a certain level of mutual respect and reciprocity, allowing individuals the space to explore and question their beliefs without fear of retribution or ostracism. In this environment, the journey into disbelief can be a more subtle and gradual process rather than a sudden and dramatic break from the past.

This is not to say that the experiences of Indian sceptics are without challenge or struggle. Many still grapple with societal expectations and norms; some face criticism or judgement from friends and family. However, these challenges are often tempered by the larger cultural context, allowing for greater understanding and acceptance than in other, more dogmatic societies.

In addition to examining the experiences of sceptics in India, this book will also explore the role of social media in shaping our conversations about faith and disbelief. While social media has undoubtedly provided a platform for individuals to share their stories and connect with like-minded individuals, it has also fostered a culture of recreational outrage that can sometimes overshadow the more nuanced and relatable aspects of the human experience.

Ultimately, this book celebrates human progress; it is a testament to the power of introspection, questioning, and self-discovery and a reminder that sometimes the most profound transformations occur not in the spotlight but in the quiet corners of our hearts and minds. So, as you delve into the pages of this book, I invite you to set aside your expectations — do not assume that you are watching a debate anchored by some Indian mainstream media anchor — and instead approach these stories like you are watching a well-curated serious debate or discussion on Doordarshan.

The first chapter of this book aims to explore the differences between Nāstika, Nirīśvaravāda, and atheism in the West. While both the terms, Nāstika and Nirīśvaravāda, refer to rejecting belief in a divine creator or deity, they originate from vastly different cultural and philosophical backgrounds. Nirīśvaravāda, a term from Indian philosophy, is often misunderstood and conflated with atheism. By examining these two concepts in greater detail, we can better understand the nuances and distinctions between Eastern and Western approaches to disbelief in the divine. While atheism is primarily concerned with the rejection of belief in gods, Nāstika and Nirīśvaravāda encompass a broader range of philosophical positions that critique various aspects of Hinduism, including the authority of the Vedas, the concept of karma, and the cycle of birth, death, and rebirth. This broader scope allows for the existence of spiritual and metaphysical beliefs within the Nāstika and Nirīśvaravādi traditions.

In contrast, atheism is more focused on the non-existence of divine entities. While both perspectives share a critical approach to religious dogma, their epistemological foundations are distinct, reflecting the unique cultural and historical contexts in which they emerged. Despite their rejection of certain Āstīka beliefs, they often maintain a connection to Hindu cultural practices, core beliefs like reincarnation in the case of Jainism, and rituals. For example, individuals who identify as Nāstika and/or Nirīśvaravādi may still participate in Hindu festivals, observe dietary restrictions, and engage in meditation or yoga. In contrast, atheism often entails a complete disassociation from religious practices and rituals, as these are seen as grounded in theistic beliefs that the atheist rejects.

The second chapter of this book talks about New Atheism and how the rise of neo-atheism in the West has been a significant cultural and intellectual movement. However, it has not been without its shortcomings. In this chapter, we will delve into the reasons behind the failure of neo-atheism as a movement, highlighting its aggressive, confrontational approach, and lack of engagement with religious thought and spirituality. By examining these issues, we can better understand the limitations of neo-atheism and explore alternative paths to understanding and engaging with religious beliefs and practices. The chapter begins by defining neo-atheism as a movement characterised by its aggressive critique of religious beliefs and its promotion of secularism, science, and rationality. Neo-atheism emerged in the early 21st century, with prominent figures such as Richard Dawkins, Christopher Hitchens, Sam Harris, and Daniel Dennett leading the charge. It highlights the success of neo-atheism in challenging religious authority and contributing to the decline of religion in the West. This decline is evidenced by decreasing church attendance, a growing number of religiously unaffiliated individuals, and increased secular values. The chapter argues that the effectiveness of neo-atheism in dismantling religious dogma led to its ironic downfall, as it created a vacuum of meaning and purpose in society. While neo-atheism excels at critiquing religious beliefs, it often fails to offer a satisfying alternative for those seeking a sense of purpose and identity. The chapter contends that this failure left many individuals searching for a new belief system that could provide meaning and a sense of belonging in a post-religious world. Atheism+ or 'wokeism' is the response to the void left by religion's decline and neo-atheism's shortcomings. Wokeism is characterised by its emphasis on social justice, intersectionality, and activism, with its adherents seeking to address systemic inequalities and promote a more inclusive and equitable society. Wokeism fills the gap left by neo-atheism by providing a sense of meaning, purpose, and identity rooted in activism and social change. The chapter contends that the emergence of wokeism highlights the enduring human need for meaning and identity, even as traditional religious structures continue to decline.

The third chapter of this book focuses on the dual nature of religion. Religion can be both good and bad. Religion has long been a source of both solace and strife for humanity. Religion can be both beneficial and detrimental to society. By recognising the inherent complexities and contradictions within religious institutions and practices, we can appreciate the need for a more nuanced and balanced perspective on religion's role in our lives. By examining religion's historical, social, and psychological aspects, the chapter contends that religion is a complex and necessary component of human experience, deeply encoded in our evolutionary upbringing. The chapter begins by discussing the positive aspects of religion, emphasising its role in providing meaning, purpose, and a sense of belonging. Religion has been a cornerstone of human culture, shaping art, literature, and morality and fostering a sense of community and shared values. It promotes altruism and compassion and gives a framework for coping with life's challenges and the inevitability of death. But religion also has a dark side that has significantly fuelled conflict, division, and suffering throughout history. Religion has been used to justify wars, persecution, and discrimination, as well as the suppression of scientific progress and critical thinking. The chapter argues that certain religious beliefs' dogmatic and uncompromising nature can lead to intolerance, fanaticism, and violence. Scientific studies suggest that religious impulse is deeply encoded in our evolutionary upbringing. Multiple cognitive and evolutionary psychologists argue that religion may have evolved as an adaptive mechanism, facilitating social cohesion, cooperation, and the transmission of cultural norms. In light of the paradoxical nature of religion, it is both good and bad but ultimately necessary. It is a fundamental aspect of human culture and experience that cannot be separated from our collective history and psychological makeup. Recognising and accepting the dual nature of religion allows us to better understand its impact on our lives and society and to harness its potential for fostering connection, meaning, and understanding.

In Chapter 4, we will examine the unique experiences of sceptics from a dharmic background. Growing up within a tradition that emphasises the importance of questioning and critical thinking, dharmic sceptics often find themselves at a crossroads between their cultural heritage and the modern world. We'll talk about how a unique fusion of tradition and modernity exists in the moral code of dharmic sceptics, which draws inspiration from both ancient scriptures and modern ideals. The moral code of Eastern atheists presents an interesting contrast compared to their Western counterparts. At a superficial level, both groups share common ground in rejecting traditional religious beliefs. However, upon closer examination, the two groups diverge significantly in their epistemological frameworks and the sources from which they derive their moral principles. Eastern atheists often maintain a solid connection to their native faiths and cultural traditions despite rejecting specific unsubstantiated claims or theistic components of these belief systems. For example, Buddhism emphasises mindfulness, and Confucianism, focusing on social harmony, filial piety, and ethical behaviour, provides another set of moral principles that Eastern atheists can adopt. In contrast, Western atheists derive their moral codes from secular humanism, emphasising the importance of reason, empathy, and human-centred ethics. Understanding these nuances and appreciating the diverse approaches to morality among atheists around the world can foster greater empathy, tolerance, and cross-cultural understanding.

Chapter 5 will focus on broader Indian society and its relationship with religion. We look at the various religious traditions in India and examine their strengths and weaknesses from an Indian epistemological perspective. By adopting this approach, we can better understand the complex interplay between religion, culture, and societal norms in India. While Indian religions and philosophies have produced profound insights and wisdom, they have also contributed to developing and maintaining harmful social structures and beliefs. In this critique, we will focus on the issues of *jati varna* (caste), belief in *punarjanma* (reincarnation), and other unsubstantiated claims that plague Indian society. The caste system, or jati varna, is one of the most deeply entrenched and problematic aspects of Indian culture. Rooted in ancient Hindu and Buddhist texts such as the *Smriti*s and *Sutta*s, the caste system has resulted in centuries of discrimination, social stratification, and untold suffering for millions of people. Despite legal efforts to dismantle the caste system, it persists in various forms, perpetuating inequality and hindering social mobility. Confronting the problematic origins of the caste system within our religious texts is an essential step towards dismantling this oppressive structure. While the caste system may have been conceived of as a division of labour in ancient Indian society, its transformation into an immutable, hereditary social hierarchy has had devastating consequences. It is crucial that, as a society, we recognise the harm the caste system causes, reject its religious justifications, and work to create a more equitable and inclusive society. The belief in an afterlife, familiar to many Indian religions, has problems. While the concept of reincarnation and the transmigration of souls may offer some a sense of comfort and purpose, it can also contribute to perpetuating social inequalities. In some interpretations, one's birth in a particular jati/varna or social position is seen as a result of one's karma from past lives, thereby justifying and reinforcing the jati/varna hierarchy. By confronting and critically examining the belief in an afterlife, we can challenge the narratives perpetuating social inequality and promote a more just society. Indian religious texts, whether Hindu, Jain, Buddhist, or Sikh, contain deeply problematic claims that need to be confronted and scrutinised. For example, the *Smritis* prescribe harsher punishments for transgressions made by people from the Shudra varna, while some Buddhist *Suttas* justify the jati/varna system based on the purity of one's birth. In the Sikh tradition, the Guru Granth Sahib speaks of the transmigration of souls. This belief can indirectly reinforce the jati/varna system and the notion of karma. The Jains claim that the earth is flat, which is easily falsifiable. We must not avoid examining these texts and their problematic claims, even if they hold a revered status in our cultural and religious history.

Finally, in Chapter 6, we will explore the notion of identity for Nāstikas and/or Nirīśvaravādis. Unlike atheists from Abrahamic backgrounds, who often feel the need to entirely abandon their religious identity, their Eastern counterparts can maintain a connection to their dharmic roots. We will discuss how disbelief in the divine can coexist with a sense of cultural belonging and identity, offering a unique perspective on the relationship between religion and personal identity. The term 'Hindu' has significantly changed meaning and scope throughout history. Today, it is often used as a broad label for the religious and cultural traditions that emerged in the Indian subcontinent, encompassing diverse beliefs, practices, and philosophical systems. However, defining Hinduism solely based on the Āstika darśanas (orthodox schools of Indian philosophy) overlooks the rich plurality and heterodoxy that have been integral to the development of the dharmic tradition. Nāstikas and/or Nirīśvaravādis, despite denying many claims put forth by Āstika darśanas, are still considered part of the larger Hindu/dharmic family. Understanding that 'Hindu' fundamentally differs from the identity labels associated with Christianity and Islam is crucial. The Christian and Muslim identities are rooted in specific religious doctrines, texts, and beliefs in a single God or deity.

In contrast, Hinduism is an umbrella term encompassing many diverse religious and philosophical systems, many of which do not adhere to a singular doctrine or deity. The term 'Hindu' itself originated long after the foundations of Eastern philosophy had been established. It was initially used as a geographical and cultural descriptor for the people living beyond the Indus river rather than as a religious identifier. The term encompasses a variety of belief systems that have contributed to the rich tapestry of Indian thought and culture.

The Nāstika schools of thought, such as Jainism, Buddhism, and the Cārvāka schools, reject the authority of the Vedas and other fundamental tenets of the Āstika darśanas. Similarly, Nirīśvaravādis deny the existence of a personal creator deity (Īśvara). Despite these differences, these philosophical systems are considered part of the broader dharmic tradition because they share common cultural and historical roots and a commitment to the pursuit of knowledge and spiritual growth. The assertion that Nāstikas and/or Nirīśvaravādis are 'ex-Hindus' constitutes a category error, as it assumes a rigid and exclusivist definition of Hinduism that is not reflective of the tradition's inherent diversity and fluidity. The attempt by some neo-atheists to impose their rigid views on Nirīśvaravādis in India replicates the same kind of exclusivist thinking they critique in the Abrahamic religious context. It reflects their fundamental misunderstanding of the tradition's inclusive and pluralistic nature. In this context, neo-atheism is a mirror image of Abrahamism, albeit without a creator God.

Through this book, I hope to offer readers an insightful and thought-provoking exploration of the complexities surrounding atheism, scepticism, and religious belief. By examining the unique experiences and perspectives of Āstikas, Nāstikas, Nirīśvaravādis, and sceptics from a dharmic background, we can gain a deeper understanding of the many paths that lead individuals to question and ultimately reject the divine. In doing so, we may also discover that there is more common ground between believers and non-believers than we might have initially thought and that the human experience of grappling with questions of faith and spirituality transcends cultural, religious, and geographical boundaries.

As you embark on this journey through the pages of *Nāstika: Why I Am Not an Atheist*, I encourage you to approach the subject matter with an open mind and a willingness to challenge your beliefs and assumptions. I hope this book will serve as a catalyst for meaningful conversations and a deeper understanding of our world's diverse perspectives. So, let us begin this journey together, exploring the intricacies of faith, disbelief, and everything in between.

1

Nāstika, Nirīśvaravāda, and Atheism in the West

Human diversity is not just about physical characteristics, languages, and civilisations but also about thinking and beliefs. The range of this diversity is found in the variety of perspectives that people have, providing a wide range of ideas, philosophies, and worldviews. This diversity affects the sphere of disbelief (atheism), where diverse individuals and cultures offer their interpretations and understanding of the lack of belief in a greater force.

One of the most scintillating parts of human thought, diversity is the chance for debate and the interchange of ideas. When people with different viewpoints get together, they can have meaningful dialogues that question preconceptions, extend horizons, and stimulate intellectual progress. This also extends to atheism. There are numerous perspectives within atheistic philosophy, from philosophical and scientific opinions to moral and ethical considerations. Dialogue with atheists from varied backgrounds allows for investigating these ideas, leading to a fuller knowledge of atheism and its various facets.

Furthermore, this diversity of atheism reflects the complexities of the human experience and the various routes that have led people to question the existence of a superior entity. Some atheists may have concluded by critically examining religious texts, scientific investigations, or personal experiences. Others may have become atheists due to peer pressure, cultural influences, or other societal issues. This variety of paths enhances atheistic thought and demonstrates the complex nature of human reasoning and the various forces that create our opinions.

The beauty of human thought, diversity is also evident in the numerous philosophical frameworks that atheists use to make sense of the world. Atheism can coexist with multiple philosophical positions, such as secular humanism, existentialism, naturalism, and scepticism. Each framework contributes insights and contributions to the study of existence, ethics, and the human predicament. Accepting variety allows for a thorough examination of the implications and applications of atheism, resulting in a more robust intellectual conversation.

Furthermore, the beauty of diversity in the human mind is its ability to question preconceived assumptions and promote personal progress. When we encounter different points of view, we are encouraged to challenge our opinions and biases, which fosters empathy and promotes a more inclusive worldview. This also applies to atheism. Engaging with different atheistic perspectives allows us to rethink our assumptions, critically examine our beliefs, and broaden our understanding of the world. As a result, we have a more extensive and more nuanced understanding of the complexity of atheism and the human experience.

Atheism is a critical aspect of the enormous tapestry of human beliefs and ideologies, undermining the fabric of religious concepts. Atheism, typically regarded as a rejection of the presence of deities, manifests itself in various ways throughout civilisation. In this chapter, we will look at the fascinating contrast between the Āstika and Nāstika schools (of darśana) and Nirīśvaravāda from the ancient Indian tradition and then compare it to Western atheism, examining their philosophical foundations and shedding light on their unique perspectives and some key differences.

The Different Kinds of Atheism in the West

Rejecting the existence of a higher power, atheism in the West is characterised by a rich diversity of philosophical, scientific, and cultural perspectives. From ancient Greece to the Enlightenment and beyond, Western civilisation has witnessed the emergence of various types of atheism, each of which has contributed to the ongoing discussion regarding the nature of reality, ethics, and the human experience.

There is no consensus when it comes to the ideal classification of atheism. Stephen Le Drew, in his book *The Evolution of Atheism: The Politics of a Modern Movement*, says, 'Atheism is a modern movement of thought and practice emerging from political turmoil and revolutions in various intellectual fields, and a form of belief—rather than a lack of belief—shaped by its socio-historical context.'[1] Le Drew claims atheism is 'inextricably bound up with a tradition of Enlightenment principles' and bolsters his claim by using David Berman's *A History of Atheism in Britain* and Michael J. Buckley's twin volumes *At the Origins of Modern Atheism* and *Denying and Disclosing God: The Ambiguous Progress of Modern Atheism.*[2]

Simon Glendinning, in his article 'Three Cultures of Atheism: on Serious Doubts about the Existence of God'[3] takes a very different approach as he divides Western atheism into three broad categories that he likes to call 'religious theists, modern atheists, and (replacing the category of the more or less woolly-minded indifferent) a-theists'. As per Glendinning, the first category 'comprises people who, for the most part, do not have any thoughts at all about God, positive or negative'. The second one

> comprises people who, while not full-blown atheists, would avow (if asked) that they do not believe in a God who hears our prayers. Some among them may (if asked) avow that they believe in Something, and may even call it 'God,' but this is not a religious theism: these people do not live a life that cleaves to religious creeds, and in particular they do not believe in a God able to hear our prayers.

He finds it hard to define the third category as the 'a-theist' category can 'be thought to lie on a continuum of indifference between religious theism and atheism', but should be classified differently.

Here are some reasons or ways that lead to atheism in the Western world: These categories are not absolute, and many of the qualities stated in one can be found in atheists in the other:

Scientific Exploration

Scientific atheism is based on the principles of scientific investigation and naturalism. It rejects supernatural explanations in favour of empirical evidence, observation, and the scientific method to explain the universe. Advocates of scientific atheism highlight the significance of reason and evidence-based reasoning in comprehending the natural world, challenging religious claims that lack empirical support.

Philosophical Argumentation

Philosophical atheism explores the concept of God and the existence of a higher power through intellectual inquiry. It encompasses various schools of thought, such as rationalism, scepticism, and existentialism. Rationalist atheists employ logical reasoning to question the coherence and consistency of religious doctrines. Sceptical atheists question the verifiability and reliability of religious claims. Existentialist atheists delve into the meaning and purpose of human existence without a divine framework.

Secular Humanism

While not strictly atheistic, secular humanism promotes a naturalistic worldview that prioritises human dignity, ethics, and the pursuit of happiness without relying on religious beliefs. It highlights the importance of logic, compassion, and societal progress. Secular humanists fight for the separation of church and state, highlighting the value of human agency and ethical responsibility in constructing a just and compassionate society.

New Atheism

New atheism emerged in the late 20th and early 21st centuries as a response to the perceived societal influence of religion and the impact of religious fundamentalism. It is characterised by a more aggressive approach, advocating for the open critique and rejection of religious beliefs. Prominent new atheist authors[4] and speakers,[5] such as Richard Dawkins, Sam Harris, Daniel Dennett, and Christopher Hitchens, have been influential in promoting atheistic ideas and engaging in public debates on the role of religion in society.

Spiritual not Religious

While atheism is traditionally associated with a lack of belief in gods, some individuals identify as spiritual atheists. Spiritual atheism emphasises personal experiences of awe, wonder, and transcendence without invoking supernatural explanations. It often draws inspiration from nature, art, and the human capacity for meaning-making. Spiritual atheists find value in exploring the depths of consciousness and seeking a sense of interconnectedness with the world around them. Spiritual atheists also tend to hold many 'New Age' beliefs (reincarnation, astrology, psychics, and the presence of spiritual energy in physical objects like mountains or trees). As per a Pew Research Center survey conducted in December 2017, 'Religiously unaffiliated Americans (those who say their religion is atheist, agnostic, or "nothing in particular") are about as likely as Christians to hold New Age beliefs.'[6]

Six-in-ten Christians, 'nones' hold at least one New Age belief

	Believe spiritual energy can be located in physical things	Believe in psychics	Believe in reincarnation	Believe in astrology	NET Believe in at least one
All U.S. adults	42%	41%	33%	29%	62%
Christian	37	40	29	26	61
Protestant	32	38	26	24	57
Evangelical	24	33	19	18	47
Mainline	43	44	33	30	67
Historically black	41	43	38	34	72
Catholic	47	46	36	33	70
Unaffiliated	47	40	38	32	62
Atheist	13	10	7	3	22
Agnostic	40	31	28	18	56
Nothing in particular	61	52	51	47	78

Source: Survey conducted Dec. 4-18, 2017, among U.S. adults.
PEW RESEARCH CENTER

Fig. 1.1: New Age beliefs common among both religious and nonreligious Americans

Finding Meaning through Art

The appreciation of beauty, art, and cultural expression as a source of meaning and fulfilment is the primary focus of aesthetic atheism. It is a celebration of human ingenuity, the beauties of the natural world, and the accomplishments of human society. Still, it does not attribute these things to a heavenly source. Atheists primarily concerned with aesthetics draw their motivation from the tremendous and transformational power that may be found in art, literature, music, and the study of the human condition.

Disbelief in India: Nirīśvaravāda in both Āstika and Nāstika Schools (Darśana)

Nirīśvaravāda is a philosophical idea that has its origins in Indian philosophy and that is roughly, albeit unsatisfyingly, translated to either 'atheism' or 'non-theism' in the English language. Within the religious traditions of Hinduism, Jainism, and Buddhism, this school of thought denies the existence of a personal *Iśvara* or a supreme entity (Brahman). In the dharmic traditions of India, the word 'Iśvara' can refer to several different concepts. Between the *Samhita*s of the *Yajurveda* and the *dharmashastra*s, not to mention other Indian scriptures, there is a significant shift in the word's meaning.

The conventional idea of an all-powerful, transcendent creator named Iśvara who rules the cosmos is called into question by the Nirīśvaravādis, which instead places its emphasis on investigating the nature of reality, the self, and the human predicament without referring to the existence of a divine being. It emphasises personal inquiry, critical thinking, and the achievement of one's potential while calling into doubt the authority of religious scriptures and teachings.

Nirīśvaravāda is a school of thought within Indian dharmic philosophy that is strongly related to the schools of thought that are found within both Āstika and Nāstika schools (darśana). In the Āstika darśanas, both Sāṃkhya and Mīmāṃsā negate the existence of a Iśvara. *Sāṃkhya Karika* verses 56, 57, and 61 (4) claim, 'God is attribute-less. Therefore, it is illogical to think that God produces this world endowed with the three gunas.' As per the *Sāṃkhya Karika*, the reality is an interplay between two fundamental principles: Purusha and Prakriti.

> Classical Sāṃkhya holds these two to be entirely distinct and independent. Purusha is static, and Prakriti is dynamic; one is being and the other becoming. Purusha is passive, while Prakriti, embedded with the three attributes (the three gunas), is the unfolding universe. There is no indication in this classical system that the two principals are derived from a higher unified principal, that is, the Supreme Cause. Because of the omission of any God as a creator of the universe, academics began to classify Sāṃkhya as atheistic.

The Mīmāṃsā school is primarily concerned with the interpretation and analysis of the Vedic texts, particularly the ritualistic and prescriptive portions known as the *karma-kāṇḍa*. The focus of Mīmāṃsā is to understand the rituals' procedures, their meanings, and their efficacy in achieving specific goals.

While the Mīmāṃsā school does not directly address the existence or non-existence of God or the concept of atheism in the same way as other philosophical schools, it approaches the Vedic rituals from a pragmatic perspective. Mīmāṃsā scholars emphasise the efficacy of the rituals themselves, emphasising the importance of proper performance and adherence to prescribed procedures.

The chapter on deities in the aphorisms of Mīmāṃsā (the fundamental text of the Prabhākara Mīmāṃsā school)[7] denies the existence of deities, and the author explains how rituals work independently without the intervention of a Īśvara.

In the Nāstika darśanas, Jaina, Baudha (Buddhist), and Cārvāka/ Lokāyata, all three negate the existence of a Īśvara. In Jainism, Nirīśvaravāda is aligned with the concept of Anekāntavāda (many-sidedness), which acknowledges the multifaceted nature of reality and rejects the existence of an omnipotent, omniscient God. Jainism emphasises the importance of individual spiritual effort, ethical living, and the pursuit of liberation from the cycle of birth and death. It says, 'If God created the world, where was he before creation? If you say he was transcendent then, and needed no support, where is he now?'[8] Jainism says, 'The universe has always existed and will always exist. It is regulated by cosmic laws and kept going by its own energy processes.'[9]

Buddhism, particularly the Mahayana tradition, also reflects elements of Nirīśvaravāda. While Buddhism[10] does not outright reject the existence of gods,[11] it emphasises the impermanence and interconnectedness of all phenomena. The focus is on the cessation of suffering through understanding the Four Noble Truths and practising the Eightfold Path rather than relying on a divine being.

The Cārvākas or Lokāyatas[12] advocate for a materialistic understanding of the universe, rejecting the existence of any supernatural or spiritual entities. It posits that the material world is the only reality and that consciousness arises from physical elements. Cārvāka denies the concept of a creator God and the notions of deities, souls, and any supernatural or metaphysical entities. It argues that such beliefs are mere fabrications and lack empirical evidence. It criticises religious rituals, sacrificial practices, and reliance on scriptural authority. It views rituals as exploitative and argues that priests propagate them to maintain power and wealth. They emphasise the importance of empirical evidence and rational inquiry in understanding the world.

It encourages critical thinking, logical reasoning, and a sceptical attitude towards unsupported claims and dogmas.

As can be seen even within the subset of Nirīśvaravāda, there is a diverse range of philosophical perspectives within Indian philosophy, highlighting the rich tapestry of thought and the diversity of ways in which individuals have grappled with questions of existence, consciousness, and the nature of reality. It emphasises the importance of personal inquiry, self-realisation, and pursuing liberation or enlightenment without relying on the belief in a personal God or a supreme being.

The Similarities and Differences between Nirīśvaravāda and Western Atheism

The Common Ground

While Nirīśvaravāda and Western atheism emerge from distinct cultural and philosophical backgrounds, they share commonalities. Both traditions challenge established religious beliefs, value empirical evidence and reason, and emphasise individual freedom and autonomy.

Epistemological Foundations (Means of Attaining Knowledge)

Rationality and Scepticism: Both Nirīśvaravāda and Western atheism place a strong emphasis on rationality and scepticism. They advocate critical thinking and question religious claims that lack empirical evidence or logical coherence. Both traditions value reason as a means to understand the natural world and reject supernatural explanations.

Empirical Evidence: Nirīśvaravāda and Western atheism rely on empirical evidence to understand reality. They reject faith-based claims and emphasise the importance of observation, experimentation, and scientific inquiry in acquiring knowledge. Both traditions value evidence-based thinking in exploring the nature of the universe and the human condition.

Ethical Implications

Secular Ethics: Nirīśvaravāda and Western atheism embrace secular ethics, emphasising human agency, compassion, and social responsibility. They argue for the importance of ethical conduct based on human well-being and promoting a just and compassionate society rather than relying on religious doctrines or divine commandments.

Ethical Pluralism: Both traditions recognise the diversity of ethical frameworks and reject the notion that morality depends solely on religious beliefs. They acknowledge that moral principles can be grounded in empathy, reason, and humanistic values rather than relying on a divine source of morality.

Human Experience and Meaning-Making

Pursuit of Meaning and Purpose: Nirīśvaravāda and Western atheism engage with questions of human existence, purpose, and meaning. They acknowledge the human quest for understanding the world and finding significance in life, independent of believing in a higher power. Both traditions explore the potential for humanistic and non-divine sources of meaning, such as relationships, personal growth, and the pursuit of knowledge.

Embracing Mortality: Both Nirīśvaravāda (Cārvākas and Lokāyatas) and Western atheism confront the reality of mortality and the absence of an afterlife. They emphasise the importance of making the most of our finite existence, cherishing human connections, and contributing to the well-being of others in present life. For example, Cārvāka promotes a hedonistic approach to ethics, asserting that pleasure and the avoidance of pain should be the ultimate goals of human life. It advocates for the pursuit of sensual pleasures and material well-being, rejecting the notion of self-denial or ascetic practices.

Nirīśvaravāda and Western atheism, despite arising from different cultural and philosophical contexts, converge on vital principles. They share a common rejection of belief in a higher power, a reliance on reason and empirical evidence, a commitment to plural ethics, and an exploration of the human experience and the pursuit of meaning. Recognising these shared grounds and similarities can foster dialogue and understanding between different philosophical traditions, ultimately contributing to a more inclusive and nuanced exploration of atheism and its implications for human thought and society.

The Differences

Both Nirīśvaravāda and Western atheism are philosophical perspectives that deny the existence of a supreme being or deity, but they come from distinct cultural and intellectual traditions. Nirīśvaravāda was developed in India, whereas Western atheism developed in Europe. In addition, these distinctions are not nearly as shallow as some Western and Indian new atheists would have you believe they are. If we were to look at the data from the 2001 census in India and compare it with the data from the 2011 census, we would see that the number of persons who fall under the category of 'religion not stated'[13] has increased from 7 lakhs to 29 lakhs over those 10 years. The Global Index of Religiosity and Atheism[14] found that between 2005 and 2012, there was a 6 per cent increase in the number of persons living in India who did not adhere to any religious faith.

This is negligible compared to the Western world,[15] where 'the unaffiliated portion of the adult population ranges from as high as 48% in the Netherlands to 15% in Ireland, Italy, and Portugal'.

Share of 'nones' in Western Europe ranges from 15% in Ireland, Italy and Portugal to 48% in the Netherlands

% who say they are atheist, agnostic or have no particular religion

▨ 0-15% ◼ 16-25% ◼ 26-39% ■ 40%+   ☐ Non-surveyed country

Note: Respondents were asked "What is your present religion, if any? Are you Christian, Muslim, Jewish, Buddhist, Hindu, atheist, agnostic, something else or nothing in particular?"
Source: Survey conducted April-August 2017 in 15 countries. See Methodology for details.
"Being Christian in Western Europe"

PEW RESEARCH CENTER

Fig. 1.2: Being Christian in Western Europe

The PEW survey further says,

> Within the unaffiliated category, those who describe
> their religious identity as 'nothing in particular' make up
> the biggest group (relative to atheists and agnostics) in
> most countries. For instance, fully three-in-ten Dutch
> adults (31%) describe their religious identity in this way,
> compared with 14% who are self-described atheists and
> 3% who consider themselves agnostics.
>
> But in some other places, such as Belgium, Denmark,
> and France, atheists are at least as numerous as those
> in the 'nothing in particular' category. Agnostics, by
> comparison, have a smaller presence throughout Western
> Europe.[16]

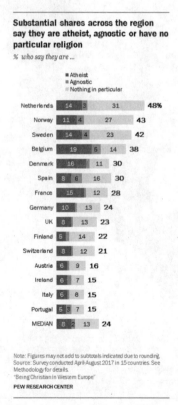

Substantial shares across the region say they are atheist, agnostic or have no particular religion

% who say they are ...

- Atheist
- Agnostic
- Nothing in particular

Country	Atheist	Agnostic	Nothing in particular	Total
Netherlands	14	3	31	48%
Norway	11	4	27	43
Sweden	14	4	23	42
Belgium	19	5	14	38
Denmark	16		11	30
Spain	8	6	16	30
France	15		12	28
Germany	10		13	24
UK	8		13	23
Finland	5		14	22
Switzerland	8		12	21
Austria	6		9	16
Ireland	6		7	15
Italy	6		8	15
Portugal	5	3	7	15
MEDIAN	8		13	24

Note: Figures may not add to subtotals indicated due to rounding.
Source: Survey conducted April-August 2017 in 15 countries. See
Methodology for details.
"Being Christian in Western Europe"

PEW RESEARCH CENTER

Fig. 1.3: Being Christian in Western Europe

Another PEW survey mentions, 'About Three-in-Ten
U.S. Adults Are Now Religiously Unaffiliated. Self-
identified Christians make up 63% of U.S. population in
2021, down from 75% a decade ago.'[17]

**In U.S., roughly three-in-ten adults now
religiously unaffiliated**

% of U.S. adults who identify with ...

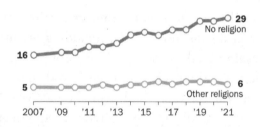

Note: Those who did not answer are not shown.
Source: Data from 2020-21 based on Pew Research Center's
National Public Opinion Reference Surveys (NPORS), conducted
online and by mail among a nationally representative group of
respondents recruited using address-based sampling. All data from
2019 and earlier from the Center's random-digit-dial telephone
surveys, including the 2007 and 2014 Religious Landscape Studies.
See Methodology for details.
"About Three-in-Ten U.S. Adults Are Now Religiously Unaffiliated"

PEW RESEARCH CENTER

When one looks at the data, it is easy to observe that
while the number of atheists has increased significantly in
Western countries, the increase in the number of 'nones'
or 'atheists' stays at a considerably lower level in India.[18]
After looking at this data, the most critical question that

has to be asked is why the percentage of 'nones' in India has remained so low. Is it possible that atheists in India, a country whose population is predominately 'Hindu', do not come forward because they fear being persecuted by society and because there is no freedom of expression in India? Or, is something essential at the heart of the dharmic traditions that prevent sceptical individuals from leaving them?[19] Is it possible that atheists and sceptics are simply a reflection of the religion from which they decided to depart? Is there something inherent to the Abrahamic religious environment that causes atheists from that fold to have a visceral reaction?

The Degree of Hostility towards the Religion of Birth

It is essential to keep in mind that generalisations made about any group of individuals, including atheists, have the potential to be deceiving and may not be accurate for any single individual. On the other hand, based on the personal interactions I've had over the past two decades as part of my activism and advocacy for scepticism, the following may be some of the possible reasons why atheists from Abrahamic religious backgrounds appear to be more hostile or critical of their religions when compared to atheists who come from Eastern religious backgrounds.

Cultural Familiarity

People who have grown up in a particular religious tradition, such as those from Abrahamic backgrounds, may have a deeper personal connection to that religion. As a result, when they become atheists, their rejection of their former beliefs can sometimes be accompanied by feelings of disappointment, betrayal, or even anger towards the religion that shaped their upbringing. This emotional attachment can contribute to a more critical stance.

Social and Cultural Context

The social and cultural environment in which individuals live can shape their attitudes and expressions of disbelief. In some predominantly Abrahamic societies, openly expressing atheistic or sceptical views about religion can be seen as more taboo or socially unacceptable compared to certain Eastern religious cultures that may be more tolerant or accepting of diverse beliefs and philosophies. This difference in societal attitudes can influence how atheists from these backgrounds interact with and criticise their respective religions.

Doctrinal Differences

There are notable differences in the theological and philosophical foundations of Abrahamic religions as compared to many Eastern religious traditions. Some atheists may find certain aspects of Abrahamic doctrines, such as the concept of a personal God, the existence of hell, or rigid moral codes, to be more objectionable or incompatible with their worldview compared to the beliefs and practices of certain Eastern religions, which may have a more flexible or non-theistic approach.

Historical and Cultural Baggage

The history of Abrahamic religions, particularly Christianity and Islam, is intertwined with political, social, and cultural conflicts throughout the centuries. This complex history, including religious wars, colonisation, persecution, and theocracy, can impact individuals' perceptions and experiences with these religions. The weight of this historical baggage might contribute to more vigorous criticism or hostility from some atheists of Abrahamic backgrounds.

Blasphemy and Apostasy

The Merriam-Webster dictionary defines blasphemy as:

1
  a: the act of insulting or showing contempt or lack of
     reverence for God accused of blasphemy
  b: the act of claiming the attributes of a deity for a mere
     man to suggest that he was ... divine could only be
     viewed ... as blasphemy—John Bright †1889
  2: irreverence toward something considered sacred or
     inviolable[20]
Apostasy is defined as:
  1: an act of refusing to continue to follow, obey, or
     recognise a religious faith
  2: abandonment of a previous loyalty: DEFECTION[21]

In the Hindu scriptures, there is the concept of *devanindā*[22]
(which more accurately fits the category of heresy[23] than
blasphemy. The neologism *īśanindā* is a term that has
recently become popular. Sanskrit scriptures contain
words like *vedanindā* or *vedanindaka*, possibly connected
to the English words blasphemy and blasphemer. But
even when it comes to just one particular truth, there are
various points of view. There is a passage in the *Manusmriti*
(2.11) which provides an illustration of vedanindā, which
reads as follows:

> (Translated by George Bühler): Every twice-born man,
> who, relying on the Institutes of dialectics, treats with
> contempt those two sources (of the law), must be cast
> out by the virtuous, as an atheist and a scorner of the
> Veda.[24]
>
> (Translated by Patrick Olivelle): If a twice-born
> disparages these two* by relying on the science of logic,
> he ought to be ostracized by good people as an infidel and
> a denigrator of the Veda.[25]

Even so, it is clear that the individual who is responsible for the vedanindā is to be shunned and excluded from society. Let's contrast this with the repercussions for committing blasphemy to Abrahamic religions. Leviticus 24.16: 'Whoever blasphemes the name of the Lord shall surely be put to death. All the congregation shall stone him. The sojourner as well as the native, when he blasphemes the Name, shall be put to death.'[26]

The Islamic concept of blasphemy is more nuanced than the Christian perspective. Different historical schools in Islam, such as the Hanafi, Maliki, Hanbali, Shaf'I, and Ja'fari, each have unique interpretations of how blasphemy should be punished. However, several schools within those groups demand the execution of individuals found guilty of blasphemy. It has been suggested by several different Islamic jurists that the *sunnah* in Sahih al-Bukhari, 3:45:687[27] and Sahih al-Bukhari, 5:59:369[28] advocate or support the imposition of the death penalty for those who commit the 'crime' of blasphemy. In the present day, the crime of blasphemy can result in death penalty in seven nations—Nigeria, Pakistan, Iran, Afghanistan, Somalia, Mauritania, and Saudi Arabia.[29] As per The Freedom of Thought Report 2021,[30] apostasy is punishable with death in at least ten countries— Afghanistan, Iran, Malaysia, the Maldives, Mauritania, Nigeria, Qatar, Saudi Arabia, the United Arab Emirates, and Yemen. As we can see, all countries with a death sentence for blasphemy or apostasy are predominantly dominated by Abrahamic religions, and their republics and governance structures are directly inspired by Abrahamic religions.[31] Blasphemy and apostasy are considered the most severe forms of religious intolerance.

Blasphemy and apostasy play significant roles in the heightened hostility that some atheists from Abrahamic backgrounds exhibit towards their religions. This is in contrast to atheists from Eastern religious backgrounds, where these concepts are either non-existent or irrelevant and diluted even if they are mentioned in random texts. The following points provide further explanation regarding the role that blasphemy and apostasy have in the rise in hostility.

Emotional and Psychological Impact

Blasphemy and apostasy carry significant emotional weight for individuals from Abrahamic backgrounds due to their cultural familiarity and personal connections to their religions. Growing up in these traditions often entails a deep-rooted religious upbringing and a strong sense of community. Rejecting one's religious beliefs can result in feelings of betrayal, disappointment, and loss. The fear of eternal punishment or damnation associated with apostasy can also generate emotional distress and anxiety. In contrast, the absence of blasphemy and apostasy concepts in Eastern religious traditions allows atheists from those backgrounds to have a more detached and less emotionally charged relationship with their former religious beliefs.

Societal and Legal Ramifications

Abrahamic societies, influenced by the concepts of blasphemy and apostasy, tend to have less tolerance for dissenting views and scepticism towards religion. Atheists from these backgrounds often face social stigma, ostracisation, and strained relationships with their families and communities. Additionally, several Abrahamic countries have laws criminalising blasphemy, which can lead to legal repercussions, including imprisonment or violence. In contrast, Eastern religious traditions generally accept diverse beliefs more, and the absence of blasphemy and apostasy laws creates a more open environment for atheists to express their views without fear of legal consequences or severe social backlash. India, a predominantly Hindu country,[32] has a blasphemy law (295A)[33] that was enacted in the early 20th century, a time when the country was under British colonial rule. The demand for a blasphemy law emerged primarily from the Muslim community, which sought to protect the sentiments of their religious beliefs. The catalyst for this demand was a controversial book, *Rangila Rasul*,[34] published in 1927, which was considered offensive by many Muslims due to its derogatory portrayal of the Prophet Muhammad. In response, the Muslim community lobbied the British government to introduce stringent measures against blasphemy to prevent such incidents.

Under pressure from the Muslim community, the British colonial administration acquiesced to their demands and enacted Section 295A as part of the Indian Penal Code in 1927. The law criminalised acts that intentionally insult or attempt to insult religious beliefs, regardless of the religion in question. However, it is noteworthy that the majority Hindu population of India had no tradition of blasphemy laws, and the concept was alien primarily to their religious and cultural beliefs. Despite this, the Indian government retained Section 295A after gaining independence in 1947, and the law remains in force today.

Doctrinal Rigidity and Consequences

Abrahamic religions often uphold strict moral codes and the belief in a personal God. The concept of apostasy challenges these religious frameworks and can be seen as rejecting divine authority. The fear of eternal punishment or damnation associated with apostasy can create additional pressure on atheists from Abrahamic backgrounds to conform to religious norms or face severe consequences. In contrast, many Eastern religious traditions adopt more flexible and pluralistic approaches, allowing for a broader range of philosophical perspectives and personal spiritual journeys. This flexibility reduces the conflict and hostility experienced by atheists from these backgrounds. For example, the first chapter of *Sarva-darśana-saṃgraha* by the 14th-century Indian scholar Mādhavāchārya[35] is the 'Cārvāka Darśana'. This clearly shows that atheism or disbelief was not considered beyond the pale of acceptance in Eastern societies.

It is essential to remember that these criteria do not necessarily apply in the same way to every person. Atheists from Abrahamic religious backgrounds may have varying animosity towards their former faiths. In contrast, atheists from Eastern religious backgrounds may have a variety of perspectives on how they used to believe in things. Individual experiences, personal journeys, and cultural nuances partly shape the attitudes of atheists of various religious origins. Each of these factors contributes in its unique way. However, on an average, atheists from Abrahamic backgrounds tend to display hostility that is absent in their counterparts from Eastern backgrounds. It is said that the fundamentalist of a religion or a meme is just like that religion or meme's fundamentals. The fundamentals of Western atheism have way more hostility per capita towards their native faith when compared to Eastern scepticism. The inbuilt hostility towards the blasphemer, apostate, or infidel in Abrahamic religions creates a particular template around which those societies are structured. When individuals in these societies reject their religions, their exit from the religion tends to mirror the overall societal standard.

The Angry, Exclusive and Jealous God of the Abrahamic Religions Is Not the Brahman or Iśvara of Eastern Philosophies

Abrahamic Concept of God

The God of Abrahamic religions (Judaism, Christianity, and Islam) is often described as an all-powerful, all-knowing, and just deity. The concept of God in these traditions emphasises a personal relationship between the divine and humanity. However, it is crucial to note that this perception can differ among adherents and interpretations of scripture. At the same time, the God of the Bible in Exodus 20.5 says, 'You must not bow down to them or worship them, for I, the LORD your God, am a jealous God who will not tolerate your affection for any other gods. I lay the sins of the parents upon their children; the entire family is affected—even children in the third and fourth generations of those who reject me.'[36] How can a just, all-knowing, all-powerful deity be jealous?

Divine Judgement and the Concept of Hell

In the Abrahamic traditions, God is often portrayed as a judge who rewards righteousness and punishes wrongdoing. Some interpret this notion as strict or hostile, particularly in contexts where sin and its consequences are emphasised. The belief in a place of eternal punishment, such as hell, is present in some interpretations of Abrahamic religions. This concept can be seen as harsh or severe, contributing to some individuals' perceptions of a potentially hostile God.

The Surah Al-Baqarah 2.39 of the Quran says, 'But those who disbelieve and deny Our signs will be the residents of the Fire. They will be there forever.'[37] Or when God in Surah Al-Baqarah 2.40 says, 'O children of Israel!

Remember My favours upon you. Fulfil your covenant and I will fulfil Mine, and stand in awe of Me alone,'[38] it indicates the very exclusive nature of the Abrahamic religions. This built-in feature makes it very hard for atheists to fit into the larger rubric of Abrahamic societies. Because the disbelievers are frowned upon, as is the case in Surah Al-Baqarah 2.98, where God says, 'Whoever is an enemy of Allah, His angels, His messengers, Gabriel, and Michael, then let them know that Allah is certainly the enemy of the disbelievers.'[39]

In Eastern religious traditions, particularly in Hinduism, the concepts of Brahman and Iśvara hold significant philosophical and theological importance. While there can be variations in interpretations and an understanding within different schools of thought, the following provides a general overview of these concepts:

Brahman

Brahman is a fundamental concept in Hindu philosophy, representing the ultimate reality or the supreme cosmic power. It is often described as the essence of all existence, transcending the physical and material worlds. Brahman is considered to be eternal, infinite, and beyond human comprehension.

Impersonal and Transcendent: Brahman is often perceived as an impersonal and formless entity that transcends human attributes and qualities. It is beyond gender, emotions, and limitations. Brahman is regarded as the source and substratum of all creation, encompassing everything in the universe. This concept is wonderfully explained in the *Br̥hadāraṇyaka Upaniṣad* (4.2.4, 4.4.22, etc.)[40] by the concept of *neti neti*.[41]

Unity and Interconnectedness: One of the key aspects of Brahman is the concept of unity and interconnectedness.

It is believed that everything in the universe, including living and non-living beings, is interconnected and derives its existence from Brahman. This understanding emphasises the underlying oneness of all creation. Rajiv Malhotra eloquently explains this in his book *Indra's Net*[42] how *Atharvaveda* 8.8.6 and 8.8.8 discuss Indra's net,

> which likens the world to a net woven by the great deity Shakra or Indra. The net is said to be infinite, and to spread in all directions with no beginning or end. At each node of the net is a jewel, so arranged that every jewel reflects all the other jewels. No jewel exists by itself independently of the rest. Everything is related to everything else; nothing is isolated.

Spiritual Liberation: In Hindu philosophy, the realisation of Brahman is considered the ultimate goal of human life. Attaining self-realisation and understanding one's true nature as an eternal soul (*atman*) is the path to realising unity with Brahman. This state of liberation (moksha) is believed to be the highest spiritual attainment.

Iśvara

Iśvara, a key concept in Hinduism, refers to the Supreme Being, or the highest deity, that represents the ultimate reality and is responsible for the universe's creation, sustenance, and dissolution. Though the concept varies across Hindu traditions, Iśvara is generally understood as a personal manifestation of the divine, possessing attributes such as omnipotence, omniscience, and benevolence. In this sense, Iśvara is often identified with specific deities like Vishnu, Shiva, or Devi, depending on the theological framework of a particular tradition. This diversity in understanding Iśvara stems from the wide range of philosophical and religious perspectives within

Hinduism, which allows for multiple interpretations of the divine.

Personal Relationship: The concept of Iśvara allows for a personal relationship between individuals and the divine. Devotees can establish a connection, devotion, and worship towards a particular deity or form of Iśvara. This relationship is characterised by love, devotion, and a sense of divine presence. Individuals can choose a form of the divine that resonates with their spiritual inclinations and aspirations. This personal deity, the *ishta devata*, becomes the focal point for the devotee's worship, meditation, and contemplation, fostering a deep and intimate connection with the divine.

This personal relationship with Iśvara is further facilitated through Bhakti Yoga, a spiritual path centred around loving devotion towards the chosen deity. Bhakti Yoga encourages the cultivation of a close, emotional bond with the divine, often expressed through prayer, meditation, chanting, rituals, and acts of selfless service. The relationship between the devotee and Iśvara is often likened to that between a parent and a child, a friend, or a lover, reflecting the profound intimacy and trust that characterises the bond. Through this personal connection, the devotee seeks to overcome the illusion of separateness, ultimately realising their true nature as one with the divine. This emphasis on a personal relationship with Iśvara enables Hinduism to accommodate diverse spiritual needs and preferences, making it an inclusive and adaptable religious tradition.

Qualities and Attributes: Iśvara is often attributed with qualities such as compassion, love, wisdom, and divine grace. Devotees seek solace, guidance, and blessings from Iśvara. The qualities associated with Iśvara can vary depending on the specific deity or form worshipped.

It is important to note that the concepts of Brahman and Iśvara can be interpreted differently within various philosophical schools and sects of Hinduism. Different perspectives exist regarding the nature of ultimate reality and the personal manifestations of the divine. In Hindu philosophy, these concepts serve as foundational principles in understanding the nature of existence, self-realisation, and the pursuit of spiritual liberation. For example, the Brahman can be both *saguṇa* (with *guna*s or qualities) and *nirguṇa* (without gunas or qualities). The Advaita Vedantins call the Brahman nirguṇa while the Dvaita of Madhava and Vishistadvaita of Ramanuja consider saguṇa Brahman the ultimate reality.[43]

The Rejection of a Personal Abrahamic God Is Much More Complicated than that of an Impersonal Eastern Brahman or Iśvara

In Abrahamic religions, the concept of God is often described as personal and separate from its believers. This perception differs from the impersonal nature of the divine in Eastern religions, and it can indeed present challenges for atheists from Abrahamic backgrounds. Here's a closer look at how the personal nature of the Abrahamic God and the impersonal nature of the Eastern God can relate to profound issues for atheists from Abrahamic backgrounds.

Personal Relationship

In Abrahamic religions, believers are encouraged to develop a personal relationship with God. This personal aspect is often emphasised through prayer, worship, and a sense of divine presence. The belief in God's involvement in human affairs, including answering prayers and providing guidance, can lead to a strong emotional and psychological attachment between believers and their understanding of God.

For atheists from Abrahamic backgrounds, rejecting the belief in a personal God can be a profound and challenging experience. It may involve questioning the sense of connection and guidance they once felt, and it can lead to a sense of loss, disconnection, or even betrayal. The Abrahamic God's personal nature can intensify the atheists' emotional struggle as they navigate their disbelief. It also leads to an outraged response from society when these individuals leave their religion, leading to an even angrier response from the one leaving their religious fold.

God as a Moral Authority

Abrahamic religions often present God as the ultimate moral authority, providing believers with a moral framework and guidelines. The belief in divine commandments and religious laws can shape individuals' ethical and moral outlook within these traditions. God's nature is often associated with His role as a judge, rewarding righteousness and punishing wrongdoing.

For atheists from Abrahamic backgrounds, rejecting the belief in God as a moral authority can present significant moral and ethical challenges. They may find themselves reevaluating their values, ethics, and the foundation of their moral compass. The personal nature of the Abrahamic God, tied to the concept of moral authority, can make this process more complex and emotionally charged.

Impersonal and Transcendent Nature of the Eastern God

In contrast, Eastern religious traditions often emphasise an impersonal and transcendent understanding of the divine. The focus is on concepts like Brahman, the ultimate reality, or the interconnectedness of all existence. These philosophical perspectives provide a broader and more abstract framework, allowing for a less personal and more detached relationship with the divine.

For atheists from Abrahamic backgrounds, the impersonal nature of the Eastern God can present a stark contrast to their previous understanding of God. It can offer an alternative perspective that allows them to explore a different way of relating to profound existential questions without the emotional baggage of a personal God. The impersonal nature of the Eastern God may resonate more with their atheistic or non-religious worldview. This is one of the reasons for the rise of Eastern religious practices like yoga and meditation in the Western world. While these practices have a religious origin, the structure of these faiths allows for a more secular approach.

This does not mean that disbelievers from Eastern backgrounds do not face any challenges or struggles. But their problems are drastically different from atheists from Abrahamic backgrounds, and bracketing them all in a single block like many Western New Atheists do is inaccurate and intellectually dishonest. Only when we develop this sense of understanding and empathy can we promote a respectful dialogue that fosters a sense of mutual understanding among individuals from different religious or non-religious backgrounds.

Abrahamic Religions Are God-obsessed in Comparison to Their Eastern Counterparts

Abrahamic religions are monotheistic, meaning they believe in the existence of a single, all-powerful God.

This monotheistic focus emphasises God's attributes, nature, and the relationship between God and humanity. In contrast, many Eastern religions encompass a more comprehensive range of beliefs, including polytheism, pantheism, or non-theistic philosophies, which may distribute religious attention among multiple deities, cosmic principles, or philosophical concepts.

In Abrahamic religions, it is believed that God communicates with humanity through an anointed prophet or messenger who serves as a conduit for divine revelation. This concept is prominent in Judaism, Christianity, and Islam. According to these traditions, prophets such as Moses, Jesus, and Muhammad received direct communication from God and conveyed God's messages, laws, and teachings to the people.

In contrast, Eastern religions, such as Hinduism, Buddhism, and Taoism, often have a different understanding of the divine and the individual's relationship to it. Rather than relying on a specific prophet or messenger, these traditions emphasise the concept of an inherent divine nature within each individual. In Hinduism, for example, the belief in Brahman asserts that the ultimate reality or divine essence permeates all existence, including human beings. These traditions often aim to realise or awaken to this divine nature within oneself. A great example of that is the famous mahāvākya *Aham Brahmāsmi*, 'I am Brahman' or 'I am Divine', from the *Brihadaranyaka Upanishad* 1.4.10[44] of the *Yajurveda*.

This distinction highlights a fundamental difference in how divine revelation and human–divine interaction are perceived in Abrahamic religions compared to many Eastern religions. In Abrahamic religions, the emphasis is on God's communication with humanity through chosen prophets, while in Eastern religions, the focus is on recognising the inherent divinity within oneself and realising one's connection to the ultimate reality or divine essence.

The history-centrism[45] of Abrahamic religions and their emphasis on the role of anointed prophets as intermediaries for divine communication compared to the Eastern religions and their focus on the recognition of the inherent sacred nature within each individual create a very god-obsessed framework within the Abrahamic traditions, unlike the Eastern religions. Add to this the concepts of blasphemy and apostasy, and we have a very toxic mix that creates many problems for atheists from Abrahamic backgrounds.

Difference Anxiety

Abrahamic religions, including Judaism, Christianity, and Islam, have historically maintained a degree of exclusivism, asserting their truth claims and often perceive themselves as the sole paths to salvation or spiritual fulfilment. However, this exclusivist outlook can give rise to various challenges in today's diverse and interconnected world.

The exclusivist nature of Abrahamic religions can contribute to a lack of religious tolerance. When adherents believe their religion is the only true path, it can foster an environment where other religious beliefs and practices are marginalised or even condemned. This intolerance may lead to discrimination, prejudice, and even religious persecution, hindering the principles of religious freedom and equality within a diverse society.

Exclusivism can hinder meaningful interfaith dialogue and understanding. When individuals and communities firmly believe their religion is the only legitimate one, they may be less inclined to engage in open, respectful conversations with people of different faiths—this lack of dialogue limits mutual learning, cooperation, and developing relationships that transcend religious boundaries.

This trait of Abrahamic religions asserts the superiority and exclusivity of their belief systems, often leaving little room for alternative perspectives, including atheism. This clash between the religious worldview and atheistic disbelief can result in frustration, resentment, and anger. Atheists may perceive themselves as marginalised or even persecuted by religious institutions and adherents, leading to an emotional response rooted in a sense of injustice. Atheists seeking intellectual freedom and autonomy may react strongly against what they perceive as the imposition of dogma, resulting in a more aggressive and angry atheistic stance. Some atheists may adopt a more vocal and aggressive approach to challenge the religious status quo as a reaction to this dominant spiritual presence.

For some atheists who were once devout followers of Abrahamic religions, the journey towards atheism can be emotionally charged. This process may involve questioning deeply held beliefs, facing personal conflicts, and potentially experiencing rejection from religious communities. The anger from this personal journey can manifest in a passionate and confrontational approach towards religion. This trait is further exacerbated by the rise of online atheist communities that have provided a platform for individuals to express their frustration and anger towards religion. Online spaces can act as echo chambers, amplifying and validating these emotions. This can further perpetuate the angry form of atheism as individuals find solace and support in like-minded communities.

The angry form of atheism, stemming from the exclusivism of Abrahamic religions, can have both positive and negative consequences. On one hand, it can catalyse critical thinking, intellectual discourse, and the promotion of secular values. On the other hand, it can perpetuate a cycle of hostility, hinder productive dialogue, and reinforce negative stereotypes about atheists.

Deep down beneath all these behavioural patterns of Abrahamic believers and disbelievers lie 'Difference Anxiety'. The Indian-American scholar Rajiv Malhotra calls difference anxiety 'the mental uneasiness caused by the perception of difference combined with a desire to diminish, conceal or eradicate it'.[46] He says, 'Difference anxiety occurs in cultural and religious contexts frequently. Such an anxiety seeks the relative comfort of homogeneous ideas, beliefs and identity.'

This process of homogenising ideas expresses itself in both atheists and theists in different ways. Theists from Abrahamic backgrounds experience a fear of the erosion of their religious values and traditions. This anxiety may lead to attempts to homogenise ideas within their religious communities, rejecting alternative viewpoints. Theists may seek to enforce strict orthodoxy, excluding dissenting voices and discouraging critical thinking. This can limit intellectual growth, hinder interfaith dialogue, and contribute to social divisions and conflicts.

On the other hand, atheists from Abrahamic backgrounds may experience difference anxiety due to their rejection of religious beliefs. They may feel marginalised or misunderstood within religious societies, leading to a desire to homogenise ideas. In their effort to establish a secular society that minimises the influence of religion, they potentially marginalise religious perspectives and stifle religious freedom. This approach overlooks the diversity of beliefs and experiences within religious communities, hindering the recognition of shared values and cooperation.

Eastern ideologies are opposed to this. The *Rigveda* 1.164.46 says, 'They say it is Indra, Mitra, Varuṇa, and Agni, and also it is the winged, well-feathered (bird) of heaven [=the Sun]. Though it is One, inspired poets speak of it in many ways. They say it is Agni, Yama, and Mātariśvan.'[47] It is the polar opposite of the numerous verses of the Bible[48] or the Quran[49] that teach that their respective God is the one real God and that followers of other gods would perish in hell.

The default character of Eastern ideologies is far more accepting of difference. This results in a much greater acceptance of sceptics and atheists inside their domain. This lack of antagonism is mirrored on the side of atheists within the dharmic universe, where sceptics are constantly seen partaking in rituals and festivals just like any other believer. The fact that it is so difficult to determine whether one is a believer or not is confirmation of this phenomenon. The irate Marxists or ex-Hindus fulminating and engaging in recreational outrage online are the exception, not the rule. And the fact that most individuals in India still identify as Hindus first and do not feel outside the societal fold is confirmation of that.

Tolerance versus Mutual Respect

Difference anxiety refers to the discomfort or fear that arises when confronted with beliefs, values, or worldviews that differ from one's own. The response to this anxiety varies, leading to different approaches in different societies. Every thought has an effect. A policy, too, has second- and third-order effects. The difference anxiety that Abrahamic theists and atheists experience has its implications. The concept of tolerance is one of these impacts. How many times have you heard religious leaders[50] or politicians[51] in the West advise us to 'embrace tolerance'?

Rajiv Malhotra's book *Being Different* effectively explains the difficulty of tolerance by narrating his experience at an interfaith meeting in the 1990s. The story is so crucial that the complete excerpt from his book must be published verbatim to understand the problem.

Malhotra says,

In the late 1990s, Prof. Karen Jo Torjesen, head of religious studies at Claremont Graduate University, invited me to the inauguration of a major interfaith initiative at her university. Claremont had decided to launch a programme in which every major world religion would be represented by a practitioner. At the same time, inter-religious dialogue and discussions would be encouraged in order to promote harmony among the world faiths. I was invited to speak on Hinduism and serve on the new initiative's Board of Advisors. Enthused at the prospect of working with peers from other religions, I accepted.

The inaugural event itself was a grand affair involving the university's top brass along with dignitaries from various religions and local communities. One of the highlights was the public endorsement by each representative of a statement written to resolve inter-religious tensions and foster better understanding among faiths. Each of the representatives endorsed the resolution which declared that there must be religious tolerance. When it was my turn to speak, I recommended that the term 'tolerance' in the resolution be replaced with the phrase 'mutual respect'. This elicited applause similar to that which had followed the remarks of the other speakers. Then I went on to explain the significance of this change and why this was not a matter of mere semantics.

As I noted, we 'tolerate' those we consider not good enough, but we do not extend our respect to them. 'Tolerance' implies control over those who do not conform to our norms by allowing them some, though not all, of the rights and privileges we enjoy. A religion which involves the worship of 'false gods' and whose adherents are referred to as 'heathens' can be tolerated, but it cannot be respected. Tolerance is a patronizing posture, whereas respect implies that we consider the other to be equally legitimate — a position which some religions routinely deny to others, instead declaring these 'others' to be 'idol worshippers' or 'infidels' and the like.

I wondered aloud if anyone in the audience would like to be told at the upcoming luncheon that he or she was being 'tolerated' at the table. No husband or wife would appreciate being told that his or her presence at home was being 'tolerated'. No self-respecting worker accepts mere tolerance from colleagues. Tolerance, in short, is an outright insult; it is simply not good enough. I pointed out that this notion of tolerance had emerged from religions built on exclusivist claims according to which other religions are false.[52]

As is visible from this incident, tolerance is a compromise for theists and atheists from Abrahamic backgrounds. After centuries of religious conflicts between Christians of various faiths, religious 'tolerance' was espoused throughout Europe. In many European countries, churches served as religious monopolies, with the mere practice of the 'wrong' faith punishable by law. 'Tolerance' was a laudable attempt to end the violence that had afflicted Christianity in Europe for ages. Still, it needed to create a sufficient foundation for true unity and collaboration, so it frequently failed.

This is the exact position adopted by atheists in the Western world, too. Western atheists, who reject theistic beliefs, may find themselves in a unique position as a mirror image of their theistic counterparts in an unusual and lopsided manner. Religion has a pervasive influence on societies. This influence has a tremendous subconscious effect on atheists, too; and, that is why the method and technique in which Abrahamic atheists respond to religion are the same. Atheists often employ tolerance as a practical strategy for coexistence with their theistic counterparts. Tolerance allows atheists to live alongside religious individuals while minimising conflicts and promoting social harmony. It acknowledges the diversity of beliefs without requiring atheists to compromise their convictions.

This approach aligns with the 'live and let live' principle, focusing on personal autonomy and respecting individual choices. However, it produces intellectual ghettos where everyone only hangs out with their 'tribe'. While tolerance serves as a pragmatic response, it has its limitations. Tolerance alone may not foster more profound understanding, empathy, or meaningful dialogue between atheists and theists. It can perpetuate a sense of indifference or apathy towards religious beliefs, hindering opportunities for mutual growth, intellectual exchange, and exploration of existential questions. Furthermore, tolerance does not address the underlying differences in worldview, philosophy of life, or existential concerns that atheists and theists may grapple with.

The Eastern philosophical worldview is the complete opposite of that. Eastern philosophies demand mutual respect. Rajiv Malhotra, in his book *Being Different*,[53] says,

In Hinduism there was no injunction against worshipping images of the divine (what the Abrahamic religions routinely and wrongly condemn as 'idolatry'). Indeed, I use images myself in my spiritual practice and felt glad that she had agreed to respect this practice. None of my practices, I reminded her, are being imposed on others. Mutual respect merely means that I am respected for my faith, with no compulsion for others to adopt or practise it. Furthermore, Hindus might view the divine in feminine form and believe in reincarnation rather than the notion of an eternal afterlife spent in either heaven or hell.

And this mutual respect is not just for fellow 'believers'. Sri Aurobindo, in *Indian Spirituality and Life*, asks, 'How again can Hinduism be called a religion when it admits all beliefs, allowing even a high-reaching atheism and agnosticism and permits all possible spiritual experiences, all kinds of religious adventures?'[54] Hindol Sengupta, in his popular book *Being Hindu*, reiterates this point when he says, 'This coexistence is not surprising to any practicing Hindu, nor even to those who are nonpracticing since even atheism is a valid theological and philosophical position in the faith.'[55]

The default style of mutual respect is why atheism is regarded as one of several paths to discovering the truth within the Eastern paradigm. And, as Western Abrahamic atheists are inspired by their original concepts and philosophies, so are their Eastern counterparts by the dharmic rule of mutual respect. They do not tolerate their opposites but admire them, and vice versa.

Skin-Deep Diversity versus Soul-Deep Diversity

Diversity has recently gained significant attention and prominence in Western societies as efforts are made to foster inclusivity, equality, and social justice. While it is true that diversity has received increased emphasis, it is essential to approach the topic with nuance and consider the underlying motivations and goals behind this focus.

Western societies' idea of diversity is built on tolerance, which leads to a very superficial effort in which people of diverse races, ethnicities, genders, and so on are encouraged. However, we find minimal disagreement when we examine the words that come out of their mouths. Tolerance alone may not necessarily lead to deeper understanding, meaningful dialogue, or genuine engagement with differing viewpoints. Here are a few points to consider.

The Superficiality of Tolerance

While tolerance is a starting point for creating inclusive societies, it should not be the goal. Simply tolerating diversity without actively seeking to understand, appreciate, and engage with differing perspectives can lead to a superficial approach. Moving beyond tolerance and fostering genuine respect, empathy, and dialogue is essential to promote deeper connections and understanding.

Echo Chambers and Confirmation Bias

Despite the emphasis on diversity, it is possible for individuals to gravitate towards like-minded individuals and communities that reinforce their existing beliefs and values. This can lead to the formation of echo chambers, where people primarily interact with others who share their perspectives. In such echo chambers, genuine disagreement and diverse viewpoints may be lacking, hindering the exploration of differing ideas.

The toxic combination of difference anxiety and tolerance results in one-sided sameness. In a world that celebrates diversity, one-sided sameness poses a significant challenge to fostering inclusive societies. One-sided sameness refers to a state where individuals or groups limit their interactions and perspectives to those that mirror their own, inadvertently creating homogeneous echo chambers that hinder the exchange of diverse ideas and perspectives. This phenomenon can be observed in various social, cultural, and political contexts. While embracing diversity has become widely accepted in Western societies, the prevalence of one-sided sameness highlights the need for genuine engagement with differing viewpoints and a willingness to challenge one's beliefs.

Abrahamism seeks homogeneity. This fundamental essence of Abrahamism, which is present in both theists and atheists, drives people to constantly erase distinctions. We shall witness Christians always attempting to 'save' the others and Muslims offering dawah[56] to members of other faiths. Abrahamic atheists exhibit similar characteristics. One of the clearest examples is a well-known book named *Manual for Creating Atheists*[57] by the Western philosopher and author Peter Boghossian.

One-sided sameness carries several pitfalls that impede the growth and progress of societies. Firstly, it perpetuates confirmation bias, where individuals seek information and engage with people who reinforce their beliefs and values. This echo chamber effect can lead to a skewed understanding of reality and hinder critical thinking. Intellectual stagnation occurs when one's viewpoints are rarely challenged, limiting opportunities for personal growth and collective progress.

Additionally, one-sided sameness fosters the exclusion of marginalised voices and perpetuates systemic inequalities. If particular perspectives dominate, those on the margins may struggle to be heard, and their unique experiences and needs may be overlooked. This exacerbates social divisions and further entrenches power imbalances within society.

Moreover, one-sided sameness stifles innovation and creativity. Diverse perspectives and experiences serve as catalysts for new ideas, problem-solving, and the development of innovative solutions. When individuals restrict their interactions to like-minded individuals, they miss the opportunity to tap into the collective wisdom and creativity that emerge from embracing diverse perspectives. A diverse society will not try to 'save' the 'other'. A truly diverse community would not 'cancel'[58] each other over disagreement. The Western theists and atheists want people who look different but think similarly.

One should cultivate empathy and promote open dialogue to address the perils of one-sided sameness, which leads to skin-deep diversity. Empathy allows individuals to step outside their own experiences and genuinely connect with the perspectives of others. By empathising with different viewpoints, individuals can develop a deeper understanding of diverse perspectives, fostering respect and appreciation for the richness that diversity brings.

Open dialogue plays a pivotal role in dismantling one-sided sameness. It creates spaces for meaningful conversations and the exploration of contrasting ideas. Engaging in respectful and constructive dialogue helps break down barriers, encourages sharing experiences, and promotes mutual learning. It enables individuals to challenge their assumptions and biases, fostering personal growth and a broader understanding of complex issues.

Actively seeking out diverse perspectives is essential to overcoming one-sided sameness. This involves deliberately engaging with individuals from different backgrounds, cultures, and beliefs without trying to convert them to your point of view. It requires stepping outside comfort zones and embracing the discomfort that may arise from encountering contrasting viewpoints.

Efforts to seek diverse perspectives should extend beyond the passive consumption of information. It involves actively participating in various communities, attending events, reading literature, and engaging in dialogue with

individuals with different opinions. Building genuine
connections and relationships across diverse communities
facilitates the exchange of ideas, challenges assumptions,
and encourages personal growth. That is what we call
soul-deep diversity.

To foster soul-deep diversity, one must cultivate the
culture of *purva paksha* (steel manning). Rajiv Malhotra
says purva paksha[59]

> is the traditional dharmic approach to rival schools. It is a
> dialectical approach, taking a thesis by an opponent (purva
> pakshin) and then providing its rebuttal (khandana) so as
> to establish the protagonist's views (siddhanta). The purva
> paksha tradition required any debater first to argue from
> the perspective of his opponent in order to test the validity
> of his understanding of the opposing position, and from
> there to realize his own shortcomings. Only after perfecting
> his understanding of opposing views would he be qualified
> to refute them. Such debates encourage individuals to
> maintain flexibility of perspective and honesty rather than
> seek victory egotistically. In this way, the dialectical process
> ensures a genuine and far-reaching shift in the individual.

> This requires direct but respectful confrontation with
> one's opponent in debate. In purva paksha, one does
> not look away, so to speak, from real differences but
> attempts to clarify them, without anxiety but also without
> the pretence of sameness. There is more to this practice
> than meets the eye. It involves not only a firm intent but
> considerable self-mastery (i.e., a movement beyond ego)
> combined with an understanding of the magnitude of the
> issues at stake. Reversing the gaze in purva paksha is not
> painless, and resistance is to be expected.

> This method was extensively applied among various
> schools of Hinduism, Buddhism and Jainism lineages.
> There are hundreds of volumes of transcripts of these
> intense debates, and they comprise an important part of

the heritage of the dharmic traditions. Advanced training in various schools of Indian philosophy includes a close study of these debates because it was through the purva paksha of the past that each school sharpened itself and evolved over time.

Societies promoting this culture of soul-deep diversity encompass a deeper understanding and appreciation of those individuals' diverse perspectives, experiences, and values. Beyond surface-level differences, soul-deep diversity fosters a prosperous and inclusive society that celebrates the complexities and nuances of human existence. For this reason, atheists are not considered the 'other' in dharmic cultures compared to their Western counterparts, and vice versa.

Atheism is an acceptable philosophical perspective within various beliefs and practises in dharmic communities. Individual spiritual journeys and the quest for truth and freedom are frequently emphasised in dharmic religions. This can foster an environment where atheistic ideas can live with other theistic beliefs without being excluded or condemned.

This reciprocity culture results in a much healthier system, and atheists in Eastern nations perceive themselves as part of the greater society rather than at odds with it, unlike their Western counterparts, who have historically had a more binary view of religious beliefs and atheism, particularly those who had a solid Christian upbringing.

Conclusion

Throughout this chapter, we have explored the differences between Western and Eastern atheism, acknowledging that these are broad generalisations and that individual perspectives can vary within each cultural context. However, there are significant distinctions between the two, stemming from various factors such as cultural heritage, philosophical traditions, and societal norms. Understanding and appreciating these differences can contribute to a more comprehensive understanding of atheism as a diverse and complex phenomenon.

One significant difference between Western and Eastern atheism lies in the cultural and historical contexts in which they emerged. The dominance of Abrahamic religions, particularly Christianity, and the subsequent cultural and intellectual struggles against religious authority and dogma have shaped Western atheism. This history has influenced the development of Western atheism as a reaction against theistic beliefs and a desire for secularism and individual autonomy. On the other hand, Eastern atheism has evolved within the cultural and philosophical traditions of dharmic religions, which have a more inclusive and pluralistic approach to beliefs and spirituality. This context allows for a wider acceptance and integration of atheistic perspectives without necessarily being seen as 'other' or deviant.

Another significant difference lies in the philosophical underpinnings and perspectives on the nature of existence. Western atheism often adopts a more materialistic and rationalistic approach rooted in scientific inquiry and empirical evidence. It tends to focus on rejecting supernatural entities and religious dogma, emphasising critical thinking and scepticism. Eastern atheism, while also valuing reason and critical inquiry, may adopt a more nuanced and holistic worldview. It draws from philosophical traditions such as Sāṁkhya, Mīmāṃsā, Buddhism, and Jainism, which emphasise the interconnectedness of all beings and the concept of self-transcendence. This perspective allows for a more fluid and multifaceted understanding of existence, which may differ from the reductionist approach often associated with Western atheism.

Furthermore, atheism's cultural and social implications differ in Western and Eastern contexts. Western atheism has often been met with resistance and social stigma, particularly in societies with strong religious traditions. It has had to navigate a complex landscape of social, political, and legal challenges to assert its visibility and rights. Although not universally accepted, Eastern atheism may face a different social environment. Dharmic traditions generally have a more tolerant and pluralistic approach, which can provide a more accommodating space for atheistic perspectives. However, it is crucial to recognise that these generalisations do not negate the existence of conservative or orthodox pockets within Eastern societies that may be less accepting of atheism.

It is essential to approach these differences with an appreciation for the diversity within atheism itself. Atheism is not a monolithic belief system, and individuals within Western and Eastern contexts can hold various perspectives and motivations for their atheistic stance. Some Western atheists may prioritise scepticism, scientific inquiry, and the separation of church and state. In contrast, some Eastern atheists may embrace a non-theistic spiritual path, focusing on personal transformation and self-realisation. These differences highlight the fluidity and complexity of atheism as a diverse set of perspectives rather than a singular ideology.

In conclusion, the differences between Western and Eastern atheism are significant, stemming from various cultural, philosophical, and social factors. Differences do not need to be negative. It can also be seen as an asset

if seen through a different lens. Understanding these
differences lets us appreciate how atheism is expressed
and experienced across different contexts. It also
highlights the importance of recognising the complexities
and nuances within atheism itself and avoiding sweeping
generalisations. By engaging in respectful dialogue and
fostering cross-cultural understanding, we can further
explore the similarities and differences between Western
and Eastern atheism, enriching our understanding of the
diverse tapestry of human beliefs and perspectives.

2

Neo-atheism
Its Success and Failure

In the vast landscape of philosophical and religious thought, many atheistic viewpoints have emerged over the centuries, each with its own unique set of principles, arguments, and ideas. While many forms of atheism exist, neo-atheism has gained significant traction and attention in the last four decades. This contemporary movement, characterised by its unapologetic critique of religion and passionate advocacy for secularism, reason, and critical thinking, has captured the imagination of a new generation of non-believers and sparked heated debates about the role of religion in society.

The rise of neo-atheism in the 21st century can be seen as a response to a changing world where advancements in science, technology, and globalisation have prompted many individuals to question the relevance and validity of religious beliefs. In this context, the arguments put forth by the key figures of neo-atheism have resonated with an increasing number of people seeking answers that are not constrained by the dogmas of traditional religious institutions. By challenging the foundations of religious thought and promoting a secular worldview, neo-atheism has emerged as a powerful intellectual and cultural force that has helped to reshape how people perceive and understand religion, spirituality, and the nature of reality.

Studying neo-atheism is essential for several reasons. First, it helps understand modern society's shifting dynamics of religious belief and non-belief. As the world becomes more secular and diverse, it is crucial to comprehend how various religious and non-religious groups interact and coexist.

Second, analysing neo-atheism provides insights into the broader debates on the role of religion in public life, education, and policy-making. It highlights the importance of promoting evidence-based reasoning and critical thinking in human life, from individual decision-making to global governance.

Lastly, examining neo-atheism allows us to explore the implications of a world without religious faith and consider alternative worldviews and ethical systems. As more people question the necessity and relevance of religion, it is vital to explore the potential consequences of a secular society and develop rational and compassionate approaches to human existence.

Historical Context and Background Leading to the Rise of Neo-atheism

The rise of neo-atheism can be understood within a broader historical context that traces the development of atheism, secularism, and scepticism over centuries. Factors such as advancements in science, philosophical inquiries, political changes, and social developments have laid the groundwork for the emergence of the New Atheist movement in the early 21st century.

One of the most significant periods in the history of atheism was the Scientific Revolution (16th to 18th centuries), which brought about significant advancements in our understanding of the natural world. The works of pioneering scientists like Galileo Galilei, Isaac Newton, and Charles Darwin provided rational explanations for natural phenomena that were once attributed to divine intervention. As scientific knowledge expanded, it challenged traditional religious beliefs and laid the foundation for a more secular and rational worldview.

Simultaneously, the Age of Enlightenment (17th to 18th centuries) saw the rise of philosophers like John Locke, Voltaire, David Hume, and Immanuel Kant, who advocated for a reason, scepticism, and the separation of the church and state. Their ideas contributed to developing secularism and religious tolerance in Western societies, paving the way for a more open and critical examination of religious beliefs.

The 19th century saw the rise of the Freethought movement, which promoted scepticism, secularism, and the rejection of religious dogma. Key figures like Robert G. Ingersoll, Charles Bradlaugh, and Annie Besant championed the separation of religion from public life and encouraged people to question religious authority and tradition. The movement also played a significant role in advancing social reforms, such as women's rights, the abolition of slavery, and the promotion of public education.

Throughout the 20th century, atheism and secularism continued to gain ground as science and technology progressed. The development of modern physics, evolutionary biology, and neuroscience challenged traditional religious explanations for the nature of the universe, human origins, and consciousness. The works of influential atheists like Bertrand Russell, Jean-Paul Sartre, and Albert Camus further questioned the existence of God and the role of religion in society.

The 20th century witnessed significant political and social changes that influenced the development of atheism and secularism. The rise of communism, particularly in the Soviet Union and China, promoted state-sponsored atheism and the suppression of religious institutions. In the Western world, the rise of secularism and religious pluralism led to a decline in religious adherence and a growing acceptance of non-religious worldviews.

The Birth of Neo-atheism

The emergence of neo-atheism in the early 21st century can be seen as a response to several factors. One of the most significant catalysts was the rise of religious fundamentalism, particularly in the form of Islamic extremism and its impact on global politics. The 11 September 2001 events and subsequent acts of terrorism perpetrated by religious extremists prompted a renewed focus on the dangers of religious dogma and the need for secularism and rationalism in public discourse.

Sam Harris, when asked 'Why did 9/11 spark your interest in religion?', says,

> Well it was two things. One, just the rather obvious liability of religious certainty was made extraordinarily clear on that day. We were having people flying planes into our buildings for explicitly religious reasons. What was also made clear was that we were going to deny the religious rationale because of our own attachment to our own religious myths. The only language we could find as a culture to comfort ourselves was to endorse our own God-talk. So I suddenly found faith playing both sides of the board in a very dangerous game where we as a nation, in prosecuting our war on terror, which was obviously the necessary thing to do, though calling it 'The War on Terror' I think is rather silly.... But we were consoling ourselves with our own religious certainties, you know,

very much in the language of Christian fundamentalism. The president comes before Congress and talks about God not being indifferent to freedom and fear. As an atheist, I hear that exactly the way I would hear someone saying, 'Zeus is not indifferent to freedom and fear.' It is an uncannily strange and empty utterance. And yet, our culture is now programmed not to notice how strange and empty it is. And it does really significant work. And so we see things like stem cell research and other causes that ... upon which the lives and happiness of millions of people really turn get subverted by religious thinking ... explicitly religious thinking.[1]

In addition to the rise of religious fundamentalism, the increasing polarisation between religious and secular worldviews in the United States also contributed to the development of the New Atheist movement. Debates over issues such as abortion, LGBTQ+ rights, and the teaching of evolution in public schools highlighted the growing divide between religious conservatives and secular progressives.

In response to the rise of religious fundamentalism, neo-atheists sought to defend reason, science, and secularism as the most reliable means of understanding the world and making informed decisions. They argued that religious dogma and faith-based thinking were irrational and incompatible with modern, pluralistic societies. By highlighting the dangers of religious fundamentalism, neo-atheists underscored the importance of critical thinking, scepticism, and the separation of the church and state.

In his book *The God Delusion*,[2] Richard Dawkins criticises the teaching of creationism or intelligent design in public schools, asserting that these ideas are not supported by scientific evidence and should not be presented as valid alternatives to the theory of evolution.

What Is 'New' in Neo-atheism?

One of the most raging debates inside intellectual circles is whether there is anything 'new' in neo-atheism. Gary Keogh, in his essay 'Theology after New Atheism', says,

> It should be noted that the new atheists bring very little new material to a debate that has been progressing earnestly for millennia. Since Aristotle for instance, theists have used logical thinking such as the first-cause argument to address the God question. Although Aristotle himself was not explicitly theistic (he did not propose one first cause identifiable with a supreme being, but rather 47 or 55 first causes) his philosophy was an example of an early attempt to articulate and address the question of who or what caused existence to be, or whether existence requires a cause. In more recent philosophical history, the prospect of a universe with no God has become an idea taken more seriously, as David Hume, Friedrich Nietzsche, Karl Marx, Sigmund Freud, and others, have presented intellectually rigorous arguments that made substantial contributions to humanity's quest for understanding. So the atheism/theism debate is certainly not new itself.[3]

While at its core the disbelief of Epicureans, Marx, and Dawkins might look similar, there is a seriously distinct element in the neo-atheistic movement that was completely lacking in atheism in the past. Neo-atheism was the first time when atheism became a collective identity. Stephen Le Drew, in 'Discovering Atheism: Heterogeneity in Trajectories to Atheist Identity and Activism', says, 'Where the New Atheists do appear to have had some effect is on the development of identity, playing an important role in the construction of a collective identity and community that appeals to atheists seeking external validation.'[4] Neo-atheism made the idea of disbelief socially acceptable.

One of the interviewees mentioned in Le Drew's essay discusses how she 'came to atheism (atheism as belief) on her own, but became an atheist (atheism as identity) through engagement with a collective'.[5]

Neo-atheism served to normalise being an open and vocal atheist. Before the rise of neo-atheism, there were individual atheists; however, their arguments were generally less aggressive and provocative than those of their New Atheist counterparts. Old atheism focused more on the intellectual aspects of the debate and was less concerned with actively challenging religious beliefs in the public sphere. Through their 'coming out' campaigns, the collective aspect of neo-atheism led to a tremendous pushback against religious dogma.

Christopher Hitchens once said,

> If someone tells me that I've hurt their feelings, I say, 'I'm still waiting to hear what your point is.' In this country, I've been told, 'That's offensive' as if those two words constitute an argument or a comment. Not to me they don't. And I'm not running for anything, so I don't have to pretend to like people when I don't.[6]

This quote captures the essence of the audacity of neo-atheism, which is unapologetic in its critique of religion and does not shy away from challenging deeply held beliefs, even when it may cause discomfort or offence. As embodied by Hitchens and other key figures, the movement encourages open and honest debate, prioritising the search for truth over the desire to avoid offending others.

The Four Horsemen

The Four Horsemen of Neo-Atheism—a term coined to describe the influential thinkers Richard Dawkins,

Christopher Hitchens, Sam Harris, and Daniel Dennett —
are widely recognised for their critique of religion
and the promotion of secularism, reason, and critical
thinking. Each of these individuals has made significant
contributions to the New Atheist movement and has
brought unique perspectives and arguments to the table.

Richard Dawkins

Richard Dawkins, born in 1941 in Nairobi, Kenya, is a
British evolutionary biologist, ethologist, and writer. He
is known for his popular science books, critical views on
religion, and contributions to the neo-atheist movement.
Dawkins studied zoology at the University of Oxford,
where he earned his bachelor's degree in 1962 and his
doctorate in 1966 under the supervision of Nobel Prize-
winning biologist Nikolaas Tinbergen. In 1995, Dawkins
became the Charles Simonyi Professor for the Public
Understanding of Science at the University of Oxford, a
position he held until 2008.

Dawkins's scientific work focuses on the gene-centred
view of evolution, which emphasises the role of genes
in shaping the traits and behaviours of organisms. This
perspective has played a significant role in the development
of evolutionary theory and has informed Dawkins's views
on religion and the nature of human culture.

Richard Dawkins has been a prominent figure in the
neo-atheist movement, known for his unapologetic and
confrontational critique of religious beliefs. Dawkins's life
can be summarised into two major phases. Phase one was
that of a scientist actively working, and phase two would
be that of a populariser of science and atheism. Dawkins's
popular science books, such as *The Selfish Gene* (1976),
The Blind Watchmaker (1986), and *The Ancestor's Tale*
(2004), have made complex scientific concepts accessible

to a broad audience. These works provide readers with a deeper understanding of evolution and biology and challenge religious explanations for the natural world. By making scientific knowledge more accessible, Dawkins has contributed to popularising atheism and ignited public interest in the debate between science and religion.

Dawkins's most famous work, *The God Delusion* (2006), is a comprehensive critique of religious beliefs and the idea of a personal God. In this book, Dawkins employs scientific, philosophical, and historical arguments to challenge the existence of God and the validity of religious doctrines. He also examines the moral implications of religious beliefs, arguing that secular humanism offers a more compassionate and rational basis for ethics. *The God Delusion* has been a bestseller and significantly popularised the neo-atheist movement. Dawkins has been a vocal proponent of 'militant atheism'.[7] This form of aggressive and in-your-face criticism and assertion of your disbelief can be summed perfectly by a direct quote from his book *The God Delusion*, where he says,

> The God of the Old Testament is arguably the most unpleasant character in all fiction: jealous and proud of it; a petty, unjust, unforgiving control-freak; a vindictive, bloodthirsty ethnic cleanser; a misogynistic, homophobic, racist, infanticidal, genocidal, filicidal, pestilential, megalomaniacal, sadomasochistic, capriciously malevolent bully.[8]

Dawkins is an outspoken advocate for secularism, arguing that government policies and public education should be based on reason and evidence rather than religious doctrines. He has been particularly critical of teaching creationism or intelligent design in public schools, asserting that these ideas are not supported by scientific evidence and should not be presented as valid alternatives to the theory of evolution. Dawkins has also spoken out against the privileging of religious beliefs in public policy, arguing that such exemptions can lead to discrimination and undermine the principle of equal treatment under the law.

He has participated in numerous public events, lectures, and debates, engaging with religious figures, philosophers, and other scientists on religion, science, and ethics topics. His appearances have helped to raise the profile of the neo-atheist movement and sparked public discussion on the role of religion in society. Dawkins's work has influenced other prominent figures in the neo-atheist movement, including Sam Harris, Christopher Hitchens, and Daniel Dennett.

Richard Dawkins has played a pivotal role in developing the neo-atheist movement. His popular science books, critique of religious beliefs, advocacy for secularism and reason, public appearances, and influence on other neo-atheists have helped to popularize atheism and promote critical thinking about religion and its role in society.

Christopher Hitchens

Christopher Hitchens, born in 1949 in Portsmouth, England, was a British-American journalist, writer, and social critic known for his sharp wit and confrontational style. He was educated at Balliol College, Oxford, where he studied philosophy, politics, and economics. Hitchens began his career as a journalist in the UK, writing for publications such as *The New Statesman* and *The Evening Standard*, before moving to the United States in the early 1980s. He contributed to various publications, including *Vanity Fair*, *The Atlantic*, and *The Nation*, and authored over a dozen books on various topics.

Along with Dawkins, Hitchens was probably the most influential public intellectual of the neo-atheist movement. He was constantly engaging in debates on politics, religion, and culture. Hitchens passed away in 2011 after a battle with oesophagal cancer.

Hitchens was known for criticising religious beliefs, institutions, and figures. His book *God Is Not Great: How Religion Poisons Everything* (2007)[9] is a comprehensive examination of the negative impact of religious beliefs on human history, politics, and culture. In the book, Hitchens argues that religion is irrational and harmful to the well-being of individuals and societies. He critiques various religious doctrines and practices, pointing out inconsistencies, moral failings, and historical inaccuracies.

Hitchens also criticised specific religious figures, such as Mother Teresa, in his book *The Missionary Position: Mother Teresa in Theory and Practice* (1995)[10] and the Dalai Lama in his various essays and articles. These critiques underscored the fallibility of religious leaders and questioned the often-unquestioned reverence for such figures.

He was a staunch advocate for secularism and the separation of church and state. He believed public policy and education should be based on reason and evidence rather than religious dogma. Hitchens also defended free speech and open debate, arguing that the freedom to criticise and challenge religious beliefs was essential for a healthy, pluralistic society.

But the one thing Hitchens is fondly remembered for is his numerous public debates, often engaging with religious figures, philosophers, and other public intellectuals on topics related to religion, ethics, and politics. His debating style was unique. Search 'Hitch Slaps' on Google, and you will be exposed to a treasure trove characterised by wit, humour, and an aggressive approach, making him a popular and engaging speaker.

He once said, 'My own opinion is enough for me, and I claim the right to have it defended against any consensus, any majority, anywhere, any place, any time. And anyone who disagrees with this can pick a number, get in line, and kiss my ass.'[11] When asked about his views on heaven, he says, '[Heaven is a] place of endless praise and adoration, limitless abnegation and abjection of self; a celestial North Korea.'[12]

His critiques of religion extended beyond theological debates, touching on political and global affairs. He argued that religious fundamentalism played a significant role in conflicts and political strife, highlighting the dangers of unquestioning adherence to religious doctrines. Hitchens was particularly critical of the role of religion in American politics and the influence of religious extremism in international terrorism and human rights abuses. In his support of the American 'war on terror', he once said, 'Terrorism is the tactic of demanding the impossible, and demanding it at gunpoint.'[13]

Hitchens stuck to his views on religion till his last days. The deathbed conversion claims made in the book, *The Faith of Christopher Hitchens: The Restless Soul of the World's Most Notorious Atheist*, by Larry Alex Taunton[14] were entirely refuted by his son Alexander Hitchens, who said,

> I spent my father's final weeks and days at his bedside and watched him draw his final breath and die, and can assure you that there was no hint of any sort of conversion (as I'm sure you have already guessed). In fact, we barely spoke about religion at all except for joint expressions of frustration at the god botherers who made the rounds in the ICU and other units where dying people could be preyed upon by vulturous Christians.[15]

Daniel Dennett

Daniel Dennett was born in Boston, Massachusetts, on 28 March 1942. He received his bachelor's degree in philosophy from Harvard University in 1963 and his doctorate from the University of Oxford in 1965. Dennett has held various academic positions throughout his career, most notably as a philosophy professor and the co-director of the Center for Cognitive Studies at Tufts University.

Dennett's work has primarily focused on the philosophy of mind, cognitive science, and the nature of consciousness. He has authored numerous books, including *Content and Consciousness* (1969), *Brainstorms: Philosophical Essays on Mind and Psychology* (1978), *The Intentional Stance* (1987), *Consciousness Explained* (1991), *Darwin's Dangerous Idea* (1995), *Freedom Evolves* (2003), and *Breaking the Spell: Religion as a Natural Phenomenon* (2006).

Dennett strongly advocates naturalism,[16] the view that the natural world is all that exists and that there is no supernatural realm. This perspective is closely related to physicalism,[17] the idea that everything in the universe, including mental states and consciousness, can be reduced to physical processes or properties.

Dennett's naturalistic approach to the mind and consciousness has been influential in developing cognitive science and artificial intelligence. He has argued that mental states, such as beliefs, desires, and intentions, can be explained in terms of physical processes in the brain. This perspective has led him to develop his theories of intentionality and consciousness.

Intentionality and the Intentional Stance: Dennett's views on intentionality are rooted in his belief that mental states can be explained in terms of physical processes.

Intentionality is the property of mental states, such as beliefs and desires, to be about or represent something. For example, the idea that the Earth is round is about the Earth and its shape.

He proposes that we can understand the behaviour of complex systems, including humans and other animals, by adopting the 'intentional stance'.[18] The intentional stance involves treating the system as if it has beliefs, desires, and intentions and then predicting its behaviour based on these assumed mental states. By adopting the intentional stance, we can make accurate predictions about the behaviour of complex systems, even if we do not fully understand the underlying physical processes.

Dennett argues that the intentional stance is a useful explanatory tool but does not imply that mental states are anything more than physical states. He believes that our everyday concepts of beliefs, desires, and intentions help us understand and predict behaviour, but they ultimately reduce it to more fundamental physical processes.

Consciousness and the Multiple Drafts Model: Dennett's views on consciousness are also rooted in his naturalistic and physicalist perspective. In his book *Consciousness Explained*, Dennett presents the Multiple Drafts Model of consciousness, which aims to provide a naturalistic account of conscious experience.

The Multiple Drafts Model proposes that our conscious experience is not a single, unified, coherent stream but a collection of multiple, parallel, and often competing 'drafts' of reality. Various cognitive processes in the brain construct these drafts, and the interactions and competition between these drafts determine our conscious experience.

Dennett's model challenges the traditional view of consciousness as a unified and coherent experience, and it emphasises the role of the brain's cognitive processes in constructing our conscious experience. The Multiple Drafts Model supports Dennett's broader commitment to physicalism and naturalism by providing a naturalistic account of consciousness.

Dennett and Neo-atheism: Daniel Dennett's work has been influential in developing the neo-atheist movement, characterised by its aggressive critique of religious beliefs and its promotion of atheism as a rational and scientifically grounded worldview. In his book *Breaking the Spell: Religion as a Natural Phenomenon*, Dennett offers a comprehensive critique of religious beliefs and practices from a naturalistic perspective. He argues that religion is a natural phenomenon that can be studied and explained scientifically without recourse to supernatural explanations.

Dennett suggests that religious beliefs and practices have evolved through natural processes, such as cultural evolution and the cognitive mechanisms of the human mind. He proposes that religion has persisted throughout human history because it serves various social, psychological, and biological functions, such as promoting group cohesion, providing comfort in the face of uncertainty, and satisfying innate cognitive tendencies.

By explaining religion as a natural phenomenon, Dennett aims to challenge the privileged status often accorded to religious beliefs and to encourage a critical examination of their truth claims and moral implications. This approach aligns with the broader neo-atheist goal of promoting a rational, evidence-based worldview that does not rely on supernatural explanations.

Advocacy of Atheism: Dennett is an outspoken advocate of atheism, and he has consistently argued that a naturalistic and scientific understanding of the world is incompatible with belief in God or other supernatural entities. For example, in his book *Darwin's Dangerous Idea*, Dennett argues that the theory of evolution by natural selection provides a powerful explanation for the complexity and diversity of life on Earth, undermining the need for a supernatural designer or creator.

In addition to critiquing religious beliefs, Dennett has defended atheism as a morally and intellectually viable worldview. He has challenged the common stereotype that atheists are necessarily nihilistic, amoral, or lacking in meaning and purpose. Instead, Dennett argues that atheism can provide a solid foundation for morality, meaning, and purpose based on rationality, empathy, and a shared commitment to improving the human condition.

Impact on the Neo-atheist Movement: Daniel Dennett's work has significantly impacted the neo-atheist movement, both through his critiques of religion and his advocacy of atheism. His naturalistic approach to the study of religion and his emphasis on the explanatory power of science has helped to shape the intellectual landscape of the movement, providing a rigorous and evidence-based foundation for atheistic arguments.

Moreover, Dennett's work in the philosophy of mind and cognitive science has bolstered the case for a naturalistic understanding of consciousness and mental states, which is central to the neo-atheist rejection of supernatural explanations. By demonstrating that complex phenomena, such as intentionality and consciousness, can be explained in terms of physical processes, Dennett has provided a compelling case for the naturalistic worldview that underlies neo-atheism.

Finally, Dennett's public engagement and advocacy of atheism have contributed to the visibility and influence of the neo-atheist movement. As a prominent intellectual and public figure, Dennett has played a crucial role in popularising atheistic ideas and fostering a critical discourse around religion and its role in society.

Daniel Dennett has made substantial contributions to philosophy, cognitive science, and artificial intelligence, but his impact on the neo-atheist movement is his most enduring legacy. Through his critiques of religion and advocacy of a naturalistic, rational, and evidence-based worldview, Dennett has played a pivotal role in shaping neo-atheism's intellectual and cultural landscape. His work continues to inspire and inform those who seek to challenge religious dogma, promote secularism, and foster a greater appreciation for the power and beauty of the natural world.

Sam Harris

Sam Harris was born in Los Angeles, California, on 9 April 1967. He received a bachelor's degree in philosophy from Stanford University and a PhD in neuroscience from the University of California, Los Angeles. Harris is a prolific author, having written numerous books, including *The End of Faith* (2004), *Letter to a Christian Nation* (2006), *The Moral Landscape* (2010), *Free Will* (2012), *Waking Up: A Guide to Spirituality without Religion* (2014), and *Making Sense: Conversations on Consciousness, Morality, and the Future of Humanity* (2020).

In addition to his writing, Harris is the co-founder and chief executive of Project Reason. This non-profit organisation promotes secularism and the separation of religion and public policy. Harris also hosts the 'Making Sense' podcast,[19] discussing topics related to philosophy, religion, ethics, neuroscience, and current events.

Critique of Religion: Harris is an outspoken critic of religious beliefs and practices, arguing that they are irrational, harmful, and incompatible with a modern, secular worldview. In his book *The End of Faith*, Harris critiques the role of faith in society and argues that religious beliefs are unjustified and dangerous. He contends that faith, as a means of acquiring knowledge, is fundamentally flawed and that reliance on faith often leads to violence, intolerance, and the suppression of critical thinking.

One of Harris's critical arguments against religion is the problem of religious diversity. He points out numerous religious traditions worldwide, each claiming access to the truth about the nature of reality, morality, and salvation. Given the vast array of conflicting religious beliefs, Harris argues that it is improbable that any particular religion accurately represents reality. Instead, he posits that religious beliefs are primarily the product of cultural and historical factors rather than divine revelation or objective truth.

Secularism and Reason: Harris is a strong advocate of secularism, the view that religious beliefs should not influence public policy or state affairs. He argues that secularism is essential for promoting social cohesion, tolerance, and rational decision-making in a pluralistic society.

Harris emphasises the importance of reason and evidence-based thinking in place of religious faith. He contends that our understanding of the world should be grounded in empirical observation, scientific inquiry, and logical reasoning rather than religious dogma or tradition. Harris's commitment to reason and secularism is a central theme of his work and a core tenet of the neo-atheist movement.

Morality and the Moral Landscape: In his book *The Moral Landscape*, Harris addresses the question of morality from a secular perspective, arguing that moral truths can be grounded in the well-being of conscious creatures. Harris proposes that moral values can be objectively determined by reference to the facts about the experiences of conscious beings and that science can play a crucial role in helping us understand and promote well-being.

Harris's views on morality challenge the often-expressed concern that atheism leads to moral relativism or nihilism. By grounding moral values in objective facts about well-being, Harris offers a secular foundation for morality compatible with a rational, evidence-based worldview.

Neuroscience and Free Will: Harris's work in neuroscience has informed his views on consciousness and free will. In his book *Free Will*, Harris argues that the concept of free will is an illusion and that a complex interplay of genetic, environmental, and neural factors determines our actions and decisions.

Harris's position on free will has implications for our understanding of moral responsibility, agency, and the criminal justice system. By challenging the notion of free will, Harris encourages a more nuanced and compassionate approach to understanding human behaviour and addressing the root causes of social problems.

Harris and Neo-atheism: Sam Harris's work has been influential in developing the neo-atheist movement, characterised by its aggressive critique of religious beliefs and its promotion of atheism as a rational and scientifically grounded worldview. Harris's critiques of religion, advocacy of secularism, and work on morality and neuroscience have helped shape the movement's intellectual landscape and advance the case for a secular, rational worldview.

Critique of Religion: Harris's critiques of religion have played a significant role in defining the neo-atheist movement. His arguments against the rationality and morality of religious belief have resonated with many atheists and have helped to galvanise opposition to religious influence in public life. Harris's focus on the dangers of faith and the problem of religious diversity has provided intellectual ammunition for the neo-atheist critique of religion. At the same time, his emphasis on secularism and reason has offered a positive alternative to religious faith.

As a prominent public intellectual, Harris has helped elevate the neo-atheist movement's profile and bring its ideas into mainstream discourse. Harris has reached a broad audience through his books, articles, podcasts, and public appearances. He has engaged in numerous high-profile debates and discussions on religion, atheism, and secularism. His willingness to engage with religious believers and to defend the neo-atheist position in public fora has contributed to the visibility and credibility of the movement.

Harris's background in philosophy and neuroscience has enabled him to bridge the gap between the scientific and philosophical aspects of the neo-atheist movement. His work on morality and free will, in particular, has demonstrated the potential for a fruitful dialogue between science and philosophy and has provided a model for other thinkers within the movement to follow. Harris's interdisciplinary approach has broadened the neo-atheist movement's scope and helped create a more robust and intellectually diverse foundation for its ideas.

While Harris has influenced the neo-atheist movement, his work has also been the subject of numerous criticisms and controversies. Some critics have accused Harris of an overly simplistic critique of religion, arguing that he fails to appreciate the diversity and complexity of religious beliefs and practices. Others have taken issue with his views on morality, arguing that his conception of well-being is too vague or subjective to provide a firm foundation for objective moral truths.

Harris has also faced criticism for his views on Islam, which some have characterised as Islamophobic or overly hostile. Harris has argued that Islam, as a religious and political system, poses unique challenges to secularism and human rights. It is essential to criticise and reform the more problematic aspects of the religion. However, some critics argue that his focus on Islam is disproportionate or unfairly singles out the religion for criticism.

Sam Harris's contributions to the neo-atheist movement have been significant and wide-ranging. Through his critiques of religion, advocacy of secularism and reason, and work on morality and neuroscience, Harris has helped to shape the intellectual landscape of the movement and to advance the case for a secular, rational worldview. While his work has not been without controversy, Harris's influence on the neo-atheist movement is undeniable, and his ideas will continue to inform and provoke debate for years to come.

Dennett and Harris would make up for the cerebral and sophisticated side of the neo-atheist movement if Dawkins and Hitchens were its more intellectually outspoken and muscular representatives. Neo-atheism has emerged as possibly one of the most influential movements of the past four decades, thanks to the contributions of these four intellectual titans.

The Successes of Neo-atheism

As I sit in a cosy café in a small town in Canada in 2023, sipping on my iced mocha latte, I find myself contemplating the successes of neo-atheism and the journey it has taken over the years. The ambient sounds of conversations and clinking cups provide a soothing background as I gather my thoughts to write this chapter. It's fascinating to think about how the landscape of religious beliefs and discourse has evolved, particularly in the West. I cannot help but wonder if this book would have been possible in 1950. The world was different back then, with its challenges and limitations.

In the mid-20th century, openly discussing atheism and challenging religious dogma would have faced considerable resistance. The West had a record of arresting people for expressing atheistic views or criticising religious institutions and their beliefs.[20] When the free speech movement began in the 1960s and gathered steam over the following decades, such conversations became more acceptable and were even encouraged in some circles.[21]

Neo-atheism rode this wave of cultural and societal change, and its successes can be seen as a testament to the power of free speech and open inquiry. As an Indian author looking at the West from the vantage point of a small Canadian town, I cannot help but acknowledge that if it weren't for the sacrifices made by people in the past, I would not be writing this book today.

The free speech movement originated in the United States and was a reaction against the repression of dissenting voices during the Cold War era. This movement helped pave the way for the rise of neo-atheism, as it provided the necessary cultural and social environment in which critical examination of religious beliefs and institutions could flourish. The works of prominent neo-atheists such as Richard Dawkins, Christopher Hitchens, Daniel Dennett, and Sam Harris would likely have faced severe backlash and possible legal consequences if published in the 1950s.

The sacrifices made by the early champions of free speech, such as the American Civil Liberties Union

(ACLU), which fought for the right to express unpopular opinions and ideas, laid the groundwork for the success of neo-atheism.[22] The ACLU's efforts in landmark cases, such as New York Times Co. v. Sullivan[23] and Tinker v. Des Moines Independent Community School District,[24] helped establish the legal framework that protects free speech and expression in the United States and influenced other Western countries as well.

The Decline of Religious Beliefs and the Rise of Secularism and Its Impact on Religious Institutions and Societal Attitudes

The emergence of neo-atheism has significantly influenced the decline of religious beliefs and the rise of secularism. Neo-atheism, a movement characterised by its vocal and public criticism of religious beliefs and institutions, has contributed to a shift in societal attitudes towards religion and has played a vital role in the growth of secularism.

One of the key factors contributing to the decline of religious beliefs in the Western world is the increased scepticism and critical examination of religious doctrines and practices. This scepticism has been fuelled mainly by the works of The Four Horsemen of Neo-atheism. These authors have written extensively on the inconsistencies and fallacies within religious texts and have encouraged readers to question the validity of religious beliefs. As Dawkins states in his book *The God Delusion*, 'The God of the Old Testament is arguably the most unpleasant character in all fiction,'[25] showcasing the level of scrutiny given to religious texts by neo-atheists.

This critical examination of religious beliefs has contributed to the decline of religious affiliation, particularly in Western countries. According to the Pew

Research Center,[26] the number of religiously unaffiliated
individuals in the United States has been steadily
increasing, with 26 per cent of the population identifying
as atheist, agnostic, or having no particular religion
in 2019. A similar trend has been observed in Western
countries, such as the United Kingdom and Australia.
While it is difficult to attribute this trend solely to the
rise of neo-atheism, it is evident that the movement has
shaped public opinion and attitudes towards religion.

As religious beliefs have declined, secularism has
gained traction in Western societies. Secularism, broadly
defined as the separation of religion from public life, has
been influenced by neo-atheist authors' philosophical and
moral arguments. For example, Harris argues in his book
The End of Faith that religious beliefs are an impediment
to reason and logic: 'Either God can do nothing to stop
catastrophes like this, or he does not care to, or he is
oblivious. God is either impotent, evil, or imaginary. Take
your pick, and choose wisely.' By presenting a rational
critique of religious beliefs, neo-atheists have encouraged
the adoption of secular perspectives on morality, ethics,
and public policy.

Moreover, secularism has been bolstered by the rise of
scientific understanding and the growing awareness of the
naturalistic explanations for phenomena previously
attributed to divine intervention. Neo-atheist authors
such as Dawkins and Dennett have argued that
advancements in biology, cosmology, and neuroscience
have rendered religious explanations for the origins of life
and the universe obsolete. Dawkins writes, 'Darwinian
natural selection, by providing a plausible explanation for
the existence of living complexity, raises our confidence
that we shall ultimately be able to understand the
whole universe in terms of rational, testable theories.'

This emphasis on scientific inquiry and naturalistic explanations has contributed to the rise of secularism and the decline of religious beliefs.

Another factor contributing to the decline of religious beliefs and the rise of secularism is the increasing emphasis on individual autonomy and personal freedom in Western societies. The secular ideal of the separation of church and state has been instrumental in protecting individual rights, particularly the freedom of speech and religion. As a result, individuals have been increasingly free to explore a variety of beliefs and ideologies, including atheism and agnosticism. Neo-atheism has been at the forefront of this shift, with authors like Hitchens advocating for the importance of individual liberty and the rejection of religious dogma: 'There is no need for us to gather every day or every seven days or on any high and auspicious day to proclaim our rectitude or to grovel and wallow in our unworthiness.'[27]

Historically, religious institutions have significantly shaped societal norms, values, and public policy.[28] However, religious institutions have seen their influence wane as secularism has gained traction. According to Taylor in his book *A Secular Age*, 'The place of religion in our collective lives has been transformed several times in the last few centuries, and each of these transformations has involved a change in the place of the churches.'[29] This decline in social influence has compelled religious institutions to adapt and evolve to maintain their relevance in the public sphere.

Religious institutions have faced increased scrutiny and criticism from neo-atheist authors and activists, so they have been compelled to adapt and evolve in response to these challenges. In some cases, this has led to a reformation of religious doctrines and practices and a renewed emphasis on social justice and community engagement. Norris and Inglehart, in *Sacred and Secular: Religion and Politics Worldwide*, argue, 'The churches that are most capable of adapting to changing cultural values are those that are more flexible in their organizational structures and doctrinal beliefs.'[30] This shift towards more progressive and inclusive religious institutions has contributed to the rise of secularism, as individuals who may have previously felt alienated or marginalised by traditional religious beliefs and practices find solace in these reformed institutions.

As individuals have been exposed to a broader range of religious beliefs and practices, they have become more accepting of religious diversity and more open to interfaith dialogue.[31] As secularism has gained traction, individuals have become more supportive of the idea that religion should be kept separate from public life and policy-making.[32] Individuals have moved away from traditional religious beliefs and increasingly turned to secular humanism and other non-religious frameworks to guide their ethical decision-making.[33] According to Grayling in his book, *The God Argument: The Case against Religion and for Humanism*, 'Secular ethics has its roots in the great tradition of moral inquiry that runs from Socrates to the present day, and which seeks to provide a rational basis for our moral judgments.'[34]

This trend has been bolstered as the internet has provided a platform for neo-atheist thinkers and activists to share their ideas with a global audience, allowing for the rapid and widespread dissemination of their arguments and critiques of religion. In particular, websites, forums, and online communities dedicated to atheism and secularism have enabled atheists to engage in discussions, debates, and collaborative projects, fostering a sense of community and shared identity among atheists worldwide.[35]

Social media platforms, such as Facebook, X, and YouTube, have played a particularly significant role in propagating neo-atheist ideas. These platforms allow for the rapid and widespread sharing of content, including articles, videos, and memes, which can quickly reach millions of users. According to a study by the Pew Research Center (2016), 'More than two-thirds of Americans now get at least some of their news from social media platforms, with younger adults being especially likely to rely on social media for news.'[36] The ease with which individuals can access and share content on social media has facilitated the spread of neo-atheist ideas, as users can quickly and easily disseminate critiques of religion and engage in discussions and debates with others.

The role of social media in propagating neo-atheist ideas has also been demonstrated through the success of various online campaigns and initiatives. For example, the annual International Blasphemy Rights Day, which aims to promote free expression and raise awareness of the importance of secularism, has gained considerable traction on social media platforms, with users sharing content in support of the campaign and engaging in discussions and debates about the role of religion in public life.[37]

Furthermore, the internet and social media have played a crucial role in forming and mobilising atheist and secularist organisations and activist groups. Online platforms like The Atheist Republic[38] have enabled these groups to coordinate efforts, share information, and mobilise supporters, fostering a sense of collective identity and purpose among atheists and secularists worldwide.

Furthermore, the rise of secularism has been facilitated by an increased focus on secular humanism and the promotion of empathy, compassion, and reason as the basis for ethical decision-making. Neo-atheist authors such as Sam Harris argue that secular humanism provides a more reliable and practical foundation for morality and ethics than religious beliefs, as it is grounded in principles that can be universally agreed upon and tested rather than relying on divine revelation or dogma. This focus on secular humanism has resonated with many individuals, leading to increased support for secularist ideals and a decline in religious affiliation.

In conclusion, the decline of religious beliefs and the rise of secularism can be partly attributed to neo-atheism's influence. The critical examination of religious doctrines and institutions, the promotion of secular humanism and scientific inquiry, and their rapid spread because of the internet have contributed to a shift in societal attitudes towards religion and the growth of secularist ideals. While it is difficult to determine the extent to which neo-atheism has directly impacted religious affiliation and secularism, it is clear that the movement has played a significant role in shaping public opinion and religious institutions' evolution.

The Impact of Neo-atheism on the Muslim World

With its diverse cultures and societies, the Muslim world has experienced a rise in atheism and secularism in recent years. This growth of atheist and secular communities in Muslim-majority countries has been facilitated by various factors, including the internet and social media, allowing like-minded individuals to connect and share their thoughts and experiences. However, the challenges faced by atheists and secularists in the Muslim world are numerous, ranging from legal restrictions and social stigma to the risk of persecution and violence.

In recent years, there has been a noticeable increase in the number of atheists and secularists in Muslim-majority countries. A 2012 WIN-Gallup International poll revealed that the number of self-identified atheists in the Arab world had increased from 8 per cent in 2005 to 14 per cent in 2012, while the number of non-religious individuals had risen from 16 per cent to 24 per cent.[39] In countries like Saudi Arabia, a 2012 survey found that 5 per cent of respondents identified as atheists.[40] This growth has led to various online and offline atheist and secular communities in Muslim-majority countries.

The reasons for this increase in atheism and secularism are multifaceted and complex. Some individuals turn away from religion due to personal experiences or intellectual questioning, while the socio-political environment influences others in their countries. For instance, the rise of political Islam and religious conservatism in some regions may have led to disillusionment and a desire for a more secular society.

The internet and social media have connected atheists and secularists in the Muslim world. In countries where openly expressing atheistic or secular views can be dangerous, the anonymity offered by the internet provides a relatively safe space for individuals to share their thoughts, experiences, and doubts. Online communities, such as Facebook groups, blogs, and forums, have become hubs for atheists and secularists to connect, discuss their views, and offer support.

In addition, the Internet has provided access to a wealth of information and resources previously unavailable to many individuals in Muslim-majority countries. This has enabled them to explore different philosophical and theological perspectives, leading some to question their religious beliefs and embrace atheism or secularism.

Richard Dawkins's book *The God Delusion* was translated
into Arabic by Iraqi translator Bassam Al-Baghdadi. It is
reported by some atheist forums that 'its pdf version has
also been downloaded 10 million times, with at least 30
per cent of all downloads being made in Saudi Arabia'.[41]

Despite the growth of atheist and secular communities
in Muslim-majority countries, these individuals continue
to face numerous challenges, both legally and socially.

In many Muslim-majority countries, apostasy (the act
of leaving one's religion) and blasphemy (speech or actions
deemed disrespectful to religious beliefs) are criminalised,
with punishments ranging from fines and imprisonment to
the death penalty. These legal restrictions make it difficult
for atheists and secularists to openly express their views,
leading many to self-censorship or conceal their true
beliefs to avoid persecution.

In addition to legal challenges, atheists and secularists
face social stigma and discrimination in the Muslim world.
The societal expectation to adhere to religious norms and
practices can be overwhelming, and those who deviate
from these norms may be ostracised or even disowned by
their families and communities.

A 2013 study conducted by the Pew Research Center
found that 88 per cent of Muslims in Egypt and 62 per
cent in Pakistan believed that leaving Islam should be
punishable by death.[42] This demonstrates the extent to
which apostasy is considered taboo and the pressure on
individuals to conform to religious expectations.

Atheists and secularists in Muslim-majority countries
also face the risk of persecution and violence. In some
cases, individuals have been targeted by vigilante groups
or even their family members for openly expressing
their atheistic or secular views. A prominent example is
the Bangladeshi blogger Avijit Roy, who was brutally

murdered in 2015 by Islamic extremists for his writings on atheism and secularism.[43]

Despite the numerous challenges atheists and secularists face in the Muslim world, there is potential for future change and growth. As the internet and social media connect like-minded individuals and provide access to diverse perspectives, more people may be encouraged to question their religious beliefs and explore alternative worldviews.

Furthermore, the growth of atheist and secular communities in Muslim-majority countries has the potential to challenge the societal norms and expectations surrounding religion. As these communities become more visible and vocal, they can help to create a space for open dialogue and critical discussion about the role of religion in society.

There is also evidence that attitudes towards atheism and secularism slowly evolve in certain regions. A 2016 study by the Arab Barometer found that support for implementing Sharia law had decreased in several countries, including Egypt, Morocco, and Jordan.[44] This suggests that there may be a growing acceptance of more secular values in some parts of the Muslim world.

The ex-Muslim movement is a growing phenomenon in the Muslim world, particularly in recent years, as more individuals have begun to leave Islam and adopt atheist or secular beliefs. This movement represents the continuation of the legacy of neo-atheism in the Muslim world, as it seeks to create a safe space for those who have left the faith while also challenging societal norms and expectations surrounding religion.

One of the earliest and most prominent examples of such a community is the Council of Ex-Muslims of Britain (CEMB),[45] founded in 2007 by Iranian-born human rights activist Maryam Namazie and other ex-Muslims living in the UK. The CEMB was formed to provide a support network for individuals who have left Islam and challenge the stigma and discrimination apostates face in Muslim-majority countries and communities.

Following the establishment of the CEMB, similar organisations and communities began to emerge in other countries, including the United States, Canada, Germany, and Australia. These groups have adopted the term 'ex-Muslim' as a self-identifier, signifying their rejection of Islam and solidarity with others who have undergone a similar journey.

In conclusion, the impact of neo-atheism on the Muslim world is multifaceted and complex. While the internet and social media have facilitated the growth of atheist and secular communities, these individuals continue to face numerous challenges, including legal restrictions, social stigma, and the risk of persecution and violence. Nevertheless, the potential for future change and growth exists as more individuals question their religious beliefs and explore alternative worldviews. For this potential to be realised, however, there must be a concerted effort to address the challenges faced by atheists and secularists and promote greater tolerance and understanding within the Muslim world.

Neo-atheism's Victory Was the Loss of Atheism

Neo-atheism, led by its prominent atheists, advocated for a secular, rationalist worldview and the rejection of religious dogma. However, it is essential to recognise that every policy decision or movement has second-order effects that are often overlooked. In the case of neo-atheism, some argue that it has inadvertently contributed to the rise of Atheism+ and 'wokeism', resulting in unintended societal consequences.

Neo-atheism initially arose with noble intentions, seeking to challenge the negative aspects of religious belief and promote reason and critical thinking. However, critics argue that in its zeal to combat religious dogma, neo-atheism may have 'thrown the baby out with the bathwater', discarding the positive aspects of religion and leaving behind a societal vacuum. This vacuum led to the emergence of Atheism+, a movement that aimed to address the perceived shortcomings of traditional atheism.

Atheism+ sought to incorporate social justice, feminism, and other progressive issues into the atheist discourse, departing from traditional atheism's focus on the non-existence of deities.[46] As religion often provides a sense of meaning and purpose, some individuals who embraced atheism turned to these progressive issues to find meaning in their lives. By incorporating social justice, feminism, and other progressive issues into its framework, Atheism+ aimed to create a more inclusive and morally engaged atheist community.[47]

The rise of wokeism, a term used to describe an increased awareness of and commitment to social justice issues, can be seen as a by-product of the shift towards Atheism+. Wokeism is a child of neo-atheism, resulting from a one-night stand that produced a new generation of activists seeking meaning in a post-religious world. Social media has played a significant role in the spread of wokeism, providing a platform for activists to share their ideas and connect with like-minded individuals.[48]

Wokeism represents a broader cultural trend that emphasises social justice and activism. With its roots in the civil rights movement, wokeism has evolved to encompass various issues, from racial and gender equality

to LGBTQ+ rights and environmental justice.[49] Some
argue that the rise of wokeism can be linked to the decline
of traditional religious institutions and the search for new
sources of meaning and community in a secular world.[50]

However, this shift in focus has yet to be universally
embraced, with some critics arguing that Atheism+ has
strayed too far from its original purpose and become
overly politicised. As individuals turn away from religion,
they may be drawn to secular movements that offer a
sense of purpose and moral guidance, such as wokeism
and Atheism+.

However, both Atheism+ and wokeism have faced
criticism for their perceived dogmatism and intolerance.
Opponents argue that these movements can sometimes
resemble the religious dogmas they claim to reject, with
rigid adherence to certain beliefs and the suppression of
dissenting voices. Jonathan Haidt and Greg Lukianoff,
in their book *The Coddling of the American Mind: How Good
Intentions and Bad Ideas Are Setting Up a Generation for
Failure*[51] have explained how the culture of safetyism,
which prioritises emotional and psychological safety, can
lead to an overemphasis on microaggressions—small,
unintentional slights that some individuals can perceive
as harmful. They suggest that constantly focusing on
microaggressions can create a hostile environment
and perpetuate a victim mentality, undermining young
people's resilience and emotional well-being.

They criticise trigger warnings, which alert people
to potentially distressing content, arguing that they
can contribute to a culture of overprotection and
limit exposure to challenging ideas. They also express
concerns about the increasing demand for censorship on
college campuses, which they argue can stifle intellectual
diversity and critical thinking.

While the authors acknowledge the importance of recognising social identities and systemic inequalities, they argue that an excessive focus on identity politics and intersectionality can lead to the formation of 'us versus them' mentalities and exacerbate social divides. They advocate for a more nuanced approach to social justice that transcends identity-based divisions and encourages empathy and understanding.

Lukianoff and Haidt express concerns about the rise of 'cancel culture', in which individuals or groups are publicly shamed or ostracised for perceived transgressions, often related to social justice issues. They argue that this phenomenon can create fear and self-censorship, stifling open dialogue and intellectual diversity. This has led to concerns about the potential erosion of free speech and intellectual diversity in the name of social justice and progressive values.

Another brilliant analysis of the quasi-religious nature of wokeism is by John McWhorter's book *Woke Racism: How a New Religion Has Betrayed Black America*.[52] McWhorter critiques the contemporary social justice movement, specifically focusing on how it intersects with race and racial issues in the United States. McWhorter, a linguist and social critic, argues that 'wokeism' is counterproductive in addressing racial inequality.

The book explains how wokeism often emphasises victimhood and systemic oppression, which McWhorter believes can distract from more constructive approaches to addressing racial inequality. McWhorter's central argument is that wokeism, despite its intentions, ultimately betrays Black America by promoting division and focusing on superficial issues rather than substantive solutions to systemic racial inequality.

The intensity of debates around neo-atheism, Atheism+, and wokeism has contributed to increased societal polarisation and division. People with opposing views are becoming more entrenched in their positions, leading to increased hostility and decreased opportunities for constructive dialogue. As progressive values gain prominence, institutions such as universities, corporations, and government agencies may prioritise diversity and inclusion initiatives. While this can lead to positive changes, it may also result in concerns about overreach, the suppression of intellectual diversity, and the potential for tokenism. The rise of Atheism+ and wokeism may impact policymaking as politicians and decision-makers respond to the demands of these movements. Policies may be implemented to address social justice issues, but they may also face criticism for being overly ideological or prioritising certain groups over others. The debate surrounding affirmative action in America is a perfect example of a policy that has led all sides to harden their stand after the Supreme Court ruling in favour of the Students for Fair Admissions in their case against Harvard and the University of North Carolina Chapel Hill.[53]

In conclusion, while neo-atheism began with laudable intentions, it has arguably given rise to unintended consequences, including Atheism+ and wokeism. By discarding the positive aspects of religion and leaving a societal void, neo-atheism may have inadvertently paved the way for a new generation of activists seeking meaning in secular progressive causes. While these movements have gained significant traction in recent years, they have also been criticised and concerned, highlighting the complexity of the relationship between atheism, religion, and social justice.

Addressing concerns about dogmatism and intolerance in movements like Atheism+, wokeism requires a multifaceted approach that promotes open dialogue, critical thinking, and empathy.

Here Are Some Potential Solutions

Promote Open Dialogue and Civil Discourse

Many thinkers emphasise the importance of engaging in open and honest conversations about controversial topics, including social justice, identity politics, and religion. By fostering a culture of civil discourse, we can better understand different perspectives and find common ground.

Encourage intellectual diversity and critical thinking: To counteract dogmatism and ideological rigidity, promoting intellectual diversity and critical thinking is essential. We can better evaluate and refine our beliefs by exposing ourselves to a wide range of ideas and perspectives.

Focus on Shared Values and Common Goals

Instead of concentrating on what divides us, it's essential to recognise our shared values and common goals. By emphasising humanism, empathy, and cooperation, we can work together to address the pressing issues that affect us all.

Defend Individual Freedoms and Autonomy

These thinkers often advocate for protecting personal freedoms and autonomy, including free speech, freedom of thought, and freedom from coercion. By defending these values, we can help create a society where diverse ideas can coexist and flourish.

Critique Ideas, Not People

To foster a more constructive and inclusive environment, it's essential to separate ideas from the people who hold them. By critiquing ideas rather than attacking individuals, we can engage in more productive conversations and avoid the pitfalls of ad hominem arguments and cancel culture.

Advocate for Evidence-based Policies and Solutions

Many thinkers emphasise the importance of evidence-based reasoning and the scientific method. By advocating for policies and solutions grounded in empirical evidence, we can more effectively address the challenges we face as a society.

Ultimately, tackling wokeism and Atheism+ involves fostering a culture of open dialogue, intellectual diversity, and critical thinking. By engaging with different perspectives, defending individual freedoms, and focusing on shared values and evidence-based solutions, we can work together to create a more inclusive, tolerant, and productive society. Implementing these strategies may address concerns about dogmatism and intolerance in movements like Atheism+ and wokeism.

3

Why Religion Is Good and Bad but Inevitable

Religion is a profoundly complex and multifaceted phenomenon that has been integral to human society since prehistoric times. Despite its ubiquity and significance, there has yet to be a consensus on a single definition of religion within the social sciences. This is primarily due to the vast diversity of religious beliefs, practices, and structures across different cultures and historical periods.

Some definitions focus on the belief aspect of religion. For instance, Emile Durkheim, a founding figure in sociology, defined religion as a unified system of beliefs and practices relative to sacred things.[1] This definition emphasises the idea of the sacred or supernatural, which is often associated with religion.

Another approach is the functionalist definition, which focuses on the role of religion in society. For instance, the renowned anthropologist Clifford Geertz defined religion as a system of symbols that establishes powerful, pervasive, and long-lasting moods and motivations in men by formulating conceptions of a general order of existence.[2] This definition highlights the role of religion in providing a framework for understanding the world and guiding human action.

However, these definitions have been critiqued for their Abrahamic bias, as they often reflect characteristics of monotheistic religions like Christianity, Judaism, and Islam. S.N. Balagangadhara, in his book *Heathen in His Blindness*,[3] argues that this bias has led to a skewed understanding of other 'religious' traditions, particularly those of India.

Balagangadhara posits that what we classify as 'religion' in India is not a religion like the Abrahamic traditions. The Indian traditions did not have a central authoritative text, a defined moral code, or an institutional structure, often seen as representing features of 'religion' in the Abrahamic sense. Instead, these traditions were diverse practices and beliefs intertwined with the broader culture, philosophy, and societal norms.

Balagangadhara further argues that this misclassification has led to the imposition of a Western religious model onto Indian cultural traditions, which can result in misunderstanding and misinterpretation. He suggests that a more fruitful approach would be understanding these traditions on their terms rather than trying to fit them into a preconceived category of 'religion'.

S.N. Balagangadhara's book *Cultures Differ Differently*[4] discusses the nature of religious and spiritual experiences, their differences, and their interpretations in different cultural contexts. He also contrasts the goals and experiences of Indian traditions with those of Abrahamic religions like Christianity. He posits that while the Abrahamic religions are indeed religions, Indian traditions like Hinduism, Buddhism, and Jainism do not fit into the same category. This is because the goal of Indian traditions is enlightenment, a fundamentally different experience from the religious or spiritual experiences in Christianity.

Enlightenment in Indian traditions involves radically reorganising one's experience and understanding of daily life. It restores the past path but doesn't dictate any specific direction for the future. The individual is left to act thoughtfully and develop his insight further.

He also discusses the role of breakdowns in religious experiences. He believes Christian traditions are more likely to induce breakdowns than Indian traditions. The Indian traditions, according to him, guide individuals towards enlightenment without causing such experiences.

Balagangadhara's interjections, while necessary, may only partially be accurate. His argument heavily relies on the goal of enlightenment as a distinguishing factor between Indian traditions and Abrahamic religions. However, this perspective needs to be more balanced with the complex, multifaceted nature of both sets of traditions. Abrahamic religions also have mystical traditions where enlightenment or direct experience of the divine is a central goal (e.g., Christian mysticism, Jewish Kabbalah, or Sufism in Islam).[5] Similarly, not all practitioners of Indian traditions seek enlightenment as their primary spiritual goal.

Labelling all Indian traditions as not being religions tends to ignore the vast diversity within these traditions. For instance, Hinduism is incredibly diverse, with various sects and philosophical schools with different beliefs, practices, and goals.[6] Some of these schools align closely with what is typically understood as 'religion'. So, to say India does not have a 'religion' as it is understood in social sciences is not entirely accurate.[7]

Some might even argue that Balagangadhara's argument ignores that religion is a universal human phenomenon that takes different forms in different cultural contexts. It appears to selectively interpret Abrahamic religions as primarily God-centric, thereby contrasting them with the enlightenment-focused

Indian traditions. This overlooks the rich and diverse traditions of mysticism and personal transformation within Christianity, Judaism, and Islam.[8] His claim that Indian traditions do not induce nervous breakdowns like Christian traditions is hard to substantiate without comprehensive comparative studies. Works like *Varieties of Religious Experience* by William James[9] may also provide a broader and more empirical exploration of religious experiences across different religions.

The significance of religion in human society is undeniable. Since prehistoric times, religion has been a means for humans to understand and interpret the world around them, find meaning and purpose in life, and establish moral and social order. Religious rituals and beliefs have often fostered social cohesion and cooperation, while religious narratives have provided a framework for understanding life, death, and the cosmos.

However, as Balagangadhara's work highlights, it's essential not to lose sight of the diversity and complexity of 'religious' phenomena across different cultures and historical periods. Recognising the limitations and biases of our definitions can help us better understand and appreciate this diversity.

The Evolutionary Origins of Religion

In attempting to decipher the evolutionary origins of religion, researchers have drawn from a vast array of disciplines, including anthropology, sociology, psychology, and biology. To begin with, we will specifically explore the perspectives within evolutionary biology and psychology to understand the emergence and persistence of religious beliefs and behaviours in human societies.

Evolutionary Biology: The Role of Natural Selection

In his seminal work *On the Origin of Species*, Charles Darwin proposed the theory of natural selection as the primary mechanism of evolution.[10] According to this theory, traits that enhance an organism's survival or reproductive success will, over time, become more prevalent within a population. Applied to the study of religion, some researchers argue that religious beliefs and behaviours were positively selected because they conferred certain adaptive advantages.[11]

One possibility is that religion promotes social cohesion and cooperation. This idea is intimately connected to the concept of 'group selection'. Darwin suggested that groups where individuals were willing to sacrifice for the common good would be more successful than groups of purely self-interested individuals.[12] Religion, with its moral codes and communal rituals, may foster such cooperation, enhancing the survival and reproductive success of the group.[13]

A second hypothesis is that religion acts as a mechanism for reducing existential anxiety and uncertainty.[14] The unpredictable nature of the environment led to the evolution of cognitive tools for detecting patterns and inferring agency, even where none exists.[15] This 'hyperactive agency detection' could have led to beliefs in supernatural agents.

Evolutionary Psychology: Religion as a By-product

While evolutionary biology focuses on the adaptive value of traits, evolutionary psychology often emphasises the by-product or spandrel view of religion. This perspective suggests that religious beliefs and behaviours are not adaptations but by-products of other cognitive and emotional mechanisms shaped by natural selection for other purposes.[16]

One central argument in this perspective is the 'theory of mind' hypothesis. Humans possess a unique cognitive ability to infer the mental states of others, which allows us to predict and explain their behaviours.[17] This capacity might have been co-opted for religious purposes, leading to beliefs in supernatural beings with minds that can be known and influenced.[18]

The 'ritual' aspect of religion could also be viewed as a by-product of our evolved cognitive capacities. Boyer and Liénard[19] argue that ritualised behaviours might be an outgrowth of our evolved precautionary systems designed to avoid danger and contamination.

Cognitive Contagion

The concept of 'cognitive contagion' is rooted in cognitive science and social psychology and has been applied to understand the spread of religious beliefs and practices.

The term 'cognitive contagion' refers to the tendency for specific ideas or behaviours to spread within a group or population, much like a virus. This phenomenon is closely related to the concept of memes, as introduced by Richard Dawkins in his book *The Selfish Gene*.[20] Dawkins used the term 'meme' to describe a unit of cultural transmission or a unit of imitation. Just as genes propagate themselves by leaping from body to body via sperm or eggs, memes propagate themselves by leaping from brain to brain via a process which, in the broad sense, can be called imitation.

Cognitive contagion could explain how specific religious ideas or practices spread and persist over time. Various factors may make some religious beliefs or practices more 'contagious' than others. For example, religious ideas that provide comfort in the face of uncertainty or fear or promote social cohesion and cooperation could be more likely to be adopted and passed on.

This concept also relates to the 'minimally counterintuitive' (MCI) hypothesis proposed by Pascal Boyer and others.[21] This hypothesis suggests that religious ideas that violate our intuitive expectations in minimal ways are particularly memorable and, thus, more likely to be transmitted. For example, a god that can see everything but is otherwise human-like is minimally counterintuitive. Such a concept might spread more effectively than a god with hundreds of eyes and who speaks in a language only understood by frogs, which is counterintuitive.

The concept of cognitive contagion has significant implications for understanding the spread of religious beliefs and practices in modern times. In an era of rapid and expansive information exchange, cognitive contagion can occur on an unprecedented scale.

Social media platforms, for instance, can serve as prime mediums for disseminating religious memes. A religious idea or practice that resonates with people can quickly go viral, spreading across geographical and cultural boundaries.[22] This process can lead to the rapid proliferation of new religious movements or the revitalisation of traditional ones.

Moreover, cognitive contagion can also explain the popularity of certain religious narratives or rituals. For example, narratives that provide a sense of purpose or identity or address existential anxieties may be particularly 'contagious'. Similarly, traditions that foster social cohesion or that give a sense of control over uncertain circumstances can also be more likely to spread.[23]

However, it's important to note that cognitive contagion is not a deterministic process. Not all religious ideas or practices that are spread will be adopted. The likelihood of adoption can be influenced by various factors, including the social and cultural context, the personal experiences and predispositions of the individuals exposed to the idea or practice, and the nature of the concept or practice itself.

In conclusion, cognitive contagion provides a valuable framework for understanding the spread of religious beliefs and practices in modern times. It highlights the dynamic and complex interplay between individual cognition, social interaction, and cultural context in shaping religious landscapes. It provides a mechanism by which religious beliefs and practices can spread within and between societies, contributing to the evolution and persistence of religion.

Costly Signalling Theory

The origin of religion is a complex and multifaceted topic, often approached from various disciplinary perspectives, including anthropology, psychology, and sociology. One prominent theory that has gained traction in recent years is the Costly Signalling theory, which provides a fascinating lens through which to view religious origins.

As we understand it today, religion is thought to have emerged around the Upper Paleolithic period, approximately 50,000 years ago.[24] This timing coincides with a surge in symbolic behaviour among *Homo sapiens*, reflected in the increased production of art, ritual burials, and other forms of symbolic expression. The exact reasons behind this surge remain hotly debated. Still, many scholars argue that developing complex social structures and the cognitive capacity for symbolic thought played a key role.[25]

The Costly Signalling theory, also known as the 'handicap principle', was first proposed by Amotz Zahavi in the context of animal behaviour.[26] The theory suggests that animals often engage in costly behaviours in terms of energy, time, or risk to prove their fitness to potential mates or rivals. It's a way of demonstrating strength by taking on a handicap, thereby signalling trustworthiness and reliability.

When applied to religion, the Costly Signalling theory suggests that religious behaviours—such as ritualistic practices, fasting, or giving away possessions—serve as signals of commitment to the group.[27] Individuals demonstrate loyalty and dedication by engaging in these costly behaviours, increasing their social capital.[28]

Various ethnographic and historical studies support this theory. For instance, Sosis and Alcorta found that religious communes tend to last longer than secular ones, possibly because demanding religious practices serve to weed out less committed members.[29] Similarly, Irons (2001) argues that the costly requirements of religious practices serve as a reliable indicator of an individual's commitment to the group.

According to the Costly Signalling theory, religion can be seen as an evolutionary adaptation that helped our ancestors navigate increasingly complex social landscapes. By providing a framework for costly signalling, religion might have helped to foster social cohesion, maintain cooperation, and manage social conflicts in large, kin-less groups.[30] This is in line with the broader perspective of 'cultural group selection', which posits that cultural traits (including religious beliefs and practices) that enhance group cohesion and cooperation can be favoured by natural selection.[31]

While the origins of religion are undoubtedly complex, the Costly Signalling theory provides a compelling perspective on why religious behaviours might have evolved. By serving as a medium for costly signalling, religion could have played a crucial role in promoting social cohesion and cooperation, thus contributing to the survival and proliferation of human societies.

However, it is crucial to remember that this is just one of the many theories regarding the origins of religion. Further research is necessary to fully understand the complex interplay of factors that led to the emergence and evolution of religious behaviours.

A Memetics Perspective

One provocative perspective on the origin of religion comes from the field of memetics, which views religion as a complex of 'memes' — ideas or behaviours that spread from person to person within a culture. This perspective provides a unique lens on the development and persistence of religious beliefs and practices.

The concept of memes was first proposed by Richard Dawkins in *The Selfish Gene* to explain how cultural information spreads.[32] Memes are akin to genes in replicating, mutating, and responding to selective pressures. They may vary from simple ideas or catchphrases to complex cultural practices or belief systems.

Applying memetics to religion, we can view religious beliefs, rituals, and structures as memes or meme complexes (also known as 'memeplexes') that have evolved and proliferated over time.[33] Just as genes propagate by helping their hosts survive and reproduce, religious memes propagate by influencing human behaviour to enhance their transmission.[34]

From a memetic perspective, the origin of religion can be seen as the emergence of certain memeplexes with high transmission fidelity, longevity, and fecundity. These religious memeplexes likely provided some form of adaptive advantage, either to the individuals who adopted them or to the memes themselves. For instance, religious memes that promoted social cohesion, cooperation, or moral behaviour could have enhanced group survival, thereby enabling their spread.[35]

Many features of religious belief and practice can be seen as strategies that memes use to ensure their survival and propagation. For instance, ritual repetition, the threat of divine punishment for disbelief, and the promise of rewards in an afterlife can all be seen as mechanisms that enhance the transmission and retention of religious memes.[36]

Dawkins has suggested that religions may be 'successful' memeplexes that have evolved to be highly infectious and resilient, possibly due to their ability to tap into deep-seated psychological needs and fears. This view has been echoed by other researchers, such as Daniel Dennett, who suggests that religions may be 'superb meme machines'.[37]

The memetic view of religion is closely tied to the broader concept of cultural evolution. It posits that cultural traits, including religious beliefs and practices, can evolve in ways that resemble biological evolution. This perspective suggests that the religious memeplexes we see today are the result of countless generations of memetic variation and selection.[38]

However, some researchers caution against a simplistic application of memetics to complex cultural phenomena like religion. They argue that cultural transmission is affected by various factors, including social structures, historical events, and human agency, which may need to be adequately captured by the meme metaphor.[39]

While controversial, the memetic perspective offers an intriguing way to think about the origin and evolution of religion. It suggests that religious beliefs and practices can be viewed as memeplexes that have evolved and spread due to their ability to influence human behaviour and culture. Further research is needed to explore this perspective's potential and limitations fully.

The Origin of Religion: Archaeological and Historical Analyses

Until now, we have looked at evolutionary biology and psychology regarding religion's origin. By integrating archaeological evidence and historical analysis, we can better understand how religion evolved alongside humanity.

Examining archaeological evidence, we find early traces of religious behaviour in the Upper Paleolithic period (around 50,000–10,000 BCE). Cave paintings, such as those found in Lascaux, France, and Altamira, Spain, depict animals and humans in ways that suggest symbolic thinking.[40] These paintings may have served ritualistic or spiritual purposes, but their meanings remain speculative.

Moreover, burial practices provide significant insights into early religious behaviours. Neanderthals, for instance, are believed to have buried their dead with grave goods, indicating a belief in an afterlife or a form of ancestor worship.[41]

Development of Organised Religion

The Neolithic Revolution, which took place around 10,000 BCE, was when humans transitioned from nomadic hunting and gathering to settled agriculture. This transition led to significant changes in human society, including the development of larger, more complex societies and the emergence of social hierarchies.

With these changes came a shift in religious practices. In hunter-gatherer societies, religious beliefs were likely animistic, emphasising the spirits of the natural world. However, with the advent of settled agricultural societies, we see more complex religious systems, often centred around fertility deities or earth goddesses, reflecting the importance of farming cycles. The transition from hunter-gatherer societies to settled agricultural communities led to significant changes in religious practices.

The archaeological site of Göbekli Tepe in Turkey, dated around 9600–7300 BCE, provides intriguing evidence of early monumental religious architecture. The site consists of massive stone pillars arranged in circles, many of which are decorated with carvings of animals. This site predates the advent of settled agriculture, which challenges the traditional view that complex religious practices emerged only after the development of agricultural societies.[42]

Religion in Ancient Civilisations

The first written records of religious practices come from ancient civilisations, such as Sumer, Egypt, and the Indus Valley, around 4000–3000 BCE. These societies had complex religious systems, often centred around a pantheon of gods, rituals, and moral codes.[43]

For example, archaeological and historical evidence from ancient Egypt reveals a rich religious tradition involving belief in an afterlife, numerous deities, and elaborate rituals. The construction of pyramids as tombs for pharaohs demonstrates the significant role of religious beliefs in social and political life.[44]

The Axial Age

Historian Karl Jaspers coined the term 'Axial Age' (800–200 BCE) to describe a period in which several major world religions and philosophies emerged in different regions, like Buddhism in India, Confucianism and Taoism in China, Zoroastrianism in Persia, and monotheistic Judaism in the Levant.[45]

These religions introduced concepts such as individual morality, personal salvation, and ethical monotheism. These shifts may have been responses to the social, political, and intellectual challenges of the time.[46]

Religion in the Modern Era

The advent of monotheism, particularly Christianity and Islam, led to significant shifts in religious practices and beliefs. These religions spread rapidly through conversion and conquest, resulting in today's religious landscape.[47]

The Enlightenment in the 17th and 18th centuries brought a new emphasis on reason and scientific inquiry, which led to a questioning of religious dogma and the emergence of secular ideologies.[48]

By integrating archaeological evidence and historical analysis, we can trace the evolution of religion from prehistoric symbolic behaviours to the complex systems of beliefs and practices that exist today. The development of religion has been inextricably linked with social, economic, and political changes throughout human history. It continues to be a vital aspect of human culture worldwide.

Religion Explained by Pascal Boyer

Pascal Boyer's *Religion Explained* is a seminal work in the cognitive science of religion. Boyer, an anthropologist, attempts to explain why religious thoughts and behaviours are so pervasive across all human cultures. He argues that religion is not a cultural invention but a by-product of various cognitive predispositions.

Boyer rejects the notion that religion exists because it answers 'big questions' about life, death, and purpose. Instead, he posits that religious concepts are 'minimally counterintuitive', meaning they violate some of our intuitive understandings of the world in ways that make them particularly memorable and enticing.

For instance, a tree that talks is minimally counterintuitive because it violates our expectations that trees can't speak. However, it's still grounded in our fundamental understanding of the world (we know what trees and talking are). Such concepts are easily remembered and shared, contributing to their cultural prevalence.

Boyer also argues that religion plays on our natural cognitive predispositions. We have an innate tendency to see patterns and infer agency, which can lead to beliefs in spirits or gods. We're also predisposed to think about social relationships, which can influence our notions of interacting with supernatural agents.

Another critical point in Boyer's book is the argument that moral codes and norms associated with religions aren't the driving force behind religious belief. They're often inconsistent and can be modified depending on the context. Instead, Boyer suggests that these moral codes are a by-product of social cohesion and community structure.

Boyer's *Religion Explained* is a thought-provoking book that offers intriguing insights into the cognitive underpinnings of religious thought and behaviour. Although it doesn't answer why we're religious, it provides a compelling framework for understanding the universality and persistence of religion in human cultures.

Some of the key themes that Boyer covers are:

Minimally Counterintuitive Concepts: Boyer's idea of 'minimally counterintuitive concepts' is central to his explanation of the prevalence and memorability of religious beliefs. He suggests that religious concepts often involve entities or events that violate our intuitive expectations about the world, but only in minimal ways. For example, a virgin birth is counterintuitive because it goes against our biological understanding of reproduction. Yet, it's easy to understand because it doesn't violate every aspect of our knowledge — we already understand the concept of birth. This minimal counter-intuitiveness makes religious concepts memorable and exciting, which aids their transmission across generations. It's one reason why supernatural beings and miraculous events feature prominently in religious narratives worldwide.

Cognitive Predispositions: Boyer also delves into how our cognitive predispositions shape religious beliefs. Humans tend to anthropomorphise — attribute human characteristics to non-human entities — and infer agency — the idea that intentional agents cause events. These tendencies can lead us to perceive supernatural beings in the world around us. For instance, if our ancestors heard rustling in the grass, assuming it was a dangerous predator (an agent) rather than the wind, it would be safer. This 'hyperactive agency detection' could contribute to beliefs in spirits or gods.

Social and Moral Norms: While many consider religious moral codes central to religious belief, Boyer argues that these are a by-product of social cohesion and community structure rather than a cause of religious belief. He points out that these codes often change depending on societal context, suggesting they're more flexible and fundamental than often assumed.

Rituals and Religious Practices: Boyer also examines religious rituals, suggesting they're not just random or arbitrary actions but are deeply tied to our cognitive predispositions. They often involve costly and hard-to-fake displays (like a sacrifice or ritualistic dancing) that signal a commitment to the group and its beliefs, thereby promoting social cohesion.

In conclusion, Boyer's *Religion Explained* offers a cognitive and evolutionary perspective on religion. Instead of viewing religion as answering the 'big questions', Boyer presents it as a by-product of our cognitive predispositions and social behaviours. This perspective provides a refreshing take on understanding the psychological and social underpinnings of religious beliefs and practices.

The Good Side of Religion

Religion has been an integral part of human societies throughout history, shaping cultures, laws, and individuals around the globe. Despite vast differences in beliefs and practices, religions share common themes of seeking truth, fostering community, and providing moral guidance. While religion can be a source of contention and conflict, it also has a 'good side' that can benefit individuals and societies immensely. Let us delve into the positive aspects of religion, exploring its capacity to foster social cohesion, provide existential comfort, stimulate altruistic behaviour, and offer a rich source of cultural heritage and identity.

Religious beliefs and practices can create a strong community and social cohesion. Shared rituals, values, and symbols can bind people together, creating a sense of unity and belonging that cannot be easy to achieve otherwise.[49] This social cohesion can be essential in times of crisis, providing a supportive network to help people cope with challenges and adversity.

Religion can also offer existential comfort and psychological well-being. It can help individuals make sense of the world, answering profound questions about the nature of existence, the purpose of life, and the mystery of death.[50] This existential comfort can alleviate anxiety, provide a sense of control, and offer hope, contributing to better mental health and overall well-being.

Moreover, religion often promotes altruistic behaviour and moral conduct. Many religious teachings emphasise love, kindness, generosity, and forgiveness, encouraging followers to strive for these ideals.[51] The belief in divine monitoring and supernatural consequences can further motivate moral behaviour, fostering social harmony and cooperation.

Lastly, religion contributes to cultural diversity and identity. Each religious tradition offers a unique lens through which to understand and interpret the world, enriched by centuries of wisdom, art, music, and literature. For many, religion provides a link to their cultural heritage and a sense of identity, adding depth and richness to the human experience.[52]

This chapter will explore these aspects of religion in depth, drawing on research from psychology, sociology, history, and anthropology. We will also consider how these benefits interact with the challenges and complexities of religion, offering a nuanced perspective on the 'good side' of religion. While religion can be a source of division and conflict, it also can inspire profound goodness, resilience, and unity, enriching individual lives and societies in countless ways.

Social Cohesion

Religion can be a powerful force for building and maintaining social cohesion. Shared religious beliefs and practices can foster a sense of community and belonging, helping to weave the social fabric of a group or society. This can be particularly important in times of crisis or hardship when communal support can provide both material and emotional aid.

For example, religious congregations often organise aid for those in need, such as food drives, disaster relief efforts, or support for the bereaved. Participating in religious rituals can also create a sense of unity and shared identity, strengthening social bonds.[53]

Religion's ability to generate social solidarity is emphasised in Emile Durkheim's classic work, *The Elementary Forms of the Religious Life*, where he argued that the primary function of religion was to bind people together. This is often accomplished through rituals and communal worship experiences, which evoke powerful emotions and create a sense of unity. This cohesion benefits more than just the community as a whole. Still, it can also provide support and comfort to individuals during times of difficulty or loss.

Existential Comfort and Psychological Well-being

Religion can answer existential questions, offering a framework for understanding the world and our place in it. Many religious traditions posit an afterlife, which can alleviate the fear of death and provide comfort in times of loss.

Religious beliefs and practices can also promote psychological well-being. For example, research has found that religious people often have lower levels of depression and anxiety, higher life satisfaction, and better physical health than non-religious people.[54]

Religion can provide a sense of purpose and meaning, a key component of psychological well-being. As existential psychotherapist Irvin D. Yalom noted, grappling with life's big questions, such as the inevitability of death and meaning, can be a source of anxiety. Religion can help individuals navigate these existential concerns, offering comforting answers and a framework for understanding the world. Indeed, research has found that religious people often report higher life satisfaction and happiness.[55]

Altruistic Behaviour and Moral Conduct

Religions often promote altruism and moral conduct. Many religious teachings emphasise virtues such as compassion, honesty, and generosity and proselytise against vices such as greed, deceit, and cruelty. Religion can also foster prosocial behaviour through divine monitoring and supernatural punishment for moral transgressions. Research has found that people who believe in a morally concerned deity are likelier to behave ethically, even when no one else is watching.[56]

Religion's role in promoting altruistic behaviour and moral conduct is extensive. Many religions advocate for selflessness and helping others. For instance, the concepts of *agape* (selfless love) in Christianity, *dana* (charity) in Hinduism, and *zakat* (almsgiving) in Islam all encourage followers to care for others. This moral guidance can extend to societal levels. For example, religious organisations often engage in humanitarian efforts, providing aid to those in need, contributing to social justice causes, and promoting peace efforts.

Cultural Diversity and Identity

Religion contributes to the richness of cultural diversity. Each religious tradition has unique beliefs, rituals, texts, art, architecture, and music, adding to the tapestry of human culture. Moreover, religion can provide a sense of identity and belonging. Many people identify strongly with their religious tradition, which can be a significant part of their personal and social identity. Religion can also connect individuals to their cultural heritage, providing a link to their ancestors and a sense of continuity with the past.[57]

Religion's contribution to cultural diversity and identity is visible in tangible and intangible forms. Religious architecture, like the intricate designs of Hindu temples, the colourful frescoes in Christian cathedrals, or the grand stupas in Buddhist temples, not only serves a religious purpose but also contributes to the cultural richness of society.

At a personal level, religious beliefs and practices can significantly shape one's identity. They can provide a sense of belonging and offer a community of like-minded individuals. For many, their religious affiliation is a fundamental part of who they are and how they view the world.

In sum, religion can be a source of conflict and division, but it has many positive aspects. It can foster social cohesion, provide existential comfort, promote moral conduct, and contribute to cultural diversity and identity. As with any complex social phenomenon, the impact of religion is multifaceted and can vary greatly depending on the specific beliefs, practices, and social context. From fostering unity, providing existential comfort, and promoting moral conduct to enriching our cultural diversity and personal identities, religion's 'good side' is as multifaceted as it is influential.

Why Religion Is Necessary

Stephen Asma's *Why We Need Religion* is a thoughtful exploration of the role of religion in human life.[58] Asma, a Professor of Philosophy at Columbia College Chicago, argues that religion serves crucial emotional and ethical functions that secular equivalents cannot easily replace.

Central to Asma's argument is that religion helps us manage our emotional lives. He posits that religion provides a vital framework for individuals to process emotions such as grief, rage, and fear. Religious rituals and beliefs, Asma argues, can provide comfort and consolation in times of trauma or loss.

'The emotional life of Homo sapiens,' Asma writes, 'was well established on the African savannah long before we had any articulate forms of culture like philosophy, science, or religion.'[59] Religion, Asma argues, evolved as a way to help manage these pre-existing emotional needs. He suggests that while science can explain the world, it often falls short in providing emotional comfort, a gap that religion fills effectively.

Asma also explores the role of religion in shaping moral behaviour. He acknowledges that one can be moral without religion. Still, he suggests religion can provide a powerful incentive for ethical behaviour. Religious beliefs can motivate people to act altruistically, even when it's not in their immediate self-interest.

'Following the rules of the group, caring for kin, and treating strangers fairly ... all these behaviors can be boosted by the belief in a watchful, moralizing god,' writes Asma.[60] He suggests that the fear of divine punishment or the desire for divine reward can inspire individuals to adhere to ethical norms.

Asma also emphasises the role of religion in fostering social cohesion and community. He argues that religious rituals and shared beliefs can unite people, creating a sense of social unity and belonging.

'Religion is one of the great pattern makers,' Asma writes. 'It provides roles, rules, expectations, narratives, rituals, and goals for the community.'[61] In this way, religion can help maintain social order and promote community cooperation.

In *Why We Need Religion*, Asma presents a nuanced and empathetic case for the value of religion. His approach is not to deny the abuses or excesses associated with religious institutions but rather to highlight the psychological, ethical, and social functions that religion serves. He suggests that religion remains a fundamental aspect of human life even in an increasingly secular age. He means religion is necessary and inevitable in many ways.

The Bad Side of Religion

While religion often serves as a source of comfort, community, and moral guidance, it can also promote exclusion and discrimination. This is especially prevalent when religious texts are interpreted to marginalise certain groups, including the LGBTQ+ community, women, and racial or ethnic minorities.

Richard Dawkins says, 'The God of the Old Testament is arguably the most unpleasant character in all fiction: jealous and proud of it; a petty, unjust, unforgiving control-freak; a vindictive, bloodthirsty ethnic cleanser; a misogynistic, homophobic, racist, infanticidal, genocidal, filicidal, pestilential, megalomaniacal, sadomasochistic, capriciously malevolent bully.'[62]

As per Dawkins, 'Faith can be very very dangerous, and deliberately to implant it into the vulnerable mind of an innocent child is a grievous wrong.'[63] He further adds that 'Many of us saw religion as harmless nonsense. Beliefs might lack all supporting evidence but, we thought, if people needed a crutch for consolation, where's the harm? September 11th changed all that.'[64]

Christopher Hitchens was not someone to be left behind either. In his book, *The God Is Not Great*, he says, 'Human decency is not derived from religion. It precedes it.' In a sharp attack on the Bible he says, 'The Bible may, indeed does, contain a warrant for trafficking in humans, for ethnic cleansing, for slavery, for bride-price, and for indiscriminate massacre, but we are not bound by any of it because it was put together by crude, uncultured human mammals.'[65]

Hitchens was not convinced about the utility of religion. He says, 'We keep on being told that religion, whatever its imperfections, at least instils morality. On every side, there is conclusive evidence that the contrary is the case and that faith causes people to be more mean, more selfish, and perhaps above all, more stupid.'[66] He thought 'Voltaire was simply ludicrous when he said that if god did not exist it would be necessary to invent him. The human invention of god is the problem to begin with.'[67]

He did not like Mother Teresa, a symbol of religious generosity. He once said, 'MT [Mother Teresa] was not a friend of the poor. She was a friend of poverty. She said that suffering was a gift from God. She spent her life opposing the only known cure for poverty, which is the empowerment of women and the emancipation of them from a livestock version of compulsory reproduction.'[68]

Religion and the LGBTQ+ Community

Many religious traditions have texts or interpretations that are seen as anti-LGBTQ+. For instance, Leviticus 18:22[69] in the Bible is often interpreted as condemning homosexuality: 'You shall not lie with a male as with a woman; it is an abomination.' This and similar passages have been used to justify discrimination and exclusion of the LGBTQ+. The Quran Surah Al Araf 7.81 says, 'Indeed, you approach men with desire, instead of women. Rather, you are a transgressing people.'[70]

Some Hadiths (sayings of the Prophet Muhammad) are taken to condemn homosexuality. Such interpretations can contribute to homophobia and exclusion in Muslim communities.[71]

The impact of literal interpretations of these verses can be profound, contributing to higher rates of mental health issues, suicide, and substance abuse in the LGBTQ+ community.[72] They also raise ethical concerns as they challenge the principles of equality and human rights. These interpretations can also influence laws and public policies. In many countries, religious beliefs have been used to justify laws criminalising homosexuality violating human rights.[73] In countries like Uganda and Russia, religious beliefs have been invoked to enforce laws against 'promoting homosexuality', leading to widespread persecution of the LGBTQ+ community.[74]

In response, many scholars and activists argue for more inclusive interpretations. For instance, some Christians say that Biblical verses on homosexuality must be understood in their historical and cultural context, which does not necessarily translate to a blanket condemnation of homosexuality today.[75]

Religion as a Tool to Justify Violent Pogroms

As a powerful social and psychological force, religion has often been harnessed to justify horrific acts of violence. To understand this, let us delve into several historical events where the perpetrators of violence used religion directly to harm their opponents.

The Crusades

The Crusades (1096–1291) were a series of religious wars sanctioned by the Latin Church in the medieval period to reclaim the Holy Land from Islamic rule. The First Crusade was instigated by Pope Urban II, who invoked religious duty in a fiery speech at the Council of Clermont and promised absolution of sins for anyone who died in the Crusade.[76]

The result was a series of brutal campaigns. The most notable was the sacking of Jerusalem in 1099, where Muslim and Jewish inhabitants were massacred. Fulcher of Chartres, a chronicler of the First Crusade, wrote, 'In this temple 10,000 were killed. Indeed, if you had been there you would have seen our feet colored to our ankles with the blood of the slain. But what more shall I relate? None of them were left alive; neither women nor children were spared.'[77]

The Spanish Inquisition

The Spanish Inquisition (1478–1834) was established by Catholic Monarchs Ferdinand II of Aragon and Isabella I of Castile to maintain Catholic orthodoxy. Inquisitors targeted Jews, Muslims, and those suspected of heresy, often resorting to torture and execution.

The Alhambra Decree of 1492 justified the expulsion of Jews from Spain on religious grounds. The decree stated, 'Inasmuch as we have been informed that there were some wicked Christians who Judaized and apostatized from our Holy Catholic Faith, the great cause of this was the communication of Jews with Christians.'[78]

The Thirty Years' War

The Thirty Years' War (1618–1648) was one of the most destructive conflicts in European history, resulting in an estimated eight million deaths. While the war had significant political and territorial components, it began mainly as a religious conflict between Protestant and Catholic states in the fragmenting Holy Roman Empire.[79]

The Defenestration of Prague in 1618, which marked the start of the war, was directly tied to religious tensions. Protestant nobles threw two Catholic regents and secretaries out of a castle window in Prague in response to perceived infringements on their religious rights. This event triggered a war that would span three decades and lay waste to large swathes of Europe.

The Mughal Invasion of India

The Mughal Empire, which ruled large parts of the Indian subcontinent from 1526 to 1857, was a complex and multifaceted political entity. Its rulers were Muslims, and they sometimes used religion as a tool to legitimise their rule and even their military campaigns. However, it is important to note that the Mughals' use of Islam in this way was not uniform across all rulers or all periods of the empire.

Babur and the Battle of Khanwa

Babur, the founder of the Mughal Empire, laid the foundation of the empire through a series of military victories. In his memoirs, the *Baburnama*, Babur often invoked the language of jihad, or holy war, to justify his campaigns. For example, in the Battle of Khanwa (1527) against Rana Sanga of Mewar, Babur declared a jihad, calling it a struggle against the 'infidels'.[80]

Aurangzeb and Religious Intolerance

Aurangzeb, the sixth Mughal emperor, is often seen as the most religiously intolerant of the Mughal rulers. He implemented policies that discriminated against non-Muslims, including the jizya tax and restrictions on Hindu festivals. Aurangzeb also used religious language to justify his violent military campaigns, often against other Muslim rulers.

For example, his long and bloody war against the Maratha king Shivaji was a clear religious conflict.[81] However, some modern-day 'historians' present it as a dispute over territorial control. In his royal orders (*farman*s), Aurangzeb often invoked Islamic law to justify his actions.

India's Partition

The 1947 partition of India into two separate states — India and Pakistan — was marked by devastating violence between Hindus and Muslims. Religious differences were used to fuel hatred and justify horrific acts of violence, leading to an estimated one to two million deaths.[82]

Many leaders, including Muhammad Ali Jinnah, the founder of Pakistan, framed the partition as a necessary protection for Muslims against Hindu domination. This religious conflict and threat narrative was used to mobilise support for partition and incite violence against other religious communities.

The Troubles in Northern Ireland

The Troubles (1968–1998) in Northern Ireland were a period of ethno-nationalist conflict between mainly Protestant Unionists who wanted Northern Ireland to remain part of the United Kingdom and primarily Catholic Nationalists who wanted it to join the Republic of Ireland.

While the root cause of the conflict was political, religious identities were closely intertwined with political affiliations, and sectarian violence between Catholics and Protestants resulted in approximately 3,500 deaths.[83] The tensions were often framed in religious terms, fostering an 'us versus them' mentality that justified violence and perpetuated the conflict.

The Rwandan Genocide

Religion also played a role in the Rwandan Genocide (1994), where Hutu extremists massacred approximately 800,000 Tutsis and moderate Hutus. While the genocide was largely ethnopolitical, some Christian leaders and institutions were implicated in the violence. International courts later convicted several clergies for their active participation in the genocide.[84]

Churches often became sites of massacres, as Tutsis sought refuge in them, believing they would be safe. Bishop Augustin Misago was accused of refusing to shelter Tutsis in his church, leading to their death.[85]

Religious Privilege

Religions have played a significant role in shaping societies throughout history. They've influenced laws, moral codes, cultural norms, and social structures, often providing a foundation upon which societies build themselves. This influence of religion can be seen in legal systems, for instance, where many laws have roots in religious commandments or doctrines.[86]

In this context, religious privilege refers to the advantages individuals and groups gain from living in societies shaped by religious values and doctrines, even if they don't actively practise religion. For example, a person who adheres to the moral code of honesty, fairness, and respect for others — principles common to many faiths — may benefit from a society that values these principles, even if they don't identify with a particular religion.

Likewise, societal structures influenced by religious norms — such as the concept of a weekend, which has roots in Jewish and Christian traditions — benefit all members of society, regardless of their individual religious beliefs. These societal norms and structures, influenced by religious practices, constitute a form of religious privilege.

Much like other forms of privilege, this religious privilege often goes unrecognised. This is primarily because the influence of religion on societal structures is so pervasive and deeply ingrained that it's considered 'normal'. People take these societal norms for granted without recognising their religious origins or understanding the privilege associated with them.

Even secularists and atheists, who may reject religious doctrines, often benefit from the structures and norms of a society rooted in religious traditions. For example, they might appreciate the moral emphasis on human rights, dignity, and equality, which religious principles have strongly influenced.

However, they may also face challenges in such societies, particularly if they challenge religiously influenced norms or advocate for a more secular societal foundation. Their perspectives can also contribute to the dialogue on religious privilege, encouraging society to recognise and critically examine these ingrained structures and norms.

Understanding religious privilege in this broader context requires us to reflect on the profound influence that religion has had on our societal structures and norms. Recognising this form of privilege can help promote a more nuanced understanding of society and foster dialogue about the role of religion in public life.

Is Religion Inevitable?

The ubiquity of religion throughout human history and across cultures suggests that it may be an inevitable part of human experience. While the specific manifestations of religious belief and practice vary widely, the propensity to seek meaning, purpose, and community, all central aspects of religion, appears universal. This can be explained and analysed using the rise of 'wokeism' in the

West, occupying the space left empty by the fall of the old religious structures.

The Psychological Perspective

From a psychological perspective, religion addresses fundamental human needs. It answers existential questions, offers a moral framework, and gives individuals a sense of purpose and identity.[87] These psychological functions are not exclusive to traditional forms of religion. For example, 'wokeism', a term often used pejoratively to describe a particular strand of progressive activism, has been compared to a secular religion due to its emphasis on moral purity, original sin (privilege), and redemption through 'wokeness'.[88]

The cognitive science of religion also suggests that belief in supernatural entities and searching for purpose and meaning are natural by-products of the human mind's work.[89] Humans tend to anthropomorphise and seek patterns and agency, even where none exist. This cognitive predisposition and our social nature make us prone to religious belief.

The Sociological Perspective

Sociologically, religion has often been seen as a tool for social cohesion. Emile Durkheim, one of the founding fathers of sociology, argued that religion binds communities together by establishing shared values and norms.[90] This function is not limited to traditional religions. For instance, the shared values and standards of 'wokeism' serve to bind together a community of believers.

Religion also helps to legitimise social structures and authority. Many societies have used religious doctrines to justify social hierarchy and rules. While 'wokeism' challenges many existing social networks, it also establishes its systems of authority and hierarchy, often based on perceived levels of oppression.

The Cultural Perspective

Culturally, religion has been a significant source of art, music, and literature, shaping many of our cultural norms and traditions. Even in secular societies, many cultural practices have religious origins. The rise of 'wokeism' has also had cultural impacts, influencing language, education, and media.

Religion, 'Wokeism', and Secular Societies

The rise of 'wokeism' in the West can reflect the inevitability of religion, or at least religion-like phenomena. Despite the secularisation of many Western societies, the human need for meaning, purpose, moral guidance, and community has remained. 'Wokeism', emphasising social justice, equality, and awareness of privilege, can be seen as a response to these unmet needs. It provides a secular framework for understanding the world, a moral code, and a sense of community, much like traditional religions.

The parallels between 'wokeism' and religion hint at the inevitable nature of religious phenomena. Even without traditional religious belief, new belief systems and ideologies emerge to fulfil the same psychological, sociological, and cultural functions. This suggests that religion, or at least religion-like phenomena, is inevitable in human society.

In conclusion, the ubiquity of religion across cultures and throughout history suggests its inevitability. The psychological, sociological, and cultural functions of religion are fundamental aspects of human society. The rise of 'wokeism' in the West, despite its secular nature, echoes many elements of traditional religion, further illustrating the seemingly inevitable nature of religious phenomena.

Creating a Healthy Balance

Creating a balanced society where the excesses of traditional religion and the so-called 'wokeness epidemic' are avoided is a significant challenge, but not impossible. The goal should be a society that values open dialogue, respects differing viewpoints, and encourages critical thinking.

The foundation for a balanced society is education. Education should not just be about imparting knowledge but also equipping individuals with the tools to evaluate information and form their opinions critically. This is particularly important in a world increasingly driven by ideology.

A good education should expose students to various perspectives, including different religious and philosophical views and differing perspectives on social issues. This exposure can help students understand that there are multiple ways to interpret the world and that no one ideology has all the answers.[91]

Promoting critical thinking also involves teaching students to question authority and recognise the difference between fact and opinion. This can help individuals resist the allure of dogmatic belief systems, whether they are religious doctrines or 'woke' ideologies.

Another critical component of a balanced society is empathy. Empathy encourages us to understand and appreciate the experiences and perspectives of others, even if they differ from our own. It is the antidote to dogmatism and intolerance.

Empathy can be fostered through diverse interactions and exposure to different cultures and belief systems. This can help to break down the 'us versus them' mentality that often characterises both religious and 'woke' extremism.[92]

It's also crucial to recognise that empathy must extend to those we disagree with. Disagreement does not necessitate disdain. It is possible, and indeed necessary, to maintain respect and understanding even in the face of ideological differences.

Healthy societies encourage open dialogue and the free exchange of ideas. This can involve creating physical and virtual spaces where individuals can engage in respectful debate and discussion.

Open dialogue allows for changing one's mind, a quality often lacking in dogmatic belief systems. It also promotes a deeper understanding of complex issues, rarely as black and white as ideological narratives suggest.

To promote open dialogue, pushing back against cancel culture is essential, which stifles free speech and discourages individuals from voicing dissenting opinions. This does not mean tolerating hate speech or bigotry but rather fostering a culture where disagreement is seen as a natural and necessary part of societal discourse.[93]

Balancing the excesses of both traditional religion and 'wokeness' is no easy task. However, through education that promotes critical thinking, fosters empathy, and encourages open dialogue, it is possible to create a society that respects diversity of thought and avoids the pitfalls of dogmatism.

In such a society, religion and 'wokeness' can exist not as rigid ideologies but as malleable belief systems, open to question and capable of evolving. This requires a shift in how we view disagreement, not as a threat but as an opportunity for growth and understanding.

4

How to Live a Good Life
Without a God

A long time ago, I was at a family function where someone casually told one of my elders that I was a Nāstika. The elder looked at me with confusion and then asked me many questions. It started with, if you do not believe in a God, how do you live your life? How do you know what is good and what is evil? What stops you from harming others? What happens to you when you die? Don't you think reincarnation (*punarjanma*) is real? Do you live your life assuming that once you are dead, it is all over? If there is no God and the theory of karma is unreal, why should I not kill every person on the road? Don't you think the world would collapse if everyone stopped believing in God? So, you think you are more moral than a god-fearing person? If religions are man-made, then where does morality come from? How do I know what is good and what is evil? If God did not create this world, who did? If there is no reincarnation, what happens to our soul?

As we had analysed this in the chapter on the role of religion from an evolutionary perspective, religion has answered almost all these questions, albeit inaccurately. A giant swathe of humanity still gets their answers from religion directly by reading texts or sermons from religious preachers.

The modern secular education system has incorporated a lot of science into our everyday lives. Still, most human beings assume their religions say the same things. They have conveniently mapped one to the other without verifying any of these claims. But, in the case of some countries, they are taught unscientific claims in their schools. Let us look at evolution as a subject.

As of 2023, evolution

is widely accepted in most Western countries, despite occasional opposition. Sadly, this is not the case in most Muslim countries, where it is banned from many schools and colleges because it is thought to contradict Islamic teachings. Saudi Arabia, Oman, Algeria and Morocco have banned the teaching of evolution completely.[1]

The situation in the Indian sub-continent is also a mixed bag, where in Pakistan, 'a commonly used biology school textbook rubbishes the theory, claiming that evolution of species is tantamount to assuming that "a motor car is evolved" when two rickshaws collide'.[2]

In his 2002 article, the former Prime Minister of Pakistan, Imran Khan, blamed the West's follies upon 'philosophers like Darwin, who with his half-baked theory of evolution had supposedly disproved the creation of men and hence religion, were read and revered' (ibid.).

India has fortunately bucked the trend and still teaches evolution as a fact in schools. The Department of Plant Sciences at the Central University of Punjab conducted a questionnaire survey which included responses from 1,706 people from fourteen Indian states.[3]

Overall, 68.5% of the Indian population accepted evolution by choosing affirmatory response to the third question of the survey. A majority of the males (71.5%), females (68.8%), religious (67%), non-religious people (74%), leftists (60.6%) and rightists (65.8%) answered correctly and accepted evolution to be definitely true.[4]

However, under the current NDA government, the National Council of Education and Research (NCERT) conducted a rationalisation exercise that decided to delete 'the chapters on evolution and the chapter on the Periodic Table of Elements from the Class 9 and Class 10 science textbooks. NCERT has called these deletions a curriculum "rationalisation" exercise necessitated by the COVID pandemic'.[5] The chapters on evolution have been retained in Class 11 and 12 science curricula.

But this move by the current government has been criticised by intellectuals, who rightfully state,

> Teaching evolution to primary or secondary school children is about more than imparting scientific knowledge. It is part of the holistic scientific development which children should undergo at school. To make the child accustomed to the basics of evolution is broadening her horizon to understand the process of life beyond the realms of socio-religious cliches. It generates ideas and enhances rational thinking. It imparts the ability to question the status quo. Science helps society by asking uncomfortable questions about itself and initiating debates. The NCERT should have emphasised this inexhaustible power of science.[6]

In such a situation, we can safely assume that religion, especially a belief in God and its influence on morality, must differ worldwide. As per a spring 2022 Pew Research Centre survey, 'most Americans say it's not necessary to believe in God in order to be moral and have good values. About two-thirds of Americans say this, while about a third say belief in God is an essential component of morality (65% vs. 34%)'.[7]

Unlike America, the eight Western European publics surveyed by Pew Research in a survey conducted across thirty-four countries from 13 May 13 to 2 October 2019, totalling 38,426 respondents, 'a median of just 22% say belief in God is necessary to be moral'.[8] The rest of the results are worth sharing in their totality over here to understand the sheer variation one sees across the globe regarding the question of God and morality.

Nearly everyone surveyed in Indonesia and the Philippines (96% each) draws a connection between belief in God and having good values. And nearly eight-in-ten (79%) in India say the same. But in East Asia, South Koreans are somewhat split on this question (53% say it is necessary, 46% say it is not), while smaller shares in Japan (39%) and Australia (19%) take the view that it's necessary to believe in God to be a moral person.

Among those in the Middle East and North African nations surveyed, at least seven-in-ten in Lebanon (72%), Turkey (75%) and Tunisia (84%) think belief in God is necessary to have good values. Israelis are split on this question, with 48% of the population on either side.

Additionally, strong majorities in each of the sub-Saharan African nations surveyed say belief in God is necessary to be moral. Over nine-in-ten in Kenya and Nigeria (95% and 93%, respectively) connect belief in God with morality, while 84% of South Africans are of the same opinion.

Majorities in all three Latin American countries surveyed say that belief in God is necessary to be moral, with the highest share in Brazil (84%). Catholicism remains the largest religion in Latin America, and majorities of Catholics in all three nations surveyed think it is necessary to believe in God to be moral.[9]

The Origin of Morality: A Dance between Science, Religion, and Modernity

The origin of morality has been a subject of contention for centuries. It forms the foundation of societal norms and values and is deeply intertwined with our understanding of human nature.

The Scientific Perspective

The scientific perspective posits that morality is a product of natural selection, evolving over millennia to promote social cohesion and survival. This hypothesis is grounded in evolutionary psychology, which interprets human behaviours and psychological traits through the lens of evolution.

According to this perspective, our moral instincts, such as empathy, fairness, and reciprocity, evolved because they increased our ancestors' survival and reproductive success. Individuals who cooperated with others, shared resources, and protected their kin would have had a better chance of survival and passing on their genes.

Studies on primates support this theory. For instance, Frans de Waal, in his book *The Bonobo and the Atheist*,[10] highlights examples of empathy, fairness, and cooperation among bonobos and chimpanzees, suggesting that these moral behaviours have deep evolutionary roots.

The role of culture in shaping morality is another crucial aspect. Cultural norms and values can reinforce or modify our innate moral instincts. Anthropologist Richard Shweder's work, particularly his book *Thinking Through Cultures: Expeditions in Cultural Psychology*,[11] comprehensively explores this dynamic interaction between biology and culture.

Science, specifically evolutionary biology and psychology, explains how our moral instincts, such as empathy and reciprocity, are likely to have evolved to promote cooperation and survival within social groups.[12]

Additionally, neuroscientific research provides evidence that moral judgements are often rooted in emotional processes. For example, studies using functional magnetic resonance imaging (fMRI) have shown that moral decision-making often involves areas of the brain associated with emotion, such as the ventromedial prefrontal cortex.

The 'is-ought' problem, which David Hume popularised, states that while science can explain why we have moral instincts, it cannot alone tell us what to do. Therefore, science must be complemented by philosophical and ethical discourse to understand morality fully.[13]

While evolutionary biology provides a framework for understanding the origins of our moral instincts, it's also crucial to consider the role of our environment. The theory of gene-environment interaction suggests that our genes influence how we respond to our environment and vice versa. This interplay has significant implications for morality.

While we might have a genetic predisposition for empathy or cooperation, our upbringing, societal norms, and individual experiences can either enhance or suppress these traits. In other words, our environment both shapes and inherits our moral character.[14]

Understanding Good, Bad, and Self-restraint

When my family elder pressed me for the first time, asking me, 'How do you know what is good and what is bad? or What stops you from harming others?', I did not have a robust answer. As I type these words today, I want to thank that relative for pushing me intellectually. If it were not for that interaction, I would not have gone down the rabbit hole of reading material and eventually trying to understand why we are the way we are.

Morality—the differentiation of actions as good or bad and the understanding of what prevents us from causing harm to others—is a complex construct. Science, particularly psychology, neuroscience, and evolutionary biology, offers intriguing insights into these questions.

From an evolutionary standpoint, certain behaviours we perceive as 'good' or 'bad' can be traced back to the survival benefits they conferred on our ancestors.

For instance, behaviours such as cooperation, fairness, and altruism, generally seen as 'good', are thought to have evolved because they enhanced group cohesion and survival.[15] Conversely, behaviours considered 'bad', like deception or aggression, can also be understood in evolutionary terms, as they may have offered some survival benefits under specific circumstances.[16]

However, the evolutionary framework does not suggest that our moral judgements are merely instinctual or predetermined. Cognitive neuroscience reveals that our brain is capable of complex moral reasoning, which involves weighing different ethical considerations and potential consequences.[17]

The prefrontal cortex, in particular, plays a significant role in this process. Neuroimaging studies have shown that damage to this area can impair moral judgement, leading to decisions that most people would consider 'bad' even if the person can articulate what is generally considered 'good' or 'bad'.[18]

These findings suggest that our moral judgements result from evolved moral instincts and cognitive processes that can reflect, evaluate, and sometimes override these instincts.

The Deterrents of Harmful Actions: Neurological and Social Factors

The question of what stops us from harming others can also be explored from a scientific perspective. Again, evolutionary biology provides some answers. The capacity for empathy, which is the ability to understand and share the feelings of others, is considered a crucial factor that restrains harmful behaviours.[19] From an evolutionary perspective, empathy likely evolved to promote altruistic behaviours, enhancing group survival.

Neuroscientific research supports this view by showing that areas of the brain involved in empathy, such as the anterior insula and anterior cingulate cortex, are activated when we observe others in pain.[20] This suggests that witnessing the suffering of others can trigger empathic responses that deter us from causing harm.

Moreover, social norms and moral education play a significant role in regulating our behaviours. Violation of social norms often results in social sanctions, which serve as a deterrent to harmful actions.[21] Moral education, on the other hand, can cultivate moral virtues and reasoning skills, promoting prosocial behaviours and discouraging harmful ones.[22]

In conclusion, science provides a multifaceted understanding of what is 'good' and 'bad' and what prevents us from harming others. This understanding involves both evolutionary and cognitive factors. It highlights the interplay of biological and social influences in shaping our moral behaviour.

Moral Intuitions and Moral Reasoning

According to psychologists like Jonathan Haidt and Joshua Greene, in the Dual-process theory of morality, our moral judgements result from both intuitive and reflective processes.[23]

Moral intuitions are quick, automatic responses to ethical situations, and it is believed that our evolutionary history has shaped them. For instance, the aversion to harming others could be an intuitive response that evolved because it promoted group survival.

In contrast, moral reasoning involves conscious deliberation and reflection. This process can lead us to override our initial moral intuitions when we recognise that they lead to morally suboptimal outcomes. For example, while our intuition might lead us to favour our in-group members, reflection can help us realise the importance of treating all individuals fairly, regardless of group membership.

Additionally, research suggests that various factors, including cultural norms, individual beliefs, and emotional states, can influence these two processes, complicating our understanding of good and evil.[24]

Self-control, or the ability to regulate our impulses, is another crucial factor that stops us from harming others. Neuroscientific research has linked self-control to the prefrontal cortex, a brain region involved in executive functions such as planning, decision-making, and impulse control.[25]

A lack of self-control is associated with various forms of harmful behaviour, from aggression to criminal activity. On the other hand, individuals with high self-control are more likely to behave in prosocial ways, even when faced with situations where they might be tempted to act otherwise.[26]

Moreover, studies suggest that self-control is like a muscle: it can be strengthened with practice but can also become depleted when used extensively.[27] This underscores the importance of cultivating self-control from an early age and the role of supportive environments in promoting this skill.

Our intuitive and reflective processes, our level of self-control, and our social and cultural contexts are just a few of the many variables that affect our moral judgements of good and evil and our restraint from harming others. Science can help us better understand and navigate our moral landscape by studying these factors.

If God Is Not the Source of Morality, Does that Mean There Is Neither Good Nor Bad?

Many mistakenly perceive God or religion as the exclusive source of morality, a belief rooted in the Divine Command theory. According to this theory, a divine decree determines an act's moral value. However, this viewpoint can result in the Euthyphro Dilemma, a philosophical conundrum that Plato introduced: Is an action morally good because God commands it, or does God command it because it's ethically sound? Each side of this dilemma has significant implications and challenges.[28]

Additionally, suppose that morality only derives from divine commands. In that case, it implies that non-religious people or those who adhere to other religious doctrines cannot behave morally, contrary to empirical evidence. Studies show that non-religious individuals can be just as moral, if not more so, than their religious counterparts, demonstrating that ethical behaviour does not depend on religious belief.[29]

The idea that morality solely arises from religion can also be challenged empirically. Anthropological research reveals the presence of moral norms across various cultures, including those with different religious beliefs or none at all.[30] This universality suggests that morality isn't strictly religious but is deeply intertwined with human sociality and cognition.

A common misconception is that without religion, we plunge into moral relativism, where 'anything goes'. Before we delve any further, let us first give a few definitions. We shall rely on the *Stanford Encyclopaedia of Philosophy*:[31]

Moral Relativism and Subjectivism

Moral relativism is the view that moral judgements and beliefs about right and wrong, good and bad, not only vary greatly across time and contexts but that their correctness is dependent on or relative to individual or cultural perspectives and frameworks. Moral subjectivism is the view that moral judgements are judgements about contingent and variable features of our moral sensibilities. For the subjectivist, to say that abortion is wrong is to say something like, 'I disapprove of abortion', or 'Around here, we disapprove of abortion'. Once, the content of the subjectivist's claim is made explicit, the truth or acceptability of a subjectivist moral judgement is no longer a relative matter. Moral relativism proper, on the other hand, is the claim that facts about right and wrong vary with and are dependent on social and cultural background. Understood in this way, moral relativism could be seen as a sub-division of cultural relativism. Values may also be relativised to frameworks of assessment independent of specific cultures or social settings.

Moral Objectivism

Moral objectivism maintains that moral judgements are ordinarily true or false in an absolute or universal sense, that some of them are true, and that people are sometimes justified in accepting true moral judgements (and rejecting false ones) on the basis of the evidence available to any reasonable and well-informed person.

Mitchell Silver provides another excellent definition of moral objectivism by stating that it is a process where a single set of principles determines the permissibility of any action and the accuracy of any judgement regarding the permissibility of an action.[32]

Moral relativism is the view that moral judgements are true or false only relative to some particular standpoint and that no perspective is uniquely privileged.

However, the absence of a divine source for moral values does not necessitate moral relativism. One can reject a religious basis for morality while maintaining that specific actions are objectively right or wrong based on rational and empirical considerations.

Indeed, a significant body of research suggests the existence of universal moral principles. For instance, the anthropologist Donald Brown has documented numerous 'human universals', many of which pertain to ethical behaviour across diverse cultures.

A Scientific and Philosophical Case for an Objective Moral Framework

The Moral Foundations Theory (MFT), proposed by Jonathan Haidt, offers a psychological basis for morality that applies across cultures. Haidt suggests that five innate and universally available psychological systems provide the foundations for the world's many character traits: Harm/Care, Fairness/Reciprocity, Ingroup/Loyalty, Authority/Respect, and Purity/Sanctity.[33] These moral foundations do not depend on religious belief. They are psychological adaptations for social interactions shaped by natural selection.

Haidt identifies five (later expanded to six) such foundations:[34]

Care/Harm: This foundation is related to our long evolution as mammals with attachment systems and an ability to feel (and dislike) the pain of others. It underlies the virtues of kindness, gentleness, and nurturing.
Fairness/Cheating: This foundation is related to the evolutionary process of reciprocal altruism. It generates ideas of justice, rights, and autonomy.

Loyalty/Betrayal: This foundation is related to our history as tribal creatures able to form shifting coalitions. It underlies the virtues of patriotism and self-sacrifice for the group. It is active anytime people feel it's 'one for all and all for one'.

Authority/Subversion: Our long history of hierarchical social interactions in primates shaped this foundation. It underlies the virtues of leadership and followership, including deference to legitimate authority and respect for traditions.

Sanctity/Degradation: The psychology of disgust and contamination shaped this foundation. It underlies religious notions of striving to live in an elevated, less carnal, more noble way. It underlies the widespread idea that the body is a temple that immoral activities and contaminants can desecrate.

Liberty/Oppression: This foundation is about people's reactions and resentment towards those who dominate them and restrict their liberty. Its intuitions are often in tension with those of the authoritative foundation. The hatred of bullies and dominators motivates people to unite to oppose or take down the oppressor.

Haidt proposes that these foundations are innate in that they are the 'first draft' of our moral minds, written by the processes of biological evolution.[35] However, he emphasises that each culture and individual then edits this first draft through learning and experience to produce the final draft of their moral intuitions. This process explains the diversity of moral systems, while their shared evolutionary origins account for their commonalities.

Like all theories, Haidt's MFT has been subject to criticism and debate. Here are some notable criticisms and limitations:

Limited Number of Foundations: Some critics argue that the moral foundations proposed by Haidt are not exhaustive. For instance, some people have proposed additional foundations like honesty, restraint, or freedom that the current six foundations do not explicitly address.[36]

Cultural Bias: Critics have pointed out that MFT may be influenced by a Western, educated, industrialized, rich, and democratic (WEIRD) bias. The theory was developed primarily based on research in Western societies, and it might not fully capture moral diversity in non-Western or traditional societies.[37]

Descriptive versus Normative: MFT is primarily a descriptive theory, explaining what people believe to be moral, rather than a normative theory, prescribing what should be moral. Critics have questioned the extent to which describing people's various types of moral intuitions can help us determine what is truly moral.[38]

Moral versus Conventional Rules: Some critics argue that MFT does not clearly distinguish between moral rules (which concern fundamental rights and wrongs) and conventional rules (which are more arbitrary and culturally specific). This could potentially lead to overestimating the moral significance of particular beliefs or practices.[39]

The Role of Reasoning: Haidt's emphasis on intuition over reasoning in moral judgement has been controversial.

Some researchers argue that reason plays a more significant role in moral judgement than Haidt suggests, particularly in novel situations or when intuitions conflict.[40]

Haidt and his colleagues have responded to these criticisms and continue to refine and develop the theory. First, they have emphasised that the current set of foundations is not meant to be exhaustive or fixed. Haidt initially proposed five foundations but later expanded to include a sixth, the Liberty/Oppression Foundation, in response to observations of political discourse and additional research. This shows an openness to refining and expanding the theory as new evidence and perspectives emerge.

Secondly, Haidt and his colleagues argue that the foundations should be considered broad categories encompassing a wide range of moral concerns. For instance, the Fairness/Cheating Foundation could cover concepts like justice, rights, equality, and reciprocity. In contrast, the Authority/Subversion foundation could include respect for tradition, deference to legitimate authority, and obedience to societal rules.

They have also suggested that additional moral issues raised by critics, such as honesty or self-control, might fall under the existing foundations. For example, honesty might be considered part of the Fairness/Cheating foundation. At the same time, self-control could be related to the Sanctity/Degradation foundation regarding self-purity and discipline.

Finally, Haidt has argued that the criteria for a moral foundation should be strict to prevent the list from becoming overly inclusive, which would dilute its explanatory power. The candidate foundation should be universally relevant across cultures, align with an evolutionary explanation, and not be reducible to other foundations.

While Haidt acknowledges the potential limitations of MFT, he maintains that it provides a valuable framework for understanding a wide range of moral intuitions and their cultural variations. Despite these criticisms, MFT has influenced moral psychology, giving valuable insights into the diversity and commonality of moral judgements across different cultures and political ideologies.

The Philosophical Perspective

In *The Moral Landscape*, Sam Harris argues that moral truths exist and can be scientifically understood. He proposes that questions about values—meaning, morality, and life's larger purpose—are questions about the well-being of conscious creatures. Therefore, to understand morality, we need to use empirical methods to study the conditions that contribute to the well-being of conscious beings.[41]

In this sense, morality becomes an empirical question that falls within the purview of science, and we can, in principle, have an objective moral framework based on understanding and promoting well-being. He argues that morality pertains to the well-being of conscious creatures, suggesting that moral truths can be discovered through the scientific study of well-being. This perspective, known as moral realism, posits that there are objective moral truths independent of human belief.

According to Harris, science, particularly neuroscience and psychology, can and should play a significant role in determining what is morally right and wrong. Harris rejects the notion that science can only describe how the world is (facts) and not how it ought to be (values). His central argument is that values are a certain kind of fact— facts about the well-being of conscious creatures. He asserts that morality is about promoting well-being and minimising suffering for conscious creatures, a definition that, according to Harris, is grounded in the objective reality of conscious experiences.

Harris maintains that there are objective truths about what leads to human flourishing, just as there are objective truths about human health. In the same way that we can use science to inform us about what's healthy or unhealthy, Harris contends that we can use science to tell us what actions or policies lead to human flourishing or suffering. So let us ask ourselves this question: can there be something like The Worst Possible Misery for Everyone? Sam Harris talks about this in detail in *The Moral Landscape*.[42]

He says,

> Even if each conscious being has a unique nadir on the moral landscape, we can still conceive of a state of the universe in which everyone suffers as much as he or she (or it) possibly can. If you think we cannot say this would be 'bad,' then I don't know what you could mean by the word 'bad' (and I don't think you know what you mean by it either). Once we conceive of 'the worst possible misery for everyone,' then we can talk about taking incremental steps toward this abyss: What could it mean for life on earth to get worse for all human beings simultaneously? Notice that this need have nothing to do with people enforcing their culturally conditioned moral precepts. Perhaps a neurotoxic dust could fall to earth from space and make everyone extremely uncomfortable. All we need imagine is a scenario in which everyone loses a little, or a lot, without there being compensatory gains (i.e., no one learns any important lessons, no one profits from others' losses, etc.). It seems uncontroversial to say that a change that leaves everyone worse off, by

any rational standard, can be reasonably called 'bad,' if this word is to have any meaning at all. We simply must stand somewhere. I am arguing that, in the moral sphere, it is safe to begin with the premise that it is good to avoid behaving in such a way as to produce the worst possible misery for everyone. I am not claiming that most of us personally care about the experience of all conscious beings; I am saying that a universe in which all conscious beings suffer the worst possible misery is worse than a universe in which they experience well-being. This is all we need to speak about 'moral truth' in the context of science. Once we admit that the extremes of absolute misery and absolute flourishing—whatever these states amount to for each particular being in the end—are different and dependent on facts about the universe, then we have admitted that there are right and wrong answers to questions of morality.

To illustrate this, he often uses extreme examples that most people would agree on while acknowledging that many real-world moral questions are more complex and nuanced.

Here are a few examples he discusses:

Physical and Psychological Abuse: Harris argues that we can objectively say that societies or cultures that promote physical and psychological abuse of certain groups (for example, women, minorities, or children) are not conducive to human flourishing. He contends that science might be able to quantify the harm these practices do to both physical and psychological health.

Freedom and Autonomy: Harris also posits that freedom and autonomy promote human flourishing. For example, he suggests that societies that severely restrict freedom of thought, expression, or belief or enforce oppressive norms and laws are not maximising well-being.

Cooperation and Altruism: Drawing from research in evolutionary biology and social psychology, Harris suggests that cooperation and altruism are generally beneficial for human flourishing. He points out that societies that encourage trust, collaboration, and concern for the well-being of others tend to be more successful and stable.

Education and Intellectual Pursuits: Harris argues that access to quality education and the freedom to pursue intellectual interests are also crucial for human flourishing. He suggests that societies that value and promote education and academic pursuits generally provide better opportunities for individual and societal progress.

Harris acknowledges that defining and measuring 'well-being' precisely is a complex task and that there may be many different paths to achieving it. However, he maintains that this does not make the concept of well-being unscientific or subjective any more than the complexity and variability of health make it unscientific or subjective. In principle, he argues that science can tell us which beliefs, actions, and institutions are more likely to promote well-being and that this knowledge should inform our moral decisions.

Here are some ways Harris addresses these issues:

Comparison with Health: Harris often compares well-being to health. Health is also a complex and multifaceted concept that can be hard to define and measure precisely. Moreover, what is healthy can vary significantly among different individuals. Yet, despite these complexities and variabilities, we still consider health a valid and valuable scientific concept, and we can often make objective judgements about what is healthy or unhealthy. Harris argues that the same applies to well-being.

Many Peaks on the Moral Landscape: Harris uses the metaphor of a 'moral landscape' with multiple peaks and valleys to represent the potential complexity and variability of well-being. Each peak represents a different way to achieve high well-being, and each valley represents a state of low well-being. According to Harris, there may be many ways to achieve increased well-being (just as there are many ways to be healthy), and science can help us navigate this landscape.

Role of Empirical Research: Harris asserts that empirical research, particularly in psychology and neuroscience, can help us understand what promotes or hinders well-being. For example, research can reveal how various factors, such as social relationships, meaningful work, physical health, mental health, and economic conditions, affect well-being.

Continuing Evolution of Understanding: Just as our scientific understanding of health has evolved and improved, Harris suggests that our knowledge of well-being can also develop and improve. He acknowledges that our understanding is incomplete and that many difficult questions remain. Still, he argues that this is a reason to push forward with the scientific study of well-being, not a reason to abandon it.

In sum, while Harris acknowledges the complexities and challenges involved in defining and measuring well-being, he argues that these are not insurmountable obstacles and do not undermine well-being's objectivity or scientific validity.

Sam Harris also acknowledges that well-being can seem subjective because what makes one person thrive may not be the same for another. However, he argues that this does not mean that well-being is purely subjective or that it cannot be scientifically studied.

Here are a few of his arguments:

Well-being and Conscious Experience: Harris defines well-being in terms of conscious experience. According to him, well-being is about the experiences of sentient beings — experiences of happiness, suffering, joy, despair, fulfilment, frustration, and so on. Harris contends that although these experiences are subjective in the sense that they occur in people's minds, they are also objective in that the physical world, including our brains, impacts them and allows for scientific study.

Objective Judgements about Well-Being: Harris argues that we can often make objective judgements about well-being. For instance, a life filled with intense suffering and despair is not conducive to well-being. In contrast, a life filled with happiness, fulfilment, and meaningful relationships is conducive to well-being. According to Harris, such judgements are not merely subjective opinions but grounded in the objective reality of conscious experiences.

Harris's view is not without critics, some of whom argue that he oversimplifies the complexity of moral deliberation and overlooks the role of cultural and personal values. Here are some criticisms and limitations of Harris's theory:

Is-Ought Problem:[43] David Hume, a philosopher, first proposed what is known as the 'is-ought problem', which Harris's detractors frequently bring up. Hume argued that just because something is a certain way (an 'is' statement), it doesn't mean it ought to be that way (an 'ought' statement). Critics claim that Harris needs to address this gap adequately.

Definition of Well-Being: Critics argue that Harris's definition of morality as the well-being of conscious creatures is too simplistic and subjective. What constitutes 'well-being' can vary significantly among individuals and cultures and may not capture all of what morality encompasses.

The Role of Science: Some critics question whether science can genuinely determine moral values. They argue that while science can inform our moral decisions by providing data about the consequences of actions, it cannot make those decisions for us. According to these critics, deciding right or wrong is a philosophical or ethical question, not a scientific one.[44]

Neglect of Moral Pluralism: Critics also suggest that Harris's theory doesn't sufficiently acknowledge moral pluralism—that there may be multiple, equally valid moral truths or paths to well-being. Instead, Harris's 'moral landscape' metaphor suggests a single peak or a limited number of peaks of well-being, implying a singular or limited set of 'correct' moral values.

Nevertheless, his work represents a provocative attempt to bridge the gap between science and morality, arguing for the possibility of an objective, secular moral framework. In conclusion, while theistic beliefs can inform an individual's moral perspective, they are not the sole or primary source of morality. The evidence suggests that morality is a complex interplay of biological, psychological, and cultural factors, allowing for the possibility of an objective moral framework that transcends religious and cultural differences.

East versus West: Moral Frameworks

The Western philosophical tradition tends to dichotomise moral perspectives into objectivism or relativism. Objectivism holds that universal moral truths are applicable to all, regardless of individual or cultural perspectives. Moral relativism, on the other hand, posits that moral judgements are subjective and dependent on cultural, social, or personal contexts.

Eastern moral frameworks, particularly those from India, often present a different approach. While they acknowledge the existence of objective moral truths, they also accommodate a degree of flexibility and context sensitivity that can be misconstrued as moral relativism. However, this flexibility doesn't negate the objectivity of moral truths. Instead, it reflects an understanding of the complex interplay between unchanging reality (Brahman in Hinduism, Dharma in Buddhism) and the ever-changing phenomenal world.

Bhagwan Sri Krishna's *Niṣkāmakarma*

Sri Krishna's concept of *niṣkāmakarma* (selfless action) in the Bhagavad Gita offers a robust example of moral objectivism within an Eastern framework. Arjuna, one of the five Pandavas in the great epic Mahabharata, lays down his weapons and refuses to fight in the ongoing conflict.[45] When he sees his loved ones, especially older people, for whom he has great affection, he is overcome with sorrow.[46] The prospect of battling the innocent and killing his kin fills him with a peculiar sense of regret. He declares, 'I will not fight', leaving his charioteer, Sri Krishna, perplexed.

Sri Krishna recalls to Arjuna that this is not only a physical battlefield (Kurukshetra) but also a moral one (*dharmakṣhetra*). After all other options were exhausted, the war was fought as a last resort. Arjuna is conscious that his cause is just, but he cannot transcend his human emotions. Sri Krishna attempts multiple arguments to convince Arjuna to battle.

One of these is a genuinely original action-based moral argument. Sri Krishna recognises that Arjuna is a man of action and urges him to perform his duty regardless of the consequences. Sri Krishna says, 'You have a right to perform your prescribed duty, but you are not entitled to the fruits of action. Never consider yourself the cause of the results of your activities, and never be attached to not doing your duty.'[47] He then advises Arjuna, 'Perform your duty equipped, O Arjuna, abandoning all attachment to success or failure. Such equanimity is called yoga.'[48]

Sri Krishna advises Arjuna to perform his duty without attachment to the fruits of the action. This advice is not relative; it applies universally. Yet, it also recognises the reality of human life, where circumstances and duties vary between individuals.

Bhagwan Mahavira's *Anekāntavāda*

Similarly, Mahavira's concept of *anekāntavāda*[49] (non-one-sidedness or many-sidedness) in Jainism embraces the complexity of reality. It posits that truth and reality are complex and always have multiple aspects. While this might seem relativistic, it's a form of pluralistic objectivism, recognising multiple objective truths based on different perspectives.

The beauty of anekāntavāda, or 'non-one-sidedness'/'many-sidedness', is that it does not promote a theory of relativism or subjectivism. In its quest to know the *satya* or truth, it creates a highly flexible and plural 'conditional yes or conditional approval' of any proposition by applying the epistemology of *saptibhaṅgīnaya*. The sevenfold path goes somewhat like this:

Affirmation: *syād-asti*—in some ways, it is,
Denial: *syād-nāsti*—in some ways, it is not,
Joint but successive affirmation and denial: *syād-asti-nāsti*—in some ways, it is, and it is not,
Joint and simultaneous affirmation and denial: in some ways, it is, and it is indescribable,
Joint and simultaneous affirmation and denial: in some ways, it is not, and it is indescribable,
Joint and simultaneous affirmation and denial: in some ways, it is, it is not, and it is indescribable,
Joint and simultaneous affirmation and denial—in some ways, it is indescribable.

In its way, anekāntavāda recognises that sometimes there are no good or universal answers to particular situations or questions in morality, metaphysics, or otherwise, but that does not mean there are no good answers.

Universal Objective Moral Pluralism

By combining these Eastern concepts with the objective moral realism of thinkers like Sam Harris, who posits that moral truths can be scientifically determined, and Jonathan Haidt, who emphasises the role of intuition and social context in moral judgements, one could potentially create a robust system of 'Universal Objective Moral Pluralism'.

As Harris suggests, this framework would recognise the existence of universal moral truths and acknowledge the role of intuition and social context, as Haidt emphasises. It would embrace the flexibility inherent in niṣkāmakarma and anekāntavāda, taking into account the complexity and diversity of human experience.

Such a system would be objectivist, as it acknowledges universal moral truths. However, it would also be pluralist, recognising that these truths can manifest differently based on context and perspective. This flexibility would allow for a more nuanced, compassionate, and practical approach to moral decision-making that respects our shared humanity and our differences.

In this integrated framework, universal moral truths provide a firm foundation, while the pluralistic approach allows flexibility and adaptability. The insights of neuroscience and psychology can inform our understanding of moral truths. At the same time, the wisdom of Eastern traditions can guide their application in the complex and diverse contexts of human life.

This approach can potentially offer a more nuanced and effective way of making moral decisions, one that is grounded in both universal principles and individual and cultural realities. It can also encourage dialogue and understanding between different perspectives, fostering greater moral wisdom and compassion. However, developing such a framework would require careful thought and a willingness to engage with other philosophical traditions and scientific disciplines. It would also require a commitment to ongoing learning and reflection as our understanding of morality evolves.

Let us look at a few hypothetical examples to illustrate how this integration of Eastern and Western moral philosophies might be applied in real-life situations.

Example 1: Medical Ethics

Imagine a doctor whose patient suffers from a terminal illness and has a poor prognosis. The Western philosophy of moral objectivism might lead the doctor to tell the patient the truth about their condition, as honesty is generally considered a universal moral value. However, the patient's family might request that the doctor not disclose the full prognosis, believing that it would cause unnecessary distress.

In this case, the concept of niṣkāmakarma from the Bhagavad Gita could guide the doctor to perform their duty, which involves providing the best care possible for the patient. This might mean balancing honesty with compassion, perhaps by disclosing the diagnosis while emphasising the support and care provided.

Anekāntavāda, the Jain philosophy, could also be helpful here. It could help the doctor understand that honesty and compassion are valid ethical principles and that the challenge is finding a course of action that respects both. This might involve a nuanced conversation where the doctor gently informs the patient about their prognosis while providing emotional support and focusing on quality of life.

Example 2: Environmental Ethics

Consider a community facing the decision of whether to support the development of a new industrial project that would not only bring economic benefits but also potential environmental harm. A strict objectivist approach might argue for a clear-cut answer based on whether the project's benefits outweigh its costs. However, this might only partially capture the complexities of the situation.

Here, niṣkāmakarma could inspire community members to consider their duties to their economic well-being, the environment, and future generations. This might lead them to support sustainable practices, even if they are more costly or complicated.

Anekāntavāda could also provide a valuable perspective. It would encourage the community to consider the multiple aspects of the situation, recognising that the industrial project can bring both economic prosperity and environmental damage. This could lead to a more holistic decision, such as working with the company to implement stricter ecological safeguards or investing in renewable energy projects that could provide economic benefits without harming the environment.

Also, the concept of Anekāntavāda can be applied in various fields, including business and politics. Here are two examples:

Business Ethics

Consider a corporation facing a decision about whether to invest profits back into the business, distribute them to shareholders, or use them to improve wages and working conditions for employees. A simplistic approach might insist that there's only one correct answer, such as maximising shareholder value as the primary goal of a business.

Applying Anekāntavāda, however, the corporation could acknowledge multiple valid perspectives. While shareholders expect returns on their investments, employees also have a legitimate claim to fair compensation and good working conditions. Furthermore, reinvesting in the business can ensure its long-term growth and sustainability.

Therefore, a decision that respects all these aspects might involve a balanced approach:
- Providing reasonable dividends to shareholders
- Improving wages and working conditions
- Setting aside funds for business development

This approach would acknowledge the multifaceted nature of the corporation's responsibilities and strive for a more comprehensive form of success.

Political Ethics

In politics, anekāntavāda can also be very valuable. For instance, politicians must often navigate complex issues with multiple competing interests when forming public policies.

Take the issue of immigration policy. On one side, there's a need to maintain national security and economic stability. On the other hand, there's a humanitarian obligation to offer refuge to those fleeing violence or persecution and a financial benefit to attracting skilled immigrants.

A politician guided by Anekāntavāda would recognise that these different perspectives hold a piece of the truth. Rather than viewing the issue in black-and-white terms — either open borders or complete restriction — they would work to develop a nuanced policy that respects national security and economic concerns but also upholds humanitarian principles and recognises the potential benefits of immigration.

Why Decoloniality Is Not the Answer

Not even a day goes by when we do not get some news from Afghanistan, where, one after another, women are subjected to atrocities. In an interview with the Australian broadcaster SBS, the deputy head of the Taliban's cultural commission, Ahmadullah Wasiq, said women's sport was considered neither appropriate nor necessary.[50]

Ahmadullah Wasiq says,

I don't think women will be allowed to play cricket because it is not necessary that women should play cricket. In cricket, they might face a situation where their face and body will not be covered. Islam does not

allow women to be seen like this. It is the media era, and
there will be photos and videos, and then people watch it.
Islam and the Islamic Emirate [Afghanistan] do not allow
women to play cricket or play the kind of sports where
they get exposed.

Beheshta Arghand, covered worldwide for becoming the
first female journalist to interview a Taliban leader after
Kabul's fall, fled to Qatar as she feared for her life. 'Women
– Taliban they don't accept,' Arghand told Reuters from
Qatar. 'When a group of people don't accept you as a
human, they have some picture in their mind of you, it's
very difficult.'[51]
   As if this was not enough, 'scores of Afghan women
were forced by the Taliban to gather at Kabul University
dressed in head-to-toe black robes that they had distributed
on the anniversary of the 9/11 terrorist attacks. Those
who dared to refuse, say students, were to be expelled.'[52]
   The Taliban says women may work (in accordance
with the principles of Islam') The Talibans' new higher
education minister, Abdul Baqi Haqqani, said, 'We have
no problems in ending the mixed-education system', 'The
people are Muslims and they will accept it.'[53]
   Taliban spokesperson Sayed Zekrullah Hashimi is
quoted saying, 'A woman can't be a minister, it is like you
put something on her neck that she can't carry. It is not
necessary for women to be in the cabinet—they should
give birth. Women protesters can't represent all women in
Afghanistan.'[54]

   What are we supposed to do in such a scenario as human
   beings? Are we supposed to condemn these actions and
   decisions of the Taliban, or should we say that the Taliban
   have their worldview? While we may disagree with their
   actions personally, their judgements are contingent on

their variables and moral sensibilities, so who are we to demand they change their way of living?

This takes us to the subject of Decolonial ethics. What answers can be given if we were to look at what is happening in Afghanistan through the lens of decoloniality and its ethical framework?

As per decoloniality, 'Western modernity, and the cosmopolitan values entwined with modernity, have an inextricable darker side—coloniality.'[55] It differs from cosmopolitanism, which is a direct outcome of Western values, and it rejects the individualism and universalism of cosmopolitan thought.

Decoloniality promotes approaches that reject abstract global designs 'in favour of inter-cultural dialogue amongst multiple people(s), including peoples who deem collective and nonhuman entities to be of fundamental moral importance'.[56] In addition, decolonial global ethics rejects universality in favour of 'pluriversality'. It does this because, from a decolonial perspective, 'universalistic and individualistic forms of cosmopolitan thought occlude and ultimately reproduce the colonial matrix of power'.[57]

Pluriversality is a two-pronged process:

[Primarily,] a value is pluriversal in a first, procedural sense, if it is constructed not through the universalisation of a particular perspective, but through dialogue across plural cultures and cosmovisions. In a second sense, pluriversality connotes a substantive value itself—the value of a world in which other worlds are possible.[58]

The critical aspect of this pluriverse is that it 'would be a world in which multiple cosmovisions, worldviews, practices and livelihoods co-exist, a world where no one particular way of living shuts down others'.[59]

Now let us focus a little more on this crucial aspect of decolonial ethics, where the epistemology 'rejects universality in favour of "pluriversality".[60] It says that "pluriversal dialogue is not solely oriented towards consensus"'.[61]

How does this work out for women in Afghanistan? Is the Taliban a part of the pluriverse or not? If yes, why aren't the Taliban's dictates regarding women covering themselves from head to toe or not joining media houses or playing cricket just another cosmovision or worldview?

Decoloniality says we must aim for a world where 'no one particular way of living shuts down others'. If that is the essence of decoloniality, coupled with its outright rejection of 'universalistic and individualistic forms of cosmopolitan thought' as they 'ultimately reproduce the colonial matrix of power',[62] how does one deal with the Taliban? Do we accept them as part of the pluriverse? Do we ignore them and not deal with them? Or do we reject them and try to engage with them and promote a better and more humane worldview? And if we encourage our worldview when engaging with the Taliban, are we committing potential epistemicide?

Or do we consider the Taliban a group that produces 'subaltern knowledges and cultural practices worldwide that modernity itself shunned, suppressed, made invisible and disqualified'?[63]

Decoloniality promotes Border Thinking, which insists on giving a '"preferential option" to those on the receiving end of colonial rule'.[64] So does Afghanistan qualify as 'the British controlled Afghanistan's foreign policy for 40 years following the end of the second Anglo-Afghan War?' (Afghanistàn was never part of the British Empire.)[65]

Decoloniality wants 'a world in which many worlds fit' or 'a world in which many worlds are possible'. So, isn't the Taliban also part of that pluriverse? It also promotes 'an understanding of the inseparability of equality and

difference. "A world in which many worlds are possible …
means that people and communities have the right to be
different precisely because we are all equals"'.[66] So, are
the Taliban and Indians morally equal?

Also, 'pluriversality sets a standard of legitimacy that
would judge as morally wrong any worldview, value or
practice that does not accept the existence of, or that
works to shut down, other worlds'.[67] So, if someone
actively works to shut down the worldview espoused by
the Taliban, would they be wrong?

Another distinct aspect or trait of decoloniality is the
complete absence of the individual from the discourse. One
can read paper after paper or book after book. Still, the
decolonial worldview puts the group over the individual. The
entire discussion revolves around competing groups jostling
with each other in a world suffering from colonialism that
has been reduced to chaos due to limited resources. In such
a scenario, the individual is completely lost. Individuality is
treated as a distinct problem that arises from colonialism.
Decoloniality and its sympathisers insist that when a 'whim
is couched as a right and has the effect of adversely affecting
the interests of the group, or the interests of other groups,
or the civilisational interest, the individual's right must
necessarily be traded off against the greater good'.[68]

Let us take this claim at face value. So, in the case of
Afghanistan, what is their civilisational interest? Isn't an
Islamic state like the one in Afghanistan a civilisational
state too? Wouldn't the propagation of Islamic civilisational
rules be their priority or interest? And if that is the case,
should the individual rights of women in Afghanistan
be traded away for the 'greater good' or the Islamic
civilisation's interest?

That brings us to the tussle between group rights and
individual rights. Yes, sometimes the group precedes the

individual, as with reservations in India. But when you
put group rights over individual rights as a norm, one can
commit grave errors, as is done in the case of free speech
in India, where we have laws like 295A that say,

> Deliberate and malicious acts, intended to outrage
> religious feelings of any class by insulting its religion or
> religious beliefs. Whoever, with deliberate and malicious
> intention of outraging the religious feelings of any class
> of 273 [citizens of India], 274 [by words, either spoken
> or written, or by signs or by visible representations or
> otherwise], insults or attempts to insult the religion or
> the religious beliefs of that class, shall be punished with
> imprisonment of either description for a term which may
> extend to 4[three years], or with fine, or with both.].[69]

So what 295A does is put the rights of a religious group
over those of individuals.

Or let us take the case of the debate around the Uniform
Civil Code in India. When Muslims in India demand that
they be governed by Sharia law for civic matters, are they
imposing their whims as a group over the individual rights
of Muslim women and every other Indian citizen? The
answer would undoubtedly be no from a decolonial ethics
perspective because, in the world of decoloniality, every
negotiation or exchange happens at the level of groups,
so it leaves an individual Muslim woman no choice other
than either leaving Islam and joining another group or
accepting the norms of Sharia.

Sympathisers of decoloniality in India say, '"uniformity"
in any realm, including and especially in civil law, is
the subject of deliberation, the federal character of this
civilisation and the reasons for its survival must be borne
in mind before resorting to a European-style "national"
treatment of a federal civilisation'. They say, 'The whole

is as strong as its parts and the survival of the parts is contingent on the existence of the whole.'[70]

Is Sharia law also a subset of that whole? If it is, is the survival of this part also contingent on the existence of the whole? The Indian decolonialists say, 'Time and again, the reformers put forward the argument that uniformity is necessary, without explaining why, simply assuming that uniformity is an un-questioned good.'[71]

This is a legitimate question that needs to be kept in mind when discussing designing not just a uniform civil code but a universal objective moral pluralism. But the decolonialists also need to answer: When discussing pluralism and diversity, where do they draw the line? Will we allow every practice under the sun under the garb of group diversity? Is female genital mutilation, *nikah halala*, triple talaq, untouchability, racism, etc., allowed? Are we going to say there is no moral tenet under the sun with any universal application?

The principle of individual rights works within the framework of the harm principle. So, the final question for decolonialists is: In a world where one group is negotiating against the other, how does one function? What will be the legal framework? Will groups govern themselves under decentralised organisations like the All India Muslim Personal Law Board or Khap Panchayats? How will one seek justice? Why is a nation or civilisational state good if uniformity is terrible as a principle? Why should we not live in small groups with porous borders where different groups negotiate with each other constantly?

Conclusion

The line between uniformity and diversity is very fine. The aim of this chapter is not to promote any moral absolutism. The objective is to challenge any authoritarianism.

Decoloniality also raises some vital points when it tells us to question the epistemic foundations of things emanating from the Western world. But decoloniality, with its group obsession, also promotes another kind of moral absolutism. So let both sides, whether decoloniality or their opponents, not make the mistake of throwing the baby out with the bathwater. Intellectual isolationism can be highly harmful. Just because an idea or a meme has come from the West, we should not call it wrong by default. Let us judge it on its own merits and test it rigorously in the marketplace of ideas. Ignacy Jan Paderewski said, 'Intellectual isolation follows commercial isolation'.[72] So let a thousand flowers bloom in the marketplace of ideas, and may the best meme win.

Whether it is business and politics, the field of medicine, or environmentalism, niṣkāmakarma and anekāntavāda can help decision-makers navigate complex ethical dilemmas by acknowledging the validity of multiple perspectives. This does not mean that all views are equally suitable or that decisions should be made by compromise or consensus alone. Instead, it encourages a more nuanced understanding of complex issues, which can lead to more thoughtful, balanced, and ethical decisions.

In these examples, integrating Eastern and Western moral philosophies provides a more nuanced and flexible approach to ethical decision-making. It allows for recognising universal moral truths while also considering the complexities and multiple perspectives inherent in real-life situations. It's important to note, though, that these are just hypothetical scenarios, and the actual application of these philosophies may differ based on specific contexts and cultural norms.

Imagine this scenario: as you sit in the comfort of your house reading this book: There is a boy, in some cases as young as nine, being forced to dress as a woman and to dance seductively for an audience of older men.[73] I am talking about Bacha Bazi, a tradition in Afghanistan where wealthy Afghans, usually across southern and eastern Afghanistan's rural Pashtun heartland or within ethnic Tajiks across the northern countryside, 'buy' young men or boys for their entertainment.[74]

As per the Afghanistan Independent Human Rights Commission (AIHRC) report, 'around 87 per cent of these victims have stated that they have exploited them without their consent'.[75]

The following graph shows the result of perpetrators and victims' statements in this regard:

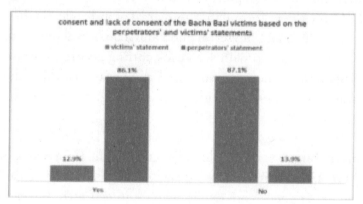

Fig. 4.1 Causes and Consequences of Bacha Bazi in Afghanistan. UNHRC report

So, is Bacha Bazi right or wrong? Is this 'cultural practice' good or bad? In other words, it is a practice where boys as young as nine years old are made to sleep with men, sexually exploited, made for dancing, entertain adults at Bachabazi parties and gatherings, serve as servants at parties and gatherings where older men touch their body organs, forcing them to massage the bodies of the perpetrators, etc., fine? [76]

Lance Cpl. Gregory Buckley Jr thought this practice was abhorrent when he told his father 'he could hear Afghan police officers sexually abusing boys they had brought to the base'. Special Forces commander Dan Quinn was relieved of his command 'after he beat up an American-backed militia commander for keeping a boy chained to his bed as a sex slave'.[77]

So was Lance Cpl. Gregory Buckley Jr and Special Forces commander Dan Quinn, right for feeling gutted when they saw young boys exploited? Or was it just another white Western Protestant Christian American imposing his worldview on another culture and multiple media outlets worldwide, then generating atrocity literature by writing articles about it?

Can we ever formulate a universal moral code? Is there such a thing as a universal good and a universal bad? Can we ever come up with scenarios cutting across the entire human race where we can comfortably say that this value practised by person A or sect B is wrong, no matter how we view it?

So, can we defend the practice of Bacha Bazi? A moral relativist or decolonialist can use the framework of M.J. Herskovits, where he says, 'Judgements are based on experience, and experience is interpreted by each individual in terms of his own enculturation.'[78] Because of that, we find the practice of Bacha Bazi morally repulsive because our cultural norms condition us to think harming young children is bad or wrong.

A moral subjectivist can say that while they might find the practice of Bacha Bazi personally wrong, it cannot be universally bad because morality directly stems from individual subjective experiences. Hence, if the Afghani think Bacha Bazi is good, they are justified in their respective belief. An Indian decolonialist might try to wiggle out of this problem by saying this is a problem of the Muslim community and Hindus should not be bothered.

Let us expand a little bit more from a meta-ethics perspective now. To understand this even better, one must understand what Mitchell Silver calls Categorical Permissibility Rules. Silver says,

> Without stirring from our armchairs, we can safely say that people are sometimes motivated by rules that they have accepted, such as 'move chess bishops only along the diagonals', or 'floss daily'. Acceptance of a rule can, in part, constitute motives for actions. Not only can rules motivate actions, they also influence judgments about the correctness of actions. The rule about chess bishops underlies my judgment that it is incorrect to move a bishop along the horizontal. While there are no precise criteria for whether or not a person has accepted a rule, or for measuring the degree of acceptance, 'acceptance' implies that the rule has some motivational force and influence on judgments. It would be nonsensical to say, 'Silver accepts the rule forbidding moving bishops horizontally, although he is not in the least inclined to follow the rule, nor does he see anything at all incorrect about moving bishops horizontally. Among the rules that can motivate actions and determine judgments are those that classify all possible actions as either permissible or impermissible.'[79]

Now Silver himself admits that 'a permissibility rule can be complex, and its application sensitive to circumstances. A permissibility rule may require that the time, place, effects, and the nature of the people involved be considered when evaluating an action. It may even take into account the acceptance of different permissibility rules by other people'.[80]

But that does not mean we cannot have a working framework. Silver says,

> For instance, I know that there are people who categorically accept the rule that one should never mistreat their holy scriptures. I accept no such rule, but my awareness of others' acceptance of the rule, combined with a rule I do accept, that everyone should show respect for others' feelings, results in me not mistreating others' holy scriptures. I do not respect the 'holy scripture rule' in itself; but I respect the holders of that rule, and in doing so I must often respect their rule. But this derivative respect for their permissibility rules does not mean I accept their rules to make my moral judgments.[81]

People often confuse differences emerging out of permissibility rules with the idea that there can be no such thing as a universal moral standard at all. Let us consider a case where we are morally dumbfounded. Jonathan Haidt explains this beautifully in his book *The Righteous Mind*, where he shares this example:

> Julie and Mark, who are sister and brother, are traveling together in France. They are both on summer vacation from college. One night they are staying alone in a cabin near the beach. They decide that it would be interesting and fun if they tried making love. At the very least it would be a new experience for each of them. Julie is already taking birth control pills, but Mark uses a condom too, just to be safe. They both enjoy it, but they decide not to do it again. They keep that night as a special secret between them, which makes them feel even closer to each other. So what do you think about this? Was it wrong for them to have sex?[82]

Now, what Haidt says is that most people find this story morally repulsive, even though they cannot rationalise their position as to why it is problematic in the face of it.

Haidt says, 'morality binds and blinds'. He tells us that 'we are products of multilevel selection, which turned us into Homo duplex. We are selfish and we are groupish. We are 90 percent chimp and 10 percent bee' and 'religion played a crucial role in our evolutionary history—our religious minds coevolved with our religious practices to create ever-larger moral communities, particularly after the advent of agriculture'.[83]

Even though we do not have good enough answers in every case, there are still good answers. In evolutionary psychology, there are proximate explanations and ultimate explanations. A proximate explanation would be the one that focuses on the immediate causes of behaviour, and an ultimate explanation would be the one that focuses on the effects for which that particular behaviour was selected. One could take a cue from evolutionary psychology and expand that worldview in morality and ethics. So, while there might be proximate differences in our morals, there has to be some ultimate moral code.

Also, one can avoid becoming an Abrahamic moral absolutist to understand that there is something like a universal moral standard. One should fight that urge to become a moral absolutist and replace it with a universal objective moral pluralism.

The beauty of Anekāntavāda is that in its quest to know the satya or truth, it creates an extraordinarily flexible and plural 'conditional yes or conditional approval' of any proposition by applying the epistemology of saptibhaṅgīnaya. It recognises that sometimes there are no good or universal answers to particular situations or questions in morality, metaphysics, or otherwise, but that does not mean there are no good answers.

If we adopt this flexible yet objective approach of saptibhaṅgīnaya, one could easily find answers to multiple moral issues like slavery, racism, birth-based *jati varna* (hereditary social structures), etc. We don't need to say that slavery might be wrong for me but suitable for someone else. We do not need to spin yarns of apologia around jati varna and its fallout by saying that we first must conduct 'epistemological decolonisation'. Until we do that, we cannot judge their results. If we do any honest analysis today, we are not Western modern Christian protestant reformists.

When someone tries to morally judge jati varna, we do not need to explain whether we have been burdened with Western Christian ethnocentrism. We do not need to make excuses and say that we have been unfairly overburdened because of the West and its newfound guilt complex around race. We can admit without any ifs or buts that discrimination has emanated out of birth-based jati varna. This practice is morally wrong, and we must reject it lock, stock and barrel.

Isaac Asimov once said, 'Never let your sense of morals prevent you from doing what is right.'[84] So, let us all work together to build a universal moral plural framework which will lead to the flourishing of our planet and all the species that are part of it.

5

The Complexity of
Indian Society

Bharat, or India as it's globally known, is a civilisation that boasts a history stretching back more than 8,000 years, with archaeological evidence potentially pushing this timeline even further. It's a nation teeming with unparalleled diversity, a mosaic of cultures, languages, religions, and philosophies that have interwoven over millennia to form a rich societal tapestry. To fully understand and critique Indian society, one must first appreciate the intricate complexity of its social fabric.

The roots of Indian society are deep and tangled in the soil of its ancient history. India's past is characterised by layers of cultural, intellectual, and spiritual evolution, from the sophisticated urban settlements of the Indus Valley Civilisation to the profound spiritual philosophies that emerged during this time. The succeeding ages, with the epics of the Mahabharata and Ramayana, the Mauryan and Gupta empires, and the advent of Buddhism and Jainism, further enriched this socio-cultural landscape.

Centuries of foreign invasions and colonial rule brought an infusion of new cultures, traditions, and religions into the Indian subcontinent. Despite the profound transformations during these periods, Indian society managed to absorb these external influences without losing its inherent character, showcasing its resilience and adaptability.

India's complexity is not only historical but also geographical. Stretching from the snow-capped peaks of the Himalayas to the tropical shores of Kanyakumari, the Indian terrain is as diverse as its people. This vast topography has given birth to myriad regional cultures, each with its own unique customs, cuisine, and language. With over 2,000 distinct ethnic groups and more than 1,600 spoken languages, India is one of the world's most ethnolinguistically diverse countries.

Religion plays a crucial role in defining Indian society. India, the birthplace of Hinduism, Buddhism, Jainism, and Sikhism, is also home to substantial populations of Muslims, Christians, and other religious communities. These religions, with their associated rituals, festivals, and moral frameworks, deeply impact the lives of their adherents and shape the country's social norms and values.

However, the Indian societal structure isn't just a simple aggregation of its diverse components. It's a complex interplay where these elements constantly interact, influence, and reshape each other, often blurring the boundaries between them. This complexity, while a source of richness and vibrancy, can also birth contradictions and conflicts.

Understanding what it means to be an Indian is no less complex. Indianness isn't a monolithic identity but a multifaceted construct that varies greatly across regions, religions, castes, and classes. Numerous factors come together to shape it, ranging from individual beliefs and personal experiences to shared historical experiences and cultural heritage. The ongoing conversation among its billion or more inhabitants and their interactions with the outside world shape the idea of Indianness, which is constantly changing.

To grasp the essence of India and its society, one must navigate this multiplicity of views, customs, beliefs, and identities. At its core, the story of India is a saga of coexistence, continuity, and change. It's a testament to the power of diversity and the resilience of the human spirit.

In the following chapter, we will delve into the intricacies of Indian society, exploring its shortcomings and challenges. We will dissect the societal norms, religious philosophies, political structures, and economic systems that govern this ancient civilisation. But before that, let's appreciate the complex, vibrant, and enduring entity that is India, or Bharat, as it has been known since time immemorial. The journey through its depths promises to be as enlightening as it is challenging.

The Deep Religious Undercurrents of Indian Society

India is a deeply religious society; its cultural fabric is intricately woven with threads of spirituality and faith. This religiosity is not merely an aspect of its societal structure but a defining attribute that permeates every facet of life in this diverse nation. From personal beliefs and community rituals to socio-political ideologies and legal frameworks, religion is central to the Indian narrative.

Diana L. Eck writes in her book *India: A Sacred Geography* that 'India is more than a land; it is an intricate tapestry of sacred stories ... a geography of faith that is itself a sacred reality'.[1]

Hinduism, the religion of the majority, is a complex and diverse faith system with a wide spectrum of beliefs, rituals, and practices. It is not a monolithic faith but a confluence of diverse religious traditions. Even Wendy Doniger writes in her book *On Hinduism* that 'Hinduism is a confluence of cultures, an array of cultures, a pluralistic narrative'.[2]

Hinduism's influence extends beyond the realm of personal faith and rituals. The religion's philosophical concepts like dharma (duty and righteousness) and karma (action and consequence) are integral to the societal and ethical frameworks of India.

Buddhism, Jainism, and Sikhism, although not as widely adhered to as Hinduism, have significantly influenced Indian thought and culture. The teachings of Buddha, Mahavira, and Guru Nanak resonate in various aspects of Indian life, from philosophy and art to social reform and politics.

Islam is the second-largest religion in India, shaping the art, architecture, cuisine, and music of the subcontinent. Christian communities, though smaller, have left their mark on education, social services, and local cultures, particularly in South India and the Northeast.

The Pew Research Centre's 2015 report stated that 95 per cent of Indians believe in God and 80 per cent pray daily, underscoring the country's deeply religious character.[3]

Religion in India is not confined to temples, mosques, or churches; it spills into the streets in the form of festivals, pilgrimages, and rituals. As stated by Pavan K. Varma in *Being Indian*, 'In India, religion is a part of life. It permeates to a significant extent all areas of public and private behavior.'[4]

Indian society is stratified along religious lines, with each community having its own distinct customs, laws, and social structures. Even though the law has tried to get rid of some of the unfair parts of the caste system, or the system of jāti and varna, it is still a big part of social rank, economic status, and job roles.

Religion also plays a pivotal role in the political landscape of India. From the politics of religious identity to policy decisions based on religious principles, the influence of religion is evident in the country's democratic processes.

The Indian individual's religiosity is often a blend of personal beliefs, community rituals, and societal norms. In *The Argumentative Indian*, Amartya Sen notes that religious identity in India, while important, is one of the many identities an individual might have in an interconnected society.[5] This complexity adds another layer to the understanding of the deeply religious character of Indian society.

India's deeply religious character is a testament to its historical, cultural, and societal complexities. As we delve deeper into the critique of Indian society in this chapter, the role of religion as a significant influence on societal norms, ethical frameworks, and individual identities will be a recurring theme.

India, with its religious diversity, has a long history of interfaith harmony and conflict. The peaceful coexistence of various religions, as well as periods of religious tension, have shaped the societal dynamics of the nation. The Mughal emperor Akbar's policy of *sulh-e-kul* (universal peace) in the 16th century exemplifies the former, promoting religious tolerance and syncretic culture. On the other hand, India has also witnessed devastating religious conflicts, from the brutal Islamic invasion of India, which led to the brutal destruction and desecration of its religious places,[6] to the eventual partition of 1947, which caused massive displacement and loss of life.

Religion profoundly influences Indian art, architecture, and literature. In her book *The Art of Ancient India*, Susan Huntington discusses how religious themes dominate Indian art forms, from classical temple architecture and sculpture to folk arts like Rangoli and Madhubani painting.[7] The epics Mahabharata and Ramayana, central to Hindu philosophy, have shaped literature, theatre, and cinema.

The Indian legal system, under the garb of recognising the 'sensitivity of religious matters', ends up accommodating religious personal laws.[8] These laws govern matters such as marriage, divorce, and inheritance among different religious communities. India is a unique case in the democratic world where its minority women are still suffering because of outdated and downright misogynistic religious norms.

Indian philosophy is intertwined with its religious thought. The schools of Hindu philosophy, Buddhist thought, Jain metaphysics, Sikh principles, Islamic Sufism, and Christian theological contributions have enriched the philosophical discourse in India.

In contemporary India, religion continues to play a significant role. It influences politics, social norms, and individual identities. While it provides a sense of identity and community, it also leads to conflicts and societal divisions. Issues like religious conversions, communal violence, and religious intolerance often feature in public debates, highlighting the challenges and complexities of being a deeply religious society.

In conclusion, the religious character of Indian society is multifaceted, deeply ingrained, and continues to evolve. As Diana Eck beautifully sums up, 'India's sacred geography does not merely represent the divine. It is the divine, ever reminding the attentive observer of the presence of the gods. In this land, the sacred and the geographical are indeed one.'[9]

Annihilate Jāti Varna

In all human societies, we encounter the phenomenon of social stratification, a structured ranking of entire groups of people that perpetuates unequal economic rewards and power. Anthropologists and sociologists have long recognised that hierarchies are a universal feature of post-agricultural societies. So, let us delve into the intricate dynamics of these hierarchies, focusing mainly on the social stratification in India.

As an economic system, agriculture has played a significant role in establishing social hierarchies. With the advent of agriculture around 10,000 years ago, human societies began transitioning from a nomadic, hunter-gatherer lifestyle to one of settled farming. This shift, often referred to as the Neolithic Revolution, brought about a sea change in human social organisation.[10]

Before agriculture, hunter-gatherer societies were characterised by a higher degree of egalitarianism. Resources were shared within the community, and social status was based on attributes such as hunting skills or wisdom. However, with the advent of agriculture, societies could produce surplus food. This surplus dramatically changed the dynamics of social organisation.[11]

The ability to produce and store surplus food led to the rise of complex societies where not everyone had to be directly involved in food production. Some people could now take on specialised roles such as crafting tools, building structures, or governing. This division of labour led to the emergence of different social classes. Those who controlled the surplus—often the landowners and rulers—became the elite, while those who worked for them formed the lower classes. Thus, agriculture sets the stage for social stratification.[12]

In his seminal work, *The Evolution of Political Society: An Essay in Political Anthropology,* Morton Fried argued that the onset of agriculture led to the development of stratified societies. He identified three types of societies: egalitarian, ranked, and stratified. According to Fried, stratification is directly related to society's surplus production and the control of that surplus.[13]

Unequal access to resources and social benefits is a characteristic of stratified societies. This inequality is institutionalised and persistently transmitted from one generation to the next. Individuals are ranked based on wealth, occupation, and education. This ranking forms the basis of social hierarchy, wherein some groups hold power, wealth, and prestige while others are denied access to these resources.

This brings us to the context of India, which has a long history of social hierarchy entrenched in its caste system. The Indian caste system, called *varna* and *jāti*, is often considered unique due to its deep religious roots and persistence over thousands of years. However, upon closer inspection, it becomes evident that it is just another manifestation of the universal social stratification in post-agricultural societies. The stratification dynamics, as seen through the lens of the caste system, will be the focus of our subsequent discussion.

From ancient to modern times, societies worldwide have implemented systems of social stratification, creating social hierarchies based on various factors such as wealth, power, occupation, and even religious purity. This is not unique to India, and understanding this can help demystify the caste system and highlight its parallels with other forms of social stratification.

Plato's *Republic* provides an early example of social stratification in ancient Greece. In his ideal city-state, Plato divides society into three distinct classes:

- The producers (artisans and farmers)
- The auxiliaries (warriors)
- The guardians (rulers or philosopher-kings)

Each class has a specific role and function, with the guardians at the top of the hierarchy.[14]

'And still easier, haply,' I said,

> is this that we mentioned before when we said that if a degenerate offspring was born to the guardians he must be sent away to the other classes, and likewise if a superior to the others he must be enrolled among the guardians; and the purport of all this was that the other citizens too must be sent to the task for which their natures were fitted, one man to one work, in order that each of them fulfilling his own function may be not many men, but one, and so the entire city may come to be not a multiplicity but a unity.[15]

This division of society into hierarchically arranged classes based on function and education bears similarities to the Indian concept of varna, where society is divided into Brahmins (scholars), Kshatriyas (warriors), Vaishyas (traders), and Shudras (labourers). In the Bhagavad Gita, Chapter 4, Verse 13, Sri Krishna says, 'According to the three modes of material nature and the work associated with them, the four divisions of human society are created by Me. And although I am the creator of this system, you should know that I am yet the nondoer, being unchangeable.'[16]

In the modern context, a similar form of social stratification can be observed in the class systems of societies like the United States and the United Kingdom, where individuals are classified into upper, middle, and lower classes based on wealth, occupation, and education.[17]

Dennis Gilbert's *The American Class Structure in an Age of Growing Inequality* shows that 'people are sorted into positions in the economic hierarchy according to their education and skills, their family background, and the jobs they hold'.[18] This is somewhat akin to the caste system as it evolved in India from its original state, where one's social position is, unfortunately, determined by birth.

Societies with feudal systems, like mediaeval Europe, had a rigid social order based on land ownership and service, with clear divisions between nobles, clergy, and peasants.[19] This resembles the Indian caste system, where social hierarchy was (and, in some places, still is) strictly adhered to.

While it may seem that the explicit rules and religious underpinnings of the caste system are unique to India, the underlying concept of social stratification is a global phenomenon. Recognising these parallels can provide a broader context for understanding the Indian caste system and the efforts towards its annihilation.

The Concept of Jāti and Varna in Ancient India

The ancient Indian social order was based on a system of varna and jāti. These concepts, though interrelated, have distinct meanings in the context of Indian society.

The term 'varna' literally means 'colour'. Still, in the social context, it represents the four principal categories or classes: Brahmins (scholars/priests), Kshatriyas (warriors/rulers), Vaishyas (farmers/traders), and Shudras (workers/servants). This classification is mentioned in ancient Indian texts like the *Rigveda* and the Bhagavad Gita.

On the other hand, 'jāti' refers to a sub-caste or a community that one is born into. There are several jātis within each varna, and each jāti has a specific occupation.

The *Rigveda*, one of the oldest Indian texts, contains a hymn known as the Purusha Sukta (*Rigveda* 10.90), which describes the cosmic being (Purusha) and the origin of the four varnas. Each varna is said to emerge from a different part of the Purusha's body: the Brahmins from the mouth, the Kshatriyas from the arms, the Vaishyas from the thighs, and the Shudras from the feet. 'The brahmin was his mouth. The ruler was made his two arms. As to his thighs—that is what the freeman was. From his two feet the servant was born.'[20]

However, in these verses, it's important to note that the *Rigveda* doesn't explicitly imply a rigid social hierarchy or a system of discrimination based on birth. The Purusha Sukta primarily has a cosmogonic and metaphysical context, describing the universe's origin and social classes as an organic division based on functions and duties (dharma) rather than a rigid status hierarchy.

Some Indian scholars argue that interpreting the feet as inferior may be flawed. They suggest that in many instances, particularly in Hindu iconography, divine beings are often depicted in a reclining posture known as the *ananta shayana* pose. In such instances, the feet are not necessarily at the 'bottom'. If the Purusha were imagined in such a posture, the varna originating from the feet wouldn't be considered 'inferior'. 'In the Anantasayana iconography, Vishnu is depicted reclining on the cosmic serpent Ananta, symbolizing the calm and patience at the beginning of creation.'[21]

This interpretation emphasises the functional division in society rather than a hierarchy of superiority or inferiority. It's a reminder that the ancient texts can be subject to different interpretations and that the current understanding of the caste system may have evolved significantly from the original concepts of varna and jāti in ancient India.

Although the original concepts of jāti and varna in the *Rigveda* did not imply a rigid, birth-based system, these concepts hardened into a system closely tied to birth and hereditary occupation over time. This transformation is reflected in later scriptures, such as the *Dharmashastras* and *Dharmasutras*.

The *Dharmashastras*, including the well-known *Manusmriti* (Laws of Manu), provide rules and regulations for social and moral conduct. These texts reflect a significant shift in the interpretation of the varna system.

In *Manusmriti*, for example, the occupational duties of the varnas are clearly defined and appear to be hereditary. The text prescribes different punishments for the same crime committed by people of different varnas, implying a hierarchical system.

The *Manusmriti* 1.91 says, 'A single activity did the Lord allot to the Sudra, however: the ungrudging service of those very social classes' (social classes being the other three varnas).[22]

The *Manusmriti* 1.92 and 1.93 deviate from the non-hierarchical Purusha of the *Rigveda* and its position by stating that

> A man is said to be purer above the navel. Therefore, the Self-existent One has declared, the mouth is his purest part. … Because he arose from the loftiest part of the body, because he is the eldest, and because he retains the Veda, the Brahmin is by Law the lord of this whole creation.[23]

The *Manusmriti* 4.60 and 4.61 advise other varnas never to reside in a Shudra-ruled kingdom. This shows how, while society still had fluidity, the *Smriti* disapproved.[24]

> He must never reside in a village full of unrighteous people or where diseases run rampant; go on a journey alone; stay long on a mountain;
> Or live in a kingdom ruled by a Shudra, teeming with unrighteous people, overrun by people belonging to heretical ascetic sects, or swamped by lowest-born people.

The *Manusmriti* 8.411 to 8.413 leave no scope for speculation when it says,

A Brahmin should support a Ksatriya or a Vaisya who is starved for a livelihood out of compassion and employ them in activities proper to them.

If a Brahmin makes twice-born men who have undergone vedic initiation do slave labor against their will through greed and to show off his power, the king should fine him.

He may, however, make a Shudra, whether he is bought or not, do slave labor; for the Shudra was created by the Self-existent One solely to do slave labor for the Brahmin. (25)

The *Dharmasutras*, like the Gautama *Dharmasutras* and Baudhayana *Dharmasutras*, also underscore a hierarchical, birth-based varna system. They provide rules for inter-varna marriages and the resulting offspring's varna, further solidifying the birth-based nature of the system. Gautama *Dharmasutras* 4.16 and 4.17 say,

(Children) born in the regular order of wives of the next, second or third lower castes (become) Savarnas, Ambasthas, Ugras, Nisādas, Dausyantas or Pārasavas.

(Children born) in the inverted order (of wives of higher castes become) Sūtas, Māgadhas, Āyogavas, Ksattrs, Vaidehakas or Candālas.[25]

Over time, the fluid and function-based varna system became rigid birth-based, as reflected in these later texts. The jāti system also became more complex, increasing the number of jātis and becoming hereditary.

Endogamy, the practice of marrying within a specific social group, caste, or ethnic group and rejecting others on such a basis is a significant aspect of the jāti and varna systems in India. This practice has had a notable impact on the genetic makeup of the Indian population, as shown in various scientific studies.

Genetic Evidence of a Strictly Enforced Social Barrier

In one study titled 'Genetic Evidence for Recent Population Mixture in India', researchers found genetic evidence that endogamy in India started around 1,900 to 4,200 years ago: 'Different groups in India today have been segregated by endogamy since about 70 generations ago, during which time there has been little gene flow between groups.'[26]

This study used sophisticated modelling methods to analyse genome-wide data from different ethnic groups in India. The researchers found that most Indian groups descend from a mixture of two genetically divergent populations: ancestral North Indians (ANI) and ancestral South Indians (ASI). However, about 70 generations ago, strict endogamy became the norm, and gene flow between groups significantly decreased.

Caste-based Differences in Genetic Makeup

Another study titled 'Genetic affinities among the lower castes and tribal groups of India: inference from Y chromosome and mitochondrial DNA' found significant differences in the genetic makeup of various castes and tribes in India: 'Our results demonstrate a common genetic origin of the Indian populations with a minor contribution of gene flow from West Eurasia. The phylogenetic analysis also suggests that the lower-ranking castes are more genetically similar to the tribal populations than to the higher-ranking castes.'[27]

This study found that lower-ranking castes and tribal populations had more genetic similarity than the lower castes had with higher-ranking castes.

These studies, along with others, provide significant genetic evidence of endogamy in India, demonstrating the jāti and varna systems' considerable impact on the genetic makeup of the Indian population.

Caste Is Not Uniquely Hindu

Buddhism, Jainism, and Sikhism are often presented as reactions against the orthodox Brahmanical Hindu traditions that rejected the caste system. They advocated for equality and rejected the birth-based systems of jāti and varna.
But the truth is far from what has been preached.

The Madhura sutta (84), the Kannakatthala sutta (90) and the Assalayana sutta (93) of the Majjhima-nikaya, the Cullavagga ix.1.4 of the Vinayapitaka, etc., all recognize the existence of four castes: Cattāro vanna, Ksatriya, Brahmana, Vaishya and Shudra. In the Kannakatthala sutta the superiority of Ksatriya and Brahmana castes is recognized: dve vannā aggam akkhāyanti: the two castes are said to be chief and therefore deserve respect and service by the other two castes.[28]

The Vinayapitaka IV.6 declares that calling an ordained monk as having come from a hina jati - Candāla, Vena, etc. — tantamounts to abusing him — calling names for which prāyascitta is essential. The word jāti in this context refers to a distinct category of human beings based on birth or descent.[29]

In the Anguttaranikāya III.57.2 the Buddha states that human beings are Kshatriya, Brāhmana, Vaishya, and Shudra, Candāla and Pukkusa (both outcastes) on the basis of their birth, jātiyam.[30]

And Buddhism is equally opposed to intercaste marriage. So, people hoping for a lack of endogamy in Buddhism are in for some terrible news.

The Buddha condemned miscegenation and upheld the virtue of caste blood purity.

In the Assalāyana sutta the Buddha explains that when a mare is mated with an ass a hybrid new jāti — a mule — is born. From this passage it appears that the Buddha did not approve of mixed marriages. The Buddha concludes:

First you (Assalāyana) went about birth, leaving birth, you went about mantras (he who knows and can recite the Vedas), leaving mantras you arrived at the purity of four castes which is just I lay down.

Here the Buddha was referring undoubtedly to purity of (caste) blood and not moral purity. And purity of blood is the most essential features of jāti vāda.

In the Anguttaranikāya iii, 221 f., the Buddha severely criticizes the Brāhmanas of his days for contracting marriages indiscriminately with women of other castes as it vitiates the purity of their blood. He observed:

In former times brāhmanas approached only a brāhmani (a Brāhmana lady), never a non-brāhmani; now they go to the brāhmani and non-brāhmani alike.[31]

And this was not just restricted to the Indian landmass. Let us look at Sri Lanka as another example.

In medieval Sri Lanka (3rd century A.D. to 15th century A.D.) the lay Buddhists were divided socially into three major groups (vargas):

(a) kulinā: those who were deemed to belong to high families, noble men.

(b) hinā kula\ commoners or ordinary folk who were considered as belonging to inferior or low families.

(c) Candālas: outcastes, now known as Rodiyas.

Occupationally also these constituted three vargas:

(a) utthaka varga consisted of landowners, farmers, Goyigama or Vellālayās, and cattle breeders Gopallā. They also included the warriors and socially were kulinā

(b) hinā varga consisted of two sub-groups:
(i) sippika: artisans, craftsmen such as weavers, oil pressers, potters, blacksmiths, etc.
(ii) those who rendered service on hire - pessika, such as barbers, washermen, workmen or labourers (kammakāra)
(c) candāla varga: those engaged in unclean, polluting jobs or jobs which caused loss of life, that is himsā Such professions or avocations are scavenging, hunting, fishing, slaughter of animals, working in hides and skins, tapping of toddy, etc.[32]

Despite the efforts of various social reformers, discrimination exists even among the Scheduled Castes and Scheduled Tribes of India. One can see hints of this in an article originally published in 1855 and reproduced in the book *A Forgotten Liberator: The Life and Struggle of Savitribai Phule*. The article's author says, 'But the mahars here, no less untouchable than the mangs, also avoid the company of mangs. They have acquired some brahmanical traits, and consider themselves to be superior to the mangs – they also get polluted by the shadow of mangs!'[33]

The Jain social organisation in India has also been unable to show signs of egalitarianism. 'It is at the later stage that the Jain community adopted this feature of socio-economic and ideological life of India and gradually castes, which existed in Hinduism, emerged in Jainism, too.'[34]

[While the] ancient Jain scriptures did not prevent the choice of marriage partners in line with the caste system. But later the 'Sajatiya' marriage with members of one's own caste or sub-caste came to prevail among the Jains. By the end of the nineteenth century, these practices increased caste sentiments and loyalties and created the cultural gulf between the castes.[35]

In his *Particulars of the Jains*, Doctor F. Buchanan, during travels in Canara, says, 'Like other Hindus, they are divided into Brahmen, Cshatriya, Vaisya and Sudra. These castes cannot intermarry together.'[36]

While he did not find such hard hierarchies in other parts of India,

> he still maintained his belief in the existence of the South: ... there is ... great reason to suspect that the proper doctrine of caste, or at least of four castes, similar to those which the orthodox Hindus suppose to have originally existed, is an innovation among the Jains, although in the South of India it now seems completely adopted in compliance with the prevailing opinions.[37]

In Sikhism, despite Guru Nanak's teachings on equality and brotherhood, castes are still prevalent among Sikhs. The Mazhabi Sikhs (scheduled caste Sikhs) often face discrimination from Jat Sikhs (a dominant caste among Sikhs).[38] However, there's a lack of explicit textual references in Sikh holy scriptures advocating caste-based discrimination.[39]

Islam and Christianity in India

In Islam and Christianity, which entered India from the outside, we are told that there is no inherent religious sanction for the caste system. Yet, over time, both these religious communities in India have absorbed caste-like features.

Muslims in India are broadly categorised into three social groupings — Ashraf (the 'noble' or 'honourable ones'), Ajlaf (backward Muslims) and Arzal (Dalit Muslims).

Ashraf Muslims are considered to be of foreign descent, while Ajlaf Muslims are of local Indian origins. The

Pasmanda Muslim movement has highlighted the caste-based discrimination among Indian Muslims:

> Leaders of Pasmanda Muslims claim that nearly 85% of the Muslim population in India is Pasmanda while the remaining are 'Ashrafs'.[40]
>
> The 2006 Sachar Committee report, which examined the state of Muslims in India, states that over 40.7 percent of Muslims in India are Muslim OBCs—nearly 16 percent of the total OBC population.[41]

Pasmanda activist Faiyaz Ahmad Faizi explains how Ashraf Muslims practice discrimination in the concept of *kufu*, or the *khutba*, before the Friday prayers. He says,

> [T]he criteria of race/caste has been considered by almost every Ashraaf ulema. This system categorically describes how only a girl from a certain caste can be an equal match to a groom belonging to a certain race/caste (both have to be kufu). This shows that racial/caste-based discrimination has complete recognition in a huge section of the Islamic society in India. Inter-caste marriages are declared anti-Islamic and those solemnised between non-kufu declared null and void. Three out of the four most widely accepted maslaks (a term commonly used by Muslims to distinguish between different Ulema-led groups) of Islamic law recognise this practice.[42]

'In khutbah as well, only people belonging to a particular tribe—Quraysh (Saiyyad and Shaikh—are hailed.'[43] As if this is not enough, 'even the description of Ansar Sahaba (Muhammad's companion from the Owais and Khajraz tribes), whose sacrifice for Islam cannot be denied by anyone, isn't brought up'.[44]

Inter-*firqa* marriages are also approved only under certain conditions. Faizi says,

> The virus of firqaparasti (loyalty to firqa) has gone so deep into the minds of the Pasmandas that they do not allow marriage between people belonging to different maslaka/firqas. That's because the Ashraaf clerics of one firqa declare those having faith in a different firqa as kafirs, and the marriage to a kafir (infidel) is considered haram in Islam.[45]

The mindset is so deeply rooted, as per Faizi, that it also influences the 'selection of the Caliph in Islam where only a Quraysh has the right. Since the departure of Prophet Muhammad, the superiority of the Quraysh tribe was made a part of Islamic faith on the basis of law.'[46]

Among Indian Christians, caste stratifications are also seen. The scheduled caste Christians often face discrimination from other Christians. Even after conversion, the status of Scheduled Castes and Scheduled Tribes usually does not change significantly.

'In Tamil Nadu, where 70 percent of Catholics are Dalits, discrimination is open.... In parishes, Dalits have separate cemeteries and are even given Holy Communion after non-Dalits.'[47]

A BBC report from 14 September 2010 narrates one such cases:

> In the town of Trichy, situated in the heart of the southern Indian state of Tamil Nadu, a wall built across the Catholic cemetery clearly illustrates how caste-based prejudice persists.
>
> Those who converted to Christianity from the formerly 'untouchable' Hindu caste groups known as Dalits are allocated space for burial on one side of the wall, while upper-caste converts are buried on the other side. The separating wall was built over six decades ago.[48]

The caste system in India, a millennia-old hierarchical social order, has had profound impacts on the socioeconomic, political, and cultural lives of the Indian population, particularly those at the bottom of this hierarchy — the Shudras and Dalits (also known as Scheduled Castes and Scheduled Tribes).

Dalits have historically been assigned roles associated with menial labour and perceived impurity, such as scavenging or manual cleaning. The socioeconomic disadvantages emerging from these assigned roles are well-documented. A study titled 'Caste and Economic Discrimination: Causes, Consequences and Remedies' highlights this:

> The caste system assigns individuals a certain economic status in the society. It is not surprising therefore that Dalits and Scheduled Tribes have always been at the lower strata of the Indian society and are characterized by poverty, illiteracy, ill-health and other social disabilities.[49]

Untouchability, the practice of ostracising a group by segregating them from the mainstream community, has been a part of the lives of the Dalits for centuries. This discrimination extends to public spaces, places of worship, and access to basic amenities:

> The constitutionally guaranteed affirmative action policies have had some positive impact in increasing the representation of Dalits in educational institutions, governmental jobs and elected positions. Notwithstanding this improvement, Dalits continue to remain the most underprivileged class of Indian society: the stigma they face remains evident to this day. Dalits in general continue to survive under inhumane, degrading conditions.[50]

Dalits also face disproportionate levels of violence. According to the National Crime Records Bureau data, crimes against Dalits have been increasing, with 45,935 registered cases of crimes against Scheduled Castes in India in 2019.[51]

> At the end of 2019, Dalits made up 21.7% of all convicts in jails across the country. The share of Scheduled Castes among undertrials languishing in jails stood at 21%. The 2011 Census put their share in the population at 16.6%.
>
> In the case of tribals, the gap was equally big. While the Scheduled Tribes made up 13.6% of the convict population, and 10.5% of all undertrials in jails, the Census put their numbers at 8.6% of the population.[52]

The caste system's impact on Shudras and Dalits extends beyond the immediate socioeconomic and physical harm. It also has profound psychological and cultural implications.

Dalits and Shudras often bear the brunt of caste-based discrimination, experiencing social exclusion, public humiliation, and harassment. This constant discrimination can lead to the internalisation of inferiority, self-deprecation, and low self-esteem, a phenomenon known as 'caste-based self-stigma'.

'A 2015 study shows that marginalised castes remain far more susceptible to chronic illnesses, specifically mental health issues.'[53]

The caste system has also influenced the cultural practices of Dalits. Over centuries, they've developed their distinct cultural traditions, dialects, folklore, music, and art forms, often reflecting their historical experiences of oppression and resistance.

For example, the 'Bahujan' literature is a literary tradition created by and for the Dalits and Shudras, portraying their lives and struggles. Similarly, the

'Ambedkarite' movement, inspired by the Dalit leader Dr B.R. Ambedkar, is a powerful cultural and political movement advocating for Dalit rights.[54]

> A subculture of Dalit music had been brewing in Punjab for the past several decades. However, since 2009 there has been a sharp rise in the popularity of what is known as 'Chamar pop'. This genre of music which is understood to be a reaction to the Jat pop music is concentrated mostly in the Doaba region of Punjab comprising the districts Jalandhar, Hoshiarpur, Nawanshahr and Kapurthala. Census reports from this region suggest that it has the highest concentration of Scheduled Castes in India.[55]

The caste system in India has been the subject of intense critique and reform efforts. While the system's roots are deeply entrenched, various social reform movements and thinkers have persistently called for its annihilation.

From the Bhakti (14th to 17th century) and Sant (15th to 18th century) movements, which advocated for spiritual egalitarianism, to the Dalit Panthers and Bahujan movements of the modern era, numerous attempts have been made to challenge caste hierarchies.[56]

The Arya Samaj movement, founded by Swami Dayanand Saraswati in the 19th century, vehemently opposed caste discrimination and untouchability, emphasising the equal worth of all humans.[57]

Dr B.R. Ambedkar led a powerful movement for Dalit rights, focusing on education, socio-economic upliftment, and conversion to Buddhism to reject the caste system.[58] Dr B.R. Ambedkar, a Dalit himself, emerged as a towering intellectual and political leader who relentlessly challenged the caste system, arguing for its annihilation.[59]

Indian Nationalist and reformist Vinayak Damodar Savarkar spoke about the seven shackles of Hindu society.

> According to Savarkar, the Hindu society was bound by seven shackles (bandi) viz. prohibition of touch (sparshabandi) of certain castes, prohibition of interdining (rotibandi) with certain castes, prohibition of intercaste marriages (betibandi), prohibition of pursuing certain occupations(vyavasayabandi), prohibition of seafaring (sindhubandi), prohibition of rites sanctioned by the Vedas (vedoktabandi), prohibition of reconversion (shuddhibandi) to the Hindu fold. Given below is an English translation of Savarkar's assorted thoughts on six shackles. The seventh shackle viz. prohibition of reconversion (shuddhibandi) has been dealt with separately.[60]

Jyotirao Phule, a radical social reformer, identified the caste system as a form of social slavery and fought for the rights of Shudras and Atishudras.[61]

India's constitution, whose drafting committee Chairman was Dr B.R. Ambedkar, contains several provisions to eradicate the caste system and promote social justice. Article 17 abolishes untouchability, and Article 15 prohibits discrimination based on religion, race, caste, sex, or place of birth.[62]

The Scheduled Castes and Scheduled Tribes (Prevention of Atrocities) Act, 1989, was enacted to prevent and punish atrocities against Dalits and tribal communities.[63] The Protection of Civil Rights Act 1955 aims to enforce the prohibition of untouchability.

Affirmative action policies in India, known as reservation policies, reserve seats in educational institutions, government jobs, and legislatures for Scheduled Castes, Scheduled Tribes, and Other Backward Classes.[64]

While significant strides have been made towards dismantling the caste system and uplifting lower castes, the struggle continues. The caste system is deeply rooted in social structures and mindsets, and its eradication requires relentless societal effort, transformative policies, and legal enforcement.

The annihilation of the caste system, or jāti and varna, in India, is an urgent necessity, not just for the sake of social justice and equality but for the overall progress and development of the nation. The caste system, which has operated for centuries, assigns social status and life opportunities based on birth, denying millions of people the chance to realise their full potential and contribute to society's advancement.

Religious figures like Karpatri Maharaj[65] and H.H. Puri Shankaracharya Nishchalanand Saraswati[66] have often defended the caste system as a divinely ordained social order. They argue that the caste system is part of the dharma or cosmic law and that each caste has its role and function in society.[67] However, such justifications overlook the system's inherent inequality and the immense suffering it causes for those at the bottom of the caste hierarchy.

The caste system's practice of endogamy, or marrying within one's caste, has resulted in various health issues due to the lack of genetic diversity. Studies have shown that endogamy can lead to a higher prevalence of certain genetic disorders in communities that practise it.[68] This is another stark reminder of the system's harmful effects on the lives of millions of people.

Economically, the caste system has been a significant barrier to social mobility and economic development. Dalits and lower-caste individuals often find themselves relegated to poorly paid manual labour and are systematically denied access to more lucrative opportunities.[69] This has resulted in the concentration of wealth and resources in the hands of the upper castes, exacerbating economic inequality.

Moreover, the caste system also wastes human potential. The caste system prevents these individuals from contributing to the country's economic growth by denying educational and economic opportunities to a significant portion of the population. Economists like Amartya Sen have argued that the caste system is a considerable hurdle to India's economic development.[70]

To call the caste system what it is — an inhuman system — is to acknowledge its devastating impact on millions of lives. It is a system that perpetuates inequality and discrimination, hampers economic development, and results in adverse health outcomes due to practices like endogamy.

Therefore, annihilating the caste system is not just a matter of social justice — it's a prerequisite for India's overall progress and development. Building a society where an individual's birth does not predetermine their social status or life opportunities is necessary. This would be a society where everyone has an equal chance to thrive and contribute to the nation's well-being.

Every Religion Gives Women a Raw Deal in Differing Ways

Religion and gender dynamics have been the subject of much scholarly debate. While it's essential to recognise the diversity and complexity within each religion, it's also true that patriarchal interpretations have often resulted in detrimental impacts on women's rights and status. When one reads religious texts as they are, they come across as manmade, patriarchal, or misogynistic, and even to date, they have been interpreted and practised in ways that often disadvantage women.

Delving deeper into the intersection of religion and gender in India requires a nuanced understanding of the diverse religious traditions and their interpretations and the social, cultural, and political factors that influence women's lives.

This chapter will divide India's social and religious landscape into two broad categories. Category one would be the dharmic pantheon, which includes Hinduism, Buddhism, Jainism, and Sikhism. Category two will be the monotheistic religions of Judaism, Christianity, and Islam. These categorisations are being done for ease of writing, and in no way is this an attempt to reduce the complexity of each of these religions into one broad brush.

The Dharmic Pantheon

Hinduism

In Hinduism, the contradiction between reverence for goddesses and the societal status of women is stark. While deities like Durga, Lakshmi, and Saraswati are worshipped, ancient texts like the *Manusmriti* contain passages that restrict women's freedoms and prescribe strict societal roles.

Gargi and Yajnavalkya's story is one of the most compelling examples of women's intellectual participation in ancient Indian philosophy. It is found in the *Brihadaranyaka Upanishad*, one of the oldest Upanishads in Hindu literature.

In the court of King Janaka of Videha, a great debate was organised where sages from all over came to discourse on the nature of reality and the ultimate truth. Yajnavalkya, an esteemed sage, was one of the participants. Gargi Vachaknavi, a renowned female philosopher, was also present.

Gargi challenged Yajnavalkya with questions about atman (the self) and brahman (the ultimate reality). She started by asking Yajnavalkya about the material composition of the world, which he responded to by outlining the order of the elements, from earth up to the ether.

Then, Gargi asked him: 'By what, O Yājñavalkya, is that pervaded which is above heaven and below the earth, which is this heaven and earth as well as between them, and which they say was, is and will be?'[71]

Yajnavalkya replied, 'That, O Gārgī, which is above heaven and below the earth, which is this heaven and earth as well as between them, and which they say was, is and will be, is pervaded by the unmanifested ether.'[72]

Next, Gargi posed two crucial metaphysical questions that led to Yajnavalkya warning her that her questions were becoming too profound and that she could risk her mental stability by pushing too far into the mysteries of the absolute. He says,

> This Immutable, O Gārgī, is never seen but is the Witness; It is never heard, but is the Hearer; It is never thought, but is the Thinker; It is never known, but is the Knower. There is no other witness but This, no other hearer but This, no other thinker but This, no other knower but This. By this Immutable, O Gārgī, is the (unmanifested) ether pervaded.[73]

Intriguingly, Gargi heeded his advice, chose to ask no further questions, and said, 'Revered Brāhmaṇas, you should consider yourselves fortunate if you can get off from him through salutations. Never shall any of you beat him in describing Brahman.' Then the daughter of Vacaknu kept silent.[74]

Gargi's dialogue with Yajnavalkya is significant for several reasons. First, it displays the respect and space given to women philosophers to participate in scholarly debates in ancient India. Gargi is present at the debate and actively engages one of the most respected sages, demonstrating her intellectual prowess and courage.

Secondly, the sophistication of Gargi's questions highlights the depth of her philosophical understanding. She navigates from the physical to the metaphysical plane, pushing Yajnavalkya to the edge of his knowledge.

Lastly, Gargi's challenge to Yajnavalkya can be seen as an assertion of women's right to question and critique spiritual and philosophical concepts. This freedom is often denied in many religious traditions.

In conclusion, the exchange between Gargi and Yajnavalkya in the Upanishads exemplifies the intellectual contribution of women in ancient Hindu texts. It reflects a time when women could actively participate in philosophical discourses and challenge established sages with their profound questions.

But the profundity and excellence of the Brihadaranyaka Upanishad are opposite of those of the *Manusmriti*, where in Chapter 5, verses 147 to 166,[75] of the section 'Laws with Respect to Women', the author of this text talks about how women cannot be independent and explain their duties towards their husbands.

Manusmriti says, 'Even in their own homes, a female — whether she is a child, a young woman, or an old lady — should never carry out any task independently.'

A woman's role is reduced to being 'cheerful, clever at housework, careful in keeping the utensils clean, and frugal in her expenditures'.

As if this were not enough, it says,

Though he may be bereft of virtue, given to lust, and totally devoid of good qualities, a good woman should always worship her husband like a god.

For women, there is no independent sacrifice, vow, or fast; a woman will be exalted in heaven by the mere fact that she has obediently served her husband.

A good woman, desiring to go to the same world as her husband, should never do anything displeasing to the man who took her hand, whether he is alive or dead.

As per the Manu Smriti, once a woman is widowed, 'she may voluntarily emaciate her body by eating pure flowers, roots, and fruits; but she must never mention even the name of another man'.

But then contradicting this very stand is Kautilya's *Arthashastra*, where in 3.2.48. Kautilya, in the section of 'Wife's Rights', says,

A wife may abandon her husband if he:
  - has a bad character;
  - is away from home for a long time in a foreign country;
  - is a traitor to the King;
  - threatens the life of his wife;
  - is declared an outcast; or
  - becomes impotent.

And then in 3.3.7-11, Kautilya says,

A wife shall be taught proper behaviour but the husband shall not use [abusive] expressions such as: 'You are lost [beyond redemption]'; 'You are thoroughly ruined'; 'You are a cripple'; 'You do not know who your father was'; 'Your mother abandoned you'. Breach of this rule is a punishable offence.

Physical punishment shall be [limited to] slapping her on her behind three times with the hand, a rope or a bamboo cane. Any beating exceeding this shall be punishable offence.

A woman who is known to abuse or beat her husband shall be subject to the same punishments as a cruel

husband. If a wife, out of jealousy, goes outside her
marital home for her pleasures, she shall be punished.[76]

It's important to note that these are not the only Hindu texts
and interpretations, and many scholars and practitioners
argue for a more equal and progressive understanding
of women's roles in Hinduism. But at the same time, we
cannot deny that Hinduism does have many problematic
utterances inside its religious pantheon, and having an open
and honest discussion about them is the only way forward.

Buddhism

Buddhism is often perceived as a path of peace,
enlightenment, and equality. However, a thorough
examination of its historical and doctrinal aspects reveals
subtle undertones of sexism and misogyny.

Archana Paudel and Qun Dong, in their paper 'The
Discrimination of Women in Buddhism: An Ethical
Analysis',[77] focus on the position and treatment of women
in Buddhism, highlighting the discriminatory aspects
present in the religion. They argue that sexism is prevalent
within Buddhism, which can be evidenced by the historical
reluctance of Gautama Buddha himself to admit women
into the sangha (the Buddhist monastic community). It
was only after the urging of his assistant Ananda that
Buddha agreed to include women, the first of whom was
his own maternal aunt, Mahaprajapati Gotami.

However, female monastics (*bhikkhuni*s) were subject
to eight weighty restrictions known as the *garudhamma*s,
which did not apply to their male counterparts (*bhikkhu*s).
These restrictions placed *bhikkhuni*s at a lower hierarchical
level, further emphasising gender inequality within the
religion. Notably, the notion that women cannot attain
enlightenment in their female form and must be reborn as

men to achieve Buddhahood is underlined as a clear act
of discrimination.

Women in Buddhism are said to face five obstacles,
including the inability to become a Brahma King, Sakra,
King Mara, Cakravartin, or Buddha. Moreover, the
authors argue that the rule, which states every nun must
bow to every monk regardless of seniority, might be a
later addition by a male-dominated society as it is found
in other religions, like Jainism.

The authors also question the interpretation of some
Buddhist teachings that blame women for the downfall
of the human race. They argue that the issue lies not
with women but with men's desires. Lastly, the authors
criticise the rule that a *bhikkhuni* should seek higher
education from *bhikkhu*s, suggesting that this is another
manifestation of sexism in Buddhism.

The Zen Studies Podcast episodes titled '221 –
Confronting the Buddha's Sexist Discourse – Part 1'[78] and
'222 – Confronting the Buddha's Sexist Discourse – Part
2'[79] take a deep dive into the Gotami Sutta. This scripture
is often interpreted as evidence of the Buddha's sexist
views. In particular, the Gotami Sutta is often quoted
as stating that a woman can't achieve enlightenment
unless she is reborn as a man. This suggests that women
are inherently inferior in their capability for spiritual
advancement, a sexist belief that has unfortunately been
perpetuated in some Buddhist traditions.

The podcast episodes also discuss the restrictions
imposed on nuns in the sangha. According to the
*garudhamma*s, nuns were subordinate to monks in all
circumstances, regardless of their experience or seniority.
This institutionalised gender inequality within the
community and these rules continue to impact Buddhist
practices today.

While Buddhism is often perceived as rational, modern, agnostic, and liberal in matters of gender and sexuality, the foundational texts of the religion contain several instances of misogyny.

The *Vinaya Pitaka*, the Buddhist scripture that outlines the rules of monastic discipline, is cited as a primary source of gender bias. It contains statements that derogate female sexuality and impose stricter rules on female monks (*bhikkunis*) compared to their male counterparts (*bhikkus*). The author Devdutt Pattanaik, in his article 'There's a misogynist aspect of Buddhism that nobody talks about', highlights how the text advises monks against succumbing to the 'lethal' charms of women and suggests that women bear additional responsibility not to arouse men's desires.[80]

Various tales and conversations from Buddhist scriptures are presented, reflecting an overarching theme of female sexuality as dangerous and enslaving and celibacy as the path to enlightenment. The depictions of women in these stories often characterise them as embodied snares of death and rebirth cycles (*samsara*). At the same time, monks are portrayed as embodiments of the path of enlightenment (*dhamma*).

Pattanaik discusses the restrictive rules regarding 'queers' (*pandakas*) and women who do not conform to traditional gender norms, stating that they are not to be ordained as monks or nuns. This is attributed to monks being courted or seduced by 'pandakas' and protecting the Buddhist way's reputation.

The *Vinaya Pitaka*, initially an oral tradition, was codified and systematised by Buddhaghosa, a monk in Sri Lanka, around 1,600 years ago. Pattanaik suggests that these rules influenced the patriarchal attitudes of other religions, including Christianity and Hinduism.

He concludes by challenging the prevailing scholarly
bias that perceives Buddhism as 'good' and other Indian
religions, particularly Hinduism, as 'bad' concerning
gender relations. Pattanaik points out that the misogynistic
aspects of Buddhism are often overlooked or silenced,
and he calls for a more nuanced understanding of the
religion's historical context and its influence on gender
norms and representations.

Jainism

Jainism, renowned for its profound respect and
consideration for all life forms, is often perceived as one
of the most peaceful religions. If there ever was a religion
of peace, it has to be Jainism. However, when it comes to
gender equality and the treatment of women, this ancient
religion, like many others, has been implicated with
instances of sexism and misogyny.

In her essay 'Chastity and Desire: Representing Women
in Jainism', Manisha Sethi talks about the positioning of
men as mendicants versus women as temptresses.[81]

She says,

[T]his theme gets an even more elaborate treatment in
some other texts: the Sutrakritanga (the second anga or
limb of the Jaina canon) and the Uttaradhyayana (the
second Mulasutra text). Dealing with a variety of subjects,
both works are guides for young initiates, instructing them
in true Jain doctrine, the correct path to the highest good,
the principal duties of a monk, but, above all, the dangers
that punctuate a monk's spiritual life.

Lecture XXXII of *Uttaradhyayana Sutra* titled the
'Causes of Carelessness' recalls some of the sanctions
we came across in the Acharanga Sutra: 'A Sramana
engaged in penance, should not allow himself to watch
the shape, beauty, coquetry, laughter, prattle, gestures,

and glances of women, nor retain a recollection of them in his mind.'

Soon enough, feminine influence comes to be identified as one of the prime causes of carelessness—and the principal source of danger—in a monk's spiritual career. Attachment to women, decrees Uttaradhyayana Sutra, is the most difficult to surmount and those who have achieved this will find it simple to sever their affections to other ties and pleasures. Forbearance and indifference to womanhood is the mark of a true monk—'Those who possess the three guptis cannot be disturbed even by well-adorned goddesses.' Yet the wholesome way for a monk is still to live alone, especially sheltered from the female presence because 'it is not safe for mice to live near the dwelling of a cat'. Thus the threat to the monk's chastity and ascetic vows derives not merely from his own lack of control and continued attachment to the pleasures a woman affords, but from the cat-like predatory female who presents an unrelenting threat to his spiritual pursuits.

The *Sutrakritanga Sutra* devotes an entire chapter to the 'Knowledge of Women'. Its principal intent is to familiarise and caution the monks about the ways of the women, their seductive tricks, their fickle nature and the terrible consequences that befall those who give in to this temptation. Part I is titled 'How Women Tempt a Monk'. Here the monk is upgraded from the status of a mouse to that of a fearless single lion. The woman though remains the entrapper who ensnares the monk/lion with a piece of flesh. The 'flesh' here is not simply allegorical, for it is her physical flesh that tempts the ascetic and misleads him from his true path. Subsequent passages regard the monk variously as an antelope, a man who drinks poisoned milk, a pot filled with lac, and the woman as hunter, poison, thorn and fire (which causes the pot of lac to melt).

A woman is defined simultaneously by stupidity and caprice: 'With clever pretences women make up to him,

however foolish they be; they know how to contrive that
some monks will become intimate with them.' Pretending
to be pious, women will, the monks are warned, attempt
to lure them by beseeching them to accept a robe, an
alms bowl, food or drink from them, or even by pleading
with the monks to teach them the law of asceticism, as if
they wish to give up their current way of life. However,
a monk should never trust a woman because 'one man
[women] have in their heart, another in their words, and
another still in their actions'.

Such views are also echoed by many contemporary
*sadhvi*s. While narrating the story of a legendary monk,
Sadhvi Prafullprabha, a Shvetambar nun, endorses the
view that women are by nature fickle-minded and bearers
of unbridled sexuality.

Sthulbhadra Muni lived with a prostitute for 12
years. But later, he was transformed and thought that
he should convert the prostitute into a pious *shravika*.
When he returned to her [with this aim], the prostitute
thought that he had come back to her for pleasure. Upon
seeing him in *muni vesh*, she exclaimed that he, who used
to look like a prince earlier, resembled a beggar now.
The muni replied that he had renounced the world and
become a Jain sadhu. The prostitute mocked him and
challenged him to observe his *chaturmas* in her pleasure
palace. So the great muni spent his rainy retreat in her
house, which had erotic pictures painted on its walls.
The prostitute danced before him and tried to ply him
with rich foods. But he remained utterly unmoved. His
was only one aim—that of converting the prostitute to
a *shravika*, to bring her to the true path. And finally,
he succeeded. His absolute control and discipline
convinced the prostitute.

Sthulbhadra's guru had four disciples: 'one spent
his *chaturmas* at the edge of a lion's den; another near a
snake's pit; the third on the periphery of a well. But upon

hearing them all, the Guru declared that Sthulbhadra's had been the most severe because he had won over the woman. So if one sees, all of these were very dangerous but Sthulbhadra had passed the most difficult test. Even great munis can fall from their greatness [because of women].'

Nalini Balbir, in her essay 'Women in Jainism'[82] points out another fascinating dichotomy in Jains: except for the Digambharas, the nuns outnumber the monks in the three major sects. But Balbir concludes her essay by stating,

[I]f one's birth depends on one's own conduct, womanhood (which is due to specific karmic matters) will never be a permanent feature of the individual through the cycle of rebirths. Thus no one is excluded from emancipation for good. The 'failure' will last as long as womanhood lasts.

Secondly, even if the theology of equivalence advocates theoretical equality of men and women, it also shares the postulate of the theology of subordination regarding the inferiority of women, although it is expressed through insinuations and not given the same extension.... Thus whatever the theology espoused, nuns have had less important positions than monks in the religious hierarchy and have been mostly denied leadership roles in spite of their large numbers.

Sikhism

Sikhism, which Guru Nanak founded in the Punjab region of India in the 15th century, has received praise for its progressive perspective on gender equality. The religion's founding principles emphasise the equality of all humans, irrespective of caste, creed, or gender.

Sikhism's holy scripture, the Guru Granth Sahib, contains numerous passages that uphold the equality and dignity of women. For example, it states:

> From woman, man is born; within woman, man is conceived; to woman he is engaged and married. Woman becomes his friend; through woman, the future generations come. When his woman dies, he seeks another woman; to woman he is bound. So why call her bad? From her, kings are born. From woman, woman is born; without woman, there would be no one at all.[83]

This passage underscores the importance of women in society and the cycle of life, challenging the notion of female inferiority. It was also opposed to the barbaric practice of Sati, as is shown in Sri Guru Granth Sahib, Ang 787, where we are told,

> Do not call them 'satee', who burn themselves along with their husbands' corpses. O Nanak, they alone are known as 'satee', who die from the shock of separation. They are also known as 'satee', who abide in modesty and contentment. They serve their Lord, and rise in the early hours to contemplate Him. The widows burn themselves in the fire, along with their husbands' corpses. If they truly knew their husbands, then they suffer terrible bodily pain. O Nanak, if they did not truly know their husbands, why should they burn themselves in the fire? Whether their husbands are alive or dead, those wives remain far away from them.[84]

However, like many other religions, Sikhism's interpretation and practice have not always aligned perfectly with its foundational ideals, and instances of sexism and misogyny have been reported. Broader cultural norms and biases have had an impact on Sikh society, like many others. This can result in a disconnect between religious principles and societal practices.

> Major E Lake, wrote to his government in 1851: 'The practice of killing newborn girls is not just prevalent among the Rajputs, but among the Sikhs too.' When the British administration started taking action to curb the practice, a delegation of Bedi Sikhs, who claimed their lineage to Guru Nanak Dev's family, approached the commissioner of 'Jullundur Doab', John Lawrence, with a petition to allow them to bury their newborn girls alive. The rationale was that the Bedis belonged to the highest caste and could not marry off their girls into any other caste, and that they had been doing it for four centuries. Lawrence, a tough administrator and reformer, was already appalled to see not even a single girl child among the 2,000 Bedi families in his division. He warned them against the practice and reminded them that their religion did not allow it. 'It will be considered murder. I will hang each one of you found involved in female infanticide.' This practice was prevalent among the Hindu Khatris as well. The census of 1854 confirmed Lawrence's fears: The number of women was recorded at 837 for 1,000 men in Punjab.[85]

The tradition of *kurimarr*[86] or the social disgrace associated with having daughters, is an example of this. Even though Sikhism itself does not endorse such a view, it is prevalent in parts of the Punjabi Sikh community due to cultural influences. Similarly, practices such as female infanticide and dowry, both expressly prohibited in Sikhism, have been reported in Sikh communities.

The findings of the National Family Health Survey (NFHS 2020–21) show the Punjab

> [S]tate's child sex ratio at birth increased to 904 from 860 in 2015–16, while the latest national average is 929.

According to the survey, the sex ratio at birth is 858 in urban pockets and 931 in rural areas of Punjab. Also, the state improved its overall sex ratio (females per 1,000 males) from 905 in 2015-16 to 938, against the country's overall figure of 1,020.[87]

Regarding religious leadership, Sikhism does not bar women from any religious roles. Yet the number of women in leadership positions within Sikh institutions is notably low, indicating a gap between religious ideals and reality. This lack of representation can perpetuate disparities and hinder progress towards gender equality.

The National Family Health Survey (NFHS 2020–21) shows Punjab

fared badly in terms of certain indicators vis-à-vis women empowerment. The percentage of women married before 18 in the state went up to 8.7% from 7.6% in the previous survey. Similarly, the percentage of women in the 15-19 age group, who were already mothers at the time of the survey, also increased to 3.1% against the earlier 2.5%. The adolescent fertility rate for women aged 15 to 19 increased to 21% from 20%.[88]

The practice of wearing the 'five Ks' (kesh—uncut hair, kara - a steel bracelet, kanga - a wooden comb, kachera - cotton underwear, and kirpan - a strapped curved sword) considered the identity of a baptised Sikh, is another area where gender disparities come into play. Although there is no scriptural prohibition against women wearing the five Ks, it is less commonly practised by women due to societal norms and expectations, a trend that reflects the influence of patriarchal cultural norms.[89]

Faux machismo has engulfed the Punjabi music industry. Sumati Thusoo and Shivangi Deshwal, in their paper, 'Exploring the Formation of Jat Masculinity in Contemporary Punjabi Music', mention so:

> In several Punjabi songs, the Jat protagonist is characterised by the ability to protect one's izzat vested in women's body and chastity, an overt display of arms and ammunition, exacting revenge, and his resistance to the state's law and order machinery. Just like Sevea's Maula, the Jat protagonist sees being apprehended as an opportunity to reassert his masculinity against the state's law and order machinery. He does not take legal recourse but deals with his enemies himself, as shown in Diljit Dosanjh's Kharku and Jat Fire Karda. The code of his masculinity is encapsulated by qualities such as the ability to bear and use weapons, outdo one's enemy in loud oratorical exchanges and, most importantly, take revenge.[90]

Punjabi Pop songs

> indicate the varying prescriptions for men and women, often eulogising masculinity in the following way: 'Khaan bakre te peen sharaaban, putt Sardaaran de' (Sons of Sardars eat meat and drink). The notion of masculinity, which has been celebrated for ages in Punjab, has been enormously reinforced in the recent past, courtesy Punjabi pop. This has revived, in a rather very aggressive manner, the masculinity of Punjabi men, mainly Jats, making women vulnerable. In the above quote, drinking alcohol and eating meat by men, a sign of affluence, is glorified.[91]

Sikh marriage is governed by the Anand Marriage Act. The problem with this act is that it 'does not make provisions for inheritance or divorce'.[92]

It's important to note that these issues do not stem from Sikhism's core teachings but rather from broader social and cultural norms that have influenced the interpretation and practice of the religion. While many Sikhs today are actively working to address these issues and promote greater gender equality within their communities, guided by the egalitarian principles of their faith, that is not unique to Sikhs, as it is the case in every religious group, and an analysis of Indian society cannot overlook the problems with Sikh society. The challenge for contemporary Sikh society is to reconcile these differences, challenge patriarchal norms, and ensure that the religion's founding principles of equality are fully realised in the daily lives of its adherents.

The Monotheistic Pantheon

We looked at the dharmic pantheon and saw how women were treated in those sects. Now, let us look at the monotheistic pantheon. This chapter will focus on the two monotheistic religions, i.e., Christianity and Islam. It does not mean that their later offshoots, like Mormonism or the first prominent monotheistic religion, Judaism, are some kind of paradise for women. But as this chapter looks at things from India's perspective, we will focus on religions, which are a large part of Indian society.

As per the census 2011,

Muslims in India are about 17.22 Crores i.e. 14.2 % of total population of India follows Islam. India is home to close to 11% of total Muslims Population of World. While its claimed that India has more Muslims than Pakistan, its not true statically. India has third highest Muslim Population after Indonesia and Pakistan. Muslims make up majority in UT Lakshadweep and Jammu & Kashmir while its population is substantial in states of Assam, West Bengal, Kerala and Uttar Pradesh.

In India, Christian Population is 2.78 Crores as per latest figure of 2011 Census which is about 2.3% of total

Indian Population. Decadal Growth rate of Christianity fell from 22.52 % to 15.5% in 2001-2011. Christianity is domninant religion in North East states of Nagaland, Mizoram, Meghalaya and Manipur while they make substaintial population in the states of Arunachal Pradesh, Kerala, Tamil Nadu, Goa and Andaman Nicobar Islands.[93]

Women in Islam

The Quran 4.3 Surah Al-A'raf says,

> If you fear you might fail to give orphan women their 'due' rights 'if you were to marry them', then marry other women of your choice—two, three, or four. But if you are afraid you will fail to maintain justice, then 'content yourselves with' one or those 'bondwomen' in your possession. This way you are less likely to commit injustice.[94]

Now, there might be multiple interpretations of this verse inside the Islamic pantheon, but when the rubber meets the road, reality comes out and is not pretty. As per a detailed report dated 10 May 2022, by the BBC on 'Polygamy: Muslim women in India fight "abhorrent"practice', we see how this practice impacts the lives of Muslim women in India.

> Reshma, who uses only one name, also wants the Delhi High Court to order the government to frame laws to regulate the 'regressive practice' of bigamy or polygamy. According to court documents, she married Md Shoeb Khan in January 2019 and in November the following year, they had a baby.
>
> Reshma accuses her husband of domestic violence, cruelty, harassment and dowry demands. He has levelled similar allegations against her. She also says that he's abandoned her and their baby and he plans to take another wife.

Describing his action as 'unconstitutional, anti-sharia, illegal, arbitrary, harsh, inhuman and barbaric', she says, 'this practice needs to be regulated to curb the plight of Muslim women'.

While the court dwells on their acrimonious relationship and the legality of polygamy, the case has stirred a debate on the practice which is illegal in India except among Muslims and some tribal communities.[95]

In India,

the Hindu Marriage Act, 1955 outlawed the practice. Buddhists, Jains, and Sikhs are also included under the Hindu Marriage Code. The Parsi Marriage and Divorce Act, 1936, had already outlawed bigamy.

IPC Section 494 ('Marrying again during lifetime of husband or wife') penalises bigamy or polygamy. The section reads: 'Whoever, having a husband or wife living, marries in any case in which such marriage is void by reason of its taking place during the life of such husband or wife, shall be punished with imprisonment of either description for a term which may extend to seven years, and shall also be liable to fine.'

Section 495 of the IPC protects the rights of the second wife in case of a bigamous marriage. It reads:

Whoever commits the offence defined in the last preceding section (i.e. Section 494) having concealed from the person with whom the subsequent marriage is contracted, the fact of the former marriage, shall be punished with imprisonment of either description for a term which may extend to ten years, and shall also be liable to fine.

Marriage in Islam is governed by the Shariat Act, 1937. Personal law allows a Muslim man to have four wives. To benefit from the Muslim personal law, many men from other religions would convert to Islam to have a second wife.

In a landmark ruling in 1995, the Supreme Court in Sarla Mudgal v. Union of India held that religious conversion for the sole purpose of committing bigamy is unconstitutional. This position was subsequently reiterated in the 2000 judgment in Lily Thomas v. Union of India.

The National Family Health Survey-5 (2019–20) showed the prevalence of polygamy was 2.1 per cent among Christians, 1.9 per cent among Muslims, 1.3 per cent among Hindus, and 1.6 per cent among other religious groups. The data showed that the highest prevalence of polygynous marriages was in the Northeastern states with tribal populations. A list of 40 districts with the highest polygyny rates was dominated by those with high tribal populations.[96]

A bright light in an otherwise dim reality for millions of Indian Muslim women in India is the Bharatiya Muslim Mahila Andolan (BMMA). This group was formed in January 2007

as 'an autonomous, secular, rights-based mass organisation led by Muslim women to fight for the citizenship rights of the Muslims in India.' The objective of the movement is to alleviate conditions of marginalisation of Muslim women through reforms internally, as well as ensure equal social, economic, political, civil, legal and religious rights as upheld by the Constitution of India.

BMMA has been actively propagating positive and liberal interpretations of Islam in line with feminist values of justice, equity, and human rights. They have been at the forefront of re-defining Muslim personal laws through their campaign to codify Muslim family law, training and equipping Muslim women in Islamic jurisprudence to adjudicate in Muslim family matters from an Islamic feminist perspective, creating centres of knowledge on Islam and women, demanding access and entry to Islamic sacred spaces such as the Haji Ali Dargah.

BMMA also focuses on issues of education, livelihood, health, and social security keeping in view the very low development indicators for Muslim women across India. It mobilises Muslim women at the grassroots and advocates for change by acting as pressure groups. BMMA activists present their plight before local authorities and demand immediate action.[97]

The BMMA has also conducted a National Study on Muslim Women's views on Reforms in Muslim Personal Law and published the findings in a 212-page compendium titled 'Seeking Justice within Family'.[98]

Here is a summary of the survey conducted by the BMMA.

Summary of the Status of Muslim Women
The annual income of 73.1% of the families is below ₹50,000
55.3% have married before the age of 18.
46.5% of the women surveyed have 1 or 2 children
53.2% of the surveyed women have faced domestic violence
78.7% of the women are home makers
95.5%, i.e., 4499 women have not heard of the All India Muslim Personal Law Board.
Summary of the Findings of the Study
Age of marriage
75.5% women want age of marriage to be above 18 years for girls
88.3% women want age of marriage to be above 21 years for boys
Mehr

85.7% want mehr to be given at the time of marriage

83.9% want his annual income to be the mehr amount

75.1% do not want woman to forego her mehr if she is giving khula

Polygamy

91.7% do not want their husbands to marry another woman in the subsistence of first marriage

Divorce

92.1% want a total ban on oral/unilateral divorce

88.3% want talaak-e-Ahsan to be the method of divorce

93% want arbitration process to be mandatory before divorce

72.3% want the arbitration process to be between 3 to 6 months

88.5% want the qazi to be punished who sends notice of oral divorce

Custody and adoption of children

88.9% want women to retain the custody of children after divorce

95.6% want ex-husband to pay for children's maintenance even if she holds their custody

92.7% want consent and well being of the child to be the deciding factor for custody

79.8% want the adopted child to be treated as a natural heir to the property

Codification and Darul Qazas

83.3% believe that codification of Muslim family law will help Muslim women get justice

87.9% feel that the activities of the darul qazas should be monitored by the state

95.4% want Muslim women to provide legal aid.[99]

Christian Women in India

In Christianity, passages from the Bible have been interpreted to suggest that women should be subservient to men. For instance, the Apostle Paul's letters to the Ephesians (Ephesians 5:22–24) say,

> Wives, submit yourselves to your own husbands as you do to the Lord. For the husband is the head of the wife as Christ is the head of the church, his body, of which he is the Savior. Now as the church submits to Christ, so also wives should submit to their husbands in everything.[100]

Timothy (Timothy 2:11–12) say, 'A woman should learn in quietness and full submission. I do not permit a woman to teach or to assume authority over a man she must be quiet.'[101]

Over the centuries, these passages have been used to justify domestic patriarchy and to bar women from religious leadership roles. Additionally, the story of Eve's creation from Adam's rib and her subsequent temptation by the serpent has been used to portray women as derivative of men and as a source of sin and temptation.

Of course, passages such as Galatians 3:28 emphasise equality: 'There is neither Jew nor Gentile, neither slave nor free, nor is there male and female, for you are all one in Christ Jesus.'[102]

But Christian women in India have been struggling and have their own set of problems. They could not obtain divorce on the grounds of adultery committed by the husband; it had to be coupled with cruelty, bestiality and sodomy. On the other hand, Christian husbands could simply declare their wives as adulteresses and divorce them. These antiquated laws were enacted in the colonial period to serve the interests of the British bureaucrats who had their legally wedded wives in England and were cohabiting with a local. Due to pressure from Christian women, the government last year cleared a proposal to amend the antiquated Christian Divorce Act 1869.[103]

Priscilla F, 48, had been married for 10 years. Eight of these had been turbulent, with domestic violence ruining her marriage. Two miscarriages, a fractured hand and a battered self-confidence, Priscilla left her married home in Mangalore and moved to live with an aunt in Mumbai. Since her parents too lived in Mangalore, the city was not an option to restart her life. Luckily for her, the man she had left behind did not follow her to Mumbai. For several years afterwards, she had thought of ending the marriage through legal recourse. She approached her Church for a solution.

Christian Catholics cannot divorce. The Catholic Church does not recognise divorce. 'I wanted a clean break from that man,' says Priscilla. After waiting for several years, Priscilla was advised by a lawyer to file for divorce in the family court. She did it and was ecstatic when the divorce came through. 'But everyone hounded me and told me I was wrong. They said I must go back to that man. My lawyer gave me the strength and I got a divorce through the court,' she says. 'Now when I want to pray, I go to any church in Mumbai.[104]

India Needs a Uniform Civil Code

One can look inside every Indian community and see one overarching reality. Women, by and large, are getting extremely unfair treatment. Religions, no matter which group you belong to, have treated women poorly and continue to do so despite multiple court judgments.

The concept of a Uniform Civil Code (UCC) in India refers to the proposal to replace the personal laws based on the scriptures and customs of each religious community in the country with a standard set governing every citizen. The UCC, as proposed, covers areas like marriage, divorce, inheritance, adoption, and maintenance.

The debate around the UCC is complex, intertwined with questions of religious freedom, constitutional rights, gender equality, and societal norms.

The need for a UCC is rooted in the Indian Constitution itself. Article 44 of the Constitution, which is part of the Directive Principles of State Policy, states, 'The State shall endeavour to secure for the citizens a Uniform Civil Code throughout the territory of India.'[105] Though the Directive Principles are not enforceable by any court, they are fundamental to the country's governance, and the state must apply these principles when making laws.

The UCC is viewed as an essential step towards ensuring gender justice. Personal laws of various religious communities often reflect patriarchal biases and may be used to perpetuate practices that are unfavourable to women.[106] For instance, issues like polygamy, triple talaq (a form of Islamic divorce), and unequal inheritance rights have been criticised for being discriminatory against women. A UCC could ensure that all citizens, regardless of religion, are subject to the same civil laws that uphold gender equality.

In a diverse country like India, a UCC could foster a sense of unity by underscoring the common citizenship that transcends religious and regional differences. A UCC could simplify the legal system by replacing the current patchwork of personal laws with a single, coherent set of laws. This would make the legal system more accessible and easier to navigate for all citizens.

However, critics argue that imposing a UCC could infringe on the right to religious freedom. They contend that it is possible to reform personal laws from within without imposing a uniform code. The ongoing debate over the UCC in India is a significant challenge in balancing constitutional principles, religious freedom, and societal norms.

But as we see in the survey by the BMMA, most of the criticism of the UCC comes from a specific section of the religious group that men dominate. Feminist activists like Amana Begam Ansari say, 'In the name of religious freedom, the State has left us at the mercy of the All India Muslim Personal Law Board (AIMPLB), a deeply patriarchal institution which, to this date, has not even codified Muslim personal laws.'[107]

Interestingly, while many Christian women favour the UCC, it is the men who seem opposed to it. Former Principal of St Xavier's College in Mumbai, Fr Frazer Mascarenhas, says that in a pluralist society like India, UCC is not required. 'This would regiment a wide variety of communities, including the majority community. There is nothing wrong with the present way the laws are functioning,' says Mascarenhas. According to him, there is no system of divorce in the Catholic Church. However, after a thorough investigation, the church would recommend either separation or an annulment of the marriage.[108]

On the Hindu side, Advocate Sai Deepak has been a vocal critic of the Uniform Civil Code.

Sai Deepak says he neither supports the Uniform Civil Code nor rejects it as the basic structure of the policy is yet to be decided. As per Sai Deepak, 'Hindus have already lost a lot due to the policies of Nehru. The diversity of Hindu culture has been destroyed by codifying Hindu personal laws. With the introduction of the Uniform Civil Code, it is the Hindu culture that will lose out,' Sai Deepak said, adding that the proposed Uniform Civil Code's fundamental nature will yet again revolve around the colonial ideas of secularism and democracy.

Sai Deepak notes that the Nehru government had codified the Hindu personal laws into four successive bills under the Hindu Code Bill. He adds that the personal laws were not only codified, but a good number of Hindu customs were completely done away with, and the community was never consulted.[109]

But is this the truth? As per the essay written by G.R. Rajagopaul for the *Journal of the Indian Law Institute*, October–December 1975, vol. 17, no. 4,

> Starting with the Hindu Widows' Re-marriage ACT of 1856 the legislature had intervened from time to time in order desirable changes in the law. For instance, the Hindu Inheritance of Disabilities Act, 1928 removed disqualifications based on mity or physical or mental defect for the purposes of succession. Gains of Learning Act, 1930 provided that any acquisition by a member of a Hindu undivided family by means of learning own property and not the property of the coparceners. The Rights to Property Act, 1937 was enacted because it was felt widow deserved better treatment than was given to her under the matter of succession. It gave the Hindu widow the son but it was a half-hearted measure because the interest on her was in the nature of a limited estate. Further, number of difficulties in construction and as time advanced ous that even this measure of reform did not correctly represent the people. Therefore, many were the Bills which were sought from time to time to give a better deal to Hindu women.
>
> One of such Bills was that of Akhil Chandra Datta. It was introduced in the central legislative assembly on February 18, 1939, and by an amendment of the Hindu Women's Rights to Property Act, 1937, it sought to give a right of inheritance to daughters. The Bill was circulated for the purpose of eliciting public opinion.[110]

The essay describes how the Indian state, first under the British and then in independent India, was constantly involved in discussing and reforming Hindu laws. And this process has been going on to date.

The BJP-led National Democratic Alliance (NDA) has been a constant proponent of bringing in a Uniform Civil Code.

> In 1996, the BJP manifesto stated, 'We will adopt a Uniform Civil Code which will be applicable to every community and foster a common Bharatiya identity, apart from ensuring gender equality. Regressive personal laws will cease to have legal validity.'[111]
>
> The government ... said in Parliament the Law Commission had initiated fresh consultations on the Uniform Civil Code due to the 'relevance and importance' of the subject and various court orders on the matter.
>
> On a question about the modalities of the UCC, Law Minister Arjun Ram Meghwal told the Rajya Sabha that since the law panel was still in the process of holding consultations, 'the question of modalities does not accrue at this stage'.[112]

Ironically, the ones opposing the Uniform Civil Code consistently have been 'secular' and 'liberal' outfits like Congress, led by the Gandhi family, the mother-son duo of Sonia Gandhi and Rahul Gandhi.

'I promise you that Congress will form government in 2019 and we will repeal this triple talaq law. This is a promise,' Congress leader Sushmita Dev said at the party's minority department national convention in Delhi.[113]

In response to the GOI's statement in the parliament in July 2023,

> top Congress leaders went into a huddle ... to discuss the government's push for Uniform Civil Code

(UCC). In the meeting, the party leaders unanimously
rejected the idea of uniformity of all laws and decided
to react only after the government brings the draft
bill.[114]

'We are clear that there can be nothing uniform about
all laws. How can the country have the same civil laws for
North East, South India, Muslims and Hindus? However,
some angularity of individual laws can be looked at,' said
a Congress leader.[115]

The debate surrounding the implementation of a
Uniform Civil Code (UCC) in India is undoubtedly
complex, considering the country's religious diversity,
pluralism, and constitutional commitments. However,
the necessity for a UCC, particularly from the
perspective of gender equality and women's rights,
cannot be overstated.

Despite the rich tapestry of cultures, religions, and
traditions that constitute Indian society, it is crucial to
remember that rights and equality should be universal
and transcendent. Women, regardless of their religion,
caste, or creed, should not have their rights curtailed by
personal laws that often reflect patriarchal biases under
the guise of religious freedom. The UCC, in essence,
seeks to uphold and guarantee these rights uniformly,
ensuring that all women are treated equally in the eyes
of the law.

Opposition to the UCC from certain liberal and
secular factions often stems from concerns about
protecting minority rights and religious freedoms.
While these concerns are partially valid, it is essential
to note that the objective of the UCC is not to impose a
majoritarian rule or to infringe upon religious freedom.
Instead, it seeks to establish a common civil law that
upholds the constitutional principles of equality and

non-discrimination, which should not be compromised under any circumstances.

The patriarchal religious orthodoxy, on the other hand, often resists changes to personal laws for fear of losing control over community norms and practices. However, preserving tradition cannot be an excuse to perpetuate blatantly discriminatory and unjust practices. The UCC, by challenging these patriarchal norms and practises, could play a pivotal role in dismantling gender hierarchies and promoting gender justice.

In this regard, it is worth noting the Supreme Court's observation that 'gender justice is constitutionally protected, and this protection can't be annulled by propagating personal laws with patriarchal ideologies'.[116] This observation underscores the constitutional commitment to gender justice, a commitment that a UCC could help fulfil.

Critics also argue that a UCC could potentially homogenise the diverse cultural practices in India. However, it is possible to draft a UCC that respects India's cultural diversity while ensuring uniformity in the principles of justice, equality, and non-discrimination. The Goa Civil Code, often cited as a model for a UCC, is a testament to this possibility.

India's progress as a nation is intrinsically linked to the status and rights of its women. By ensuring equal rights for all women, the UCC could significantly contribute to this progress. The empowerment of women through a UCC not only makes moral and constitutional sense but also economic sense, as countries with greater gender equality tend to have higher economic growth.[117]

In conclusion, while the road to implementing a UCC in India is fraught with challenges, it is a road worth travelling. The objections raised by certain liberal and religious groups, while important to consider, should not be allowed to obstruct the path to gender justice. The UCC, by ensuring equality and justice for all women, could mark a crucial step towards the realisation of a truly inclusive, egalitarian, and prosperous India.

6

Why I Am a Hindu

The exploration of identity is a complex, multifaceted journey. The complexity multiplies when this exploration ventures into the realm of religion and belief systems. Among the most intriguing aspects of this exploration is the notion of identity for Nāstikas and Nirīśvaravādis. Unlike their Abrahamic counterparts, these individuals often maintain a solid connection to their dharmic roots despite their disbelief in the divine. This intriguing coexistence of disbelief and cultural belonging offers a unique perspective on the relationship between religion and personal identity. This perspective challenges the common understanding of atheism and agnosticism in the Western context.

The term 'atheism' usually conjures images of a complete negation of religious beliefs and practices. In Abrahamic traditions, this often entails a conscious decision to entirely abandon one's religious identity. However, the Eastern counterparts of these atheists — the Nāstikas and Nirīśvaravādis — navigate a different path. Even as they reject certain doctrinal aspects of the religious tradition they were born into, they often maintain a connection to their cultural and philosophical roots. This seeming paradox can be understood only by delving deeper into the dharmic tradition's unique nature and multifaceted identity.

In his book *The God Delusion*, Richard Dawkins says,

> A child is not a Christian child, not a Muslim child, but
> a child of Christian parents or a child of Muslim parents.
> This latter nomenclature, by the way, would be an
> excellent piece of consciousness-raising for the children
> themselves. A child who is told she is a 'child of Muslim
> parents' will immediately realize that religion is something
> for her to choose—or reject—when she becomes old
> enough to do so.[1]

I agree with Professor Dawkins when it comes to this
specific aspect. I was born the child of Hindu parents. My
Hindu identity was not a conscious decision but something
that was given to me as a result of how our society works.
The government and society force our identities upon us.
We are born into this running train that is life, with its
fixed yet moving parts. And it is only when we develop
some level of cognitive freedom at a later stage that we
truly understand who we are.

But that applies to every single identity set that we
have. We did not actively choose to be born Indians, or
Americans, for that matter. One can replace the religious
identities mentioned in the Dawkins quote with a national
or regional identity, and the rest of the point remains the
same. To make it sound like there is something unique
regarding religious identity is a bit of a misnomer.

So, what does it mean to be a Hindu? The term
'Hindu', often used as a label for the religious and cultural
traditions that emerged in the Indian subcontinent, has
significantly changed its meaning and scope throughout
history. It encompasses diverse beliefs, practices, and
philosophical systems, making it fundamentally different
from the identity labels associated with Christianity and
Islam. Christian and Muslim identities are rooted in

specific religious doctrines, texts and a belief in a single God or deity. In contrast, Hinduism is an umbrella term encompassing many diverse religious and philosophical systems, many of which do not adhere to a singular doctrine or deity.

Plurality and heterodoxy have been integral to the development of the dharmic tradition. This is where the Nāstikas and Nirīśvaravādis find their place. Nāstikas, those who reject the authority of the Vedas and other fundamental tenets of the Āstika *darśana*s, and Nirīśvaravādis, those who deny the existence of a personal creator deity (Īśvara), are still considered part of the larger Hindu/dharmic family. Their disbelief does not necessitate a complete separation from their cultural roots. Instead, a distinctive fusion of continued affinities for some aspects of the tradition and disbelief in others shapes their identities.

This is a marked contrast to the identity of atheists from Abrahamic backgrounds. The Abrahamic traditions— Judaism, Christianity, and Islam—are monotheistic, worshipping a single, all-powerful God. As such, disbelief in God within these traditions is often seen as a total rejection of the faith. Atheism, in this context, is typically understood as an abandonment of one's religious identity.

However, with its inherent diversity and fluidity, the dharmic tradition allows for a more nuanced interplay between belief and disbelief. It provides a space where one can reject the existence of God or the authority of certain texts yet still identify with the tradition's philosophical, ethical, and cultural aspects. Nāstikas and Nirīśvaravādis exemplify this unique interplay. Their disbelief does not set them outside the dharmic tradition; instead, it places them within a broad spectrum of thought and practice that has evolved over millennia.

Thus, understanding the identity of Nāstikas and Nirīśvaravādis requires a shift in perspective. It requires moving away from the exclusivist definitions of religious identity prevalent in the Abrahamic context and embracing a more inclusive, pluralistic understanding. The identities of Nāstikas and Nirīśvaravādis are not defined by what they reject but by what they choose to accept and identify with within the broader dharmic tradition.

The exploration of the notion of identity for Nāstikas and Nirīśvaravādis is not just an academic exercise. It is an essential endeavour for anyone seeking to understand the rich diversity of human belief systems and the multitude of ways in which individuals relate to the divine, the cosmos, and each other. It underscores the importance of context in shaping our understanding of religion and identity, reminding us that how we make sense of the world around us is as diverse and intricate as humanity itself.

In the forthcoming discussion in this chapter, we will delve deeper into the complexities of these identities, exploring their historical evolution, their relationship with the broader dharmic tradition and how they contrast and align with other forms of atheism and agnosticism. Our aim is not to arrive at an absolutist understanding of what it means to be a Nāstika or a Nirīśvaravādi but to shed light on the myriad ways in which disbelief and cultural exploration of identity are complex, multifaceted journeys — the complexity multiplies when this exploration ventures into the realm of religion and belief systems.

The Origin and Evolution of the Term 'Hindu'

The term 'Hindu' is a complex entity that has evolved over centuries, carrying a complex history of cultural, religious, and geographical connotations. This etymological journey is intriguing, offering a glimpse into the sociocultural transformations that have shaped the Indian subcontinent.

The majority or consensus view on the origin of the term 'Hindu' is that it traces its origins to the ancient Persian language, which was used as a geographical term rather than a religious or cultural identifier. The Persians referred to the river Sindhu (known as Indus in the West) as 'Hindu', and over time, the term was used to denote the people living beyond the river Sindhu.[2] The Greeks, who came into contact with the Persians, adopted this term and transformed it into 'Indos' or 'Indoi,', which later evolved into 'India' in Latin.[3]

This view has been recently challenged by Indian author Aravindan Neelakandan in his book *Hindutva: Origin Evolution and Future*. Neelakandan says,

> While Indu and Sindhu are both related to the Soma ritual, the words Soma and Indu are usually related to the moon. Hieun Tsang, the famous Buddhist scholar-monk pilgrim to India in the seventh century CE, makes an explicit connection to this term and associates it to the name of the nation in a spiritual sense. He says that India was 'anciently called Shin-tu, also Hien-tau'. However, 'according to the right pronunciation, it is called In-tu' says the Buddhist monk from China. And then he proceeds to point out that in Chinese the term also refers to the moon. 'This is appropriate,' says the seventh-century pilgrim because 'the bright connected light of holy men and sages, guiding the world as the shining of the moon, have made this country eminent, and so it is called In-tu'. These connections provide us another way of looking at the name 'Hindu', not as a Persian pronunciation of Sindhu or Indus but as a name

that has direct roots in the Vedic-Harappan ritual as well
as with connection to the sacred geography of India. That
this Soma cult-object had become an accepted symbol
of temporal power in South India by third century BCE
shows the connections had started creating a unitary
cultural matrix that encompassed the entire land mass
from the Vedic Sapta Sindhu to South India.[4]

The religious connotation of the term 'Hindu' also
generates a lot of debate. Some scholars say it developed
much later, around the 13th–14th century CE, during the
Islamic invasions of the Indian subcontinent. During this
period, the term started being used to distinguish the
local population from the Muslim invaders.[5] The term
'Hindu' thus served as a broad categorisation for various
religious, cultural, and philosophical traditions that
were native to the Indian subcontinent but were distinct
from Islam.

Sachin Nandha and Acharya Vidyabhasker, in their
paper 'Who is a Hindu?', say,

Hindus were the people across the river Sindhu,
who revered it. The term did not differentiate
between various sects or traditions such as Shaivism,
Buddhism, Jainism or even Islam. Rumi, the 13th
century mystic and poet even classed Muslims living
across the Sindhu as essentially Hindu. Hindus never
described themselves as Hindus until as late as the 10th
century, or even later, when Muslim invaders came
and designated them by the Persian term. That is not
to say that Hindus before being designated as Hindus
did not possess a pan-Hindu cultural unity. It would
be verbal terrorism, in the words of Arun Shourie, if
anyone would class Hindu identity merely as a mental
construct and not apply the same standard to others.
One should not confuse the term with the concept.

People within a collective will refer to one another's lower identities, but when meeting with outsiders, everyone realises that something distinguishes the outsiders from all the members of the collective. This is not very problematic. Everybody within the Christian faith will seldom identify themselves as Christians when talking to other members of the collective, rather they will express that they are Catholic, Church of England, Lutherans or 7th-day Adventists. But when these same individuals meet a Hindu, they will identify themselves as Christian. In the same way, there has been a pan-Hindu consciousness amongst the people of India for many thousands of years, without ever using the word Hindu. As a further point, it seems apparent from the Rig Veda that it was the ancient Hindus who venerated the river Sindhu, from which the Persians may have drawn the line between 'Āryāvarta' and Persia. In other words, it was the Hindus who decided the demarcation line between 'them' and 'us' and not something that was imposed on them.[6]

The Hindu identity, therefore, denotes a people who originated from a specific geographical location and who possessed a common set of cultural traits, not merely a religion in an Abrahamic sense. The Hindu culture produced sub-groupings amongst its people through social groupings, guilds, languages, philosophies, and religions. Buddhism, Jainism, and Sikhism are three religions that have directly stemmed from and are rooted in the Hindu framework.

The British colonial period marked another significant transformation in using the term 'Hindu'. The British, in their endeavour to categorise and govern the diverse Indian populace, used the term 'Hindu' to distinguish the native population from the Muslim and Christian communities.[7] The colonial census further reified these

religious categories, solidifying the term 'Hindu' as a
religious identity.

Several theories have been proposed to understand the
evolution of the term 'Hindu' and its religious connotations.
One such theory is the 'Neo-Hinduism' theory proposed
by Friedrich Max Müller, which suggests that the idea of
Hinduism as a unified religion was a construct of British
colonial rule.[8]

In contrast, another theory suggests that the term
'Hindu' served as an umbrella term for various indigenous
religious and philosophical traditions even before the
arrival of the British.[9] This theory argues for Hinduism's
inherent pluralism and diversity as a religious tradition,
emphasising that 'Hindu' encompasses many spiritual
practices and beliefs that have co-existed on the Indian
subcontinent for centuries.

Indian American author Rajiv Malhotra explains this
beautifully in his book *Indra's Net*. Malhotra says,

> I see Hinduism neither as a 'fixed' religion akin to
> Christianity or Islam, nor as the modern-day remnant
> of some vaguely-defined 'perennial philosophy'. I prefer
> to see it as an open architecture framework that can be
> populated by a range of ideas, practices, symbols, rituals,
> and so on. The term 'open architecture' is, of course,
> taken from the domain of information technology. It is
> important to note that the internet is not infinitely open
> but only relatively so: its boundaries are defined by what it
> rejects—for example, viruses or abusive elements. Despite
> these rejections, the internet has abundant flexibility for
> the future.
>
> Similarly, Hinduism does not comprise all conceivable
> kinds of spirituality and religious claims, because it must
> exclude those that would destroy its underlying principles
> of integral unity, openness and flexibility. Exclusivist

religious claims, for example, run counter to the openness of Hinduism because they are incapable of offering mutual respect; the open architecture of Hinduism must reject such claims, just as the internet rejects viruses.[10]

The term 'Hindu' thus carries a complex history that reflects the sociocultural transformations of the Indian subcontinent. From a geographical term used by ancient Persians to a religious identity reinforced by colonial categorisations, the term has evolved significantly over the centuries.

However, it is essential to note that while the term 'Hindu' has come to denote a religious identity today, it stands for a diverse range of beliefs, practices, and philosophical systems. Even today, the definition of 'Hindu' can vary significantly based on context, underscoring this identity's inherent diversity and fluidity.

Therefore, in understanding the term 'Hindu', one must recognise its historical evolution and its diverse religious and philosophical traditions. It is not just a religious identity but a complex entity that reflects the rich cultural and intellectual diversity of the Indian subcontinent.

Will the Real Hindu Please Stand Up?

Rajiv Malhotra raises a very valid concern in his book *Indra's Net*, where he asks,

How elastic is Hinduism? To answer this, I start by rejecting two extreme kinds of responses. Those in the ultra-orthodox camp see Hinduism as inelastic, rigid and unchangeable; they dismiss Hindu revolutionary thinkers like Vivekananda as inauthentic for having violated its sanctity. Such a view fossilizes Hinduism and stunts its natural tendency to evolve. Those on the opposite extreme, such as the purveyors and followers of fashionable 'pop' Hinduism or 'new age spirituality' movements, see Hinduism as infinitely elastic—a kind of 'perennial philosophy' which can be interpreted as vaguely as one pleases, giving rise to an attitude of 'anything goes'. This approach heralds the slippery slope into sameness and relativism that turns Hinduism into a joke. It spawns such silly, evasive nonsequiturs as the definition of Hinduism as 'a way of life'. Neither extreme is useful.[11]

He then tries to redefine the terms Āstika and Nāstika, where he reduces Hinduism and its open architecture to being called Āstika. He says, 'The reader is reminded that I have redefined these terms in my own original way for my stated purpose. Through my exposition of nastika, I have sought to enable astika as the enormous space that remains when nastika is excluded.'[12]

He then goes on to explain 'specific aspects of nastika and astika'.[13]

Nastika	Astika
History centric exclusive canons for authority	Living enlightened masters as discoverers and as authorities
Centralized, corporate institutions	Decentralized explorations
Disembodied processes (like doctrine, reason, history)	Embodied processes (like yoga, mantra)
Speech is only linguistic, mental	Mantra has vibrational levels beyond the mind
Key Sanskrit terms digested and replaced by substitutes, thereby losing rishis' discoveries	Key Sanskrit words protected and utilized as precious discoveries.
Only one life in this world	Karma-reincarnation
Christian Good News—Jesus has come to save us from original sin	*Hindu Good News*—there is no original sin; we are all originally divine.
Synthetic unity	Integral unity
Closed canons	Open architecture
Chaos is fearful, to be controlled by controlling nature and other humans	Uncertainty, ambiguity are inherent; they do not threaten the integral unity of Indra's Net

Fig. 6.1. Specific aspects of nastika and astika

Rajiv Malhotra's categorisation has some inherent problems:

1. The term Nāstika becomes pejorative. According to him, 'Principles and characteristics of nastika lead to great instability and anxiety.'[14] While he insists, 'no religion, such as Christianity, is being classified as nastika in total',[15] the natural outcome of the categorisation of the aforementioned chart does lead to the othering of a giant swathe of Indians.

2. He makes believing in karma and reincarnation one of the prerequisites for being an Āstika. Then he says the 'definition of "nastika" is based on opposition to the open architecture'.[16] But Rajiv Malhotra does not explain in his book why a belief in karma-reincarnation is an underlying condition for an open architecture. Why can't one person reject the belief in *punarjanma* and yet support the open architecture of Hinduism?

Weirdly, Rajiv Malhotra promotes a 'closed canon' in his admirable pursuit of creating an open architecture.

Are Cārvākas Hindu?

The Cārvākas (also known as Lokāyata) constitute a fascinating part of India's philosophical heritage. Known for their materialistic and atheistic views, the Cārvākas were a radical departure from their time's religious and metaphysical traditions. A significant debate within the academic community focuses on whether the Cārvākas can be classified as 'Hindu'.

The Marxist doctrine, as articulated by scholars like Debiprasad Chattopadhyaya, argues that the Cārvākas cannot be considered Hindu because the term 'Hindu' was not in use during the time the Cārvākas existed.[17] From a strict chronological perspective, this argument is valid. The term 'Hindu', as we understand it today, is relatively recent, becoming prevalent only around the 13th–14th century CE.

However, this chronological argument can be challenged on several grounds. First, by this standard, none of that era's religious, philosophical, or cultural traditions can be classified as 'Hindu' since the term did not exist then. Secondly, if we consider 'Hinduism' as an open architecture or an operating platform akin to Android, the term 'Hindu' can be seen as a broad categorisation for diverse beliefs, practices, and philosophical systems that have originated and evolved in the Indian subcontinent. This perspective allows for the inclusion of various Āstika (orthodox) and Nāstika (heterodox) traditions, including Jainism, Buddhism, and indeed, the Cārvākas, under the umbrella of 'Hinduism'.[18]

Another argument against the inclusion of the Cārvākas within the Hindu fold relies on direct quotations from Hindu texts that express disapproval or condemnation of the Cārvākas. However, this argument can also be criticised. The tradition of philosophical debates and criticisms was a hallmark of the ancient Indian intellectual milieu. Numerous texts within the Āstika and Nāstika traditions contain strong criticisms and even condemnations of opposing views. For instance, the Brahmasutras, a foundational text of the Vedānta tradition, criticise the Sāmkhya and Yoga philosophies.[19] Similarly, the Nyāya *sūtra*s critique the views of the Buddhists and Jains.[20] This tradition of critique and debate does not necessarily imply exclusion from the broader cultural-religious milieu; on the contrary, it testifies to its vibrant intellectual diversity.

The classification of the Cārvākas as 'Hindu' remains a complex and contested issue in scholarly circles. Here are a few more arguments that have been put forth to make the argument in favour of Cārvākas being Hindu:

Basis of Textual References

The *Sarva-Darśana-Saṃgraha*, a classical Sanskrit text by the 14th-century philosopher Mādhava Vidyāraṇya, presents a critical account of the Cārvāka philosophy.[21]

Some scholars argue that the Cārvākas are referenced in various Hindu texts, such as the Mahābhārata, the Rāmāyaṇa, and the Purāṇas. These texts occasionally mention Nāstika views usually identified with the Cārvākas.[22] Some argue that this association with central Hindu texts provides a basis for classifying the Cārvākas as part of the Hindu philosophical tradition.

Basis of Philosophical Affiliation

Other scholars argue that despite their materialistic and atheistic views, the Cārvākas were part of the intellectual milieu of ancient India, engaging in debates with other philosophical schools. They were a part of the *sāmpradāyika* tradition—a system of philosophical discussion and dialectics, which included other schools like Nyāya, Vaiśeṣika, Sāṃkhya, Yoga, Mīmāṃsā, and Vedānta.[23] Despite their heterodox views, this engagement with different philosophical schools positions the Cārvākas within the Hindu intellectual tradition.

Basis of Cultural Continuity

Some scholars argue for a broader understanding of 'Hinduism' as a cultural and historical continuum that includes various philosophical and religious views. From this perspective, the Cārvākas, despite their radical departure from the mainstream, can be seen as part of the diverse and pluralistic fabric of Hindu philosophy.[24]

It is important to note that these arguments do not definitively answer whether the Cārvākas can be classified as 'Hindu'. The classification ultimately depends on one's understanding of the term 'Hindu' and the parameters used for inclusion within this category.

The Monotheistic Blindspot

The 'monotheistic blindspot' is a term that refers to a common tendency to view the world through a monotheistic lens, which tends to divide the world into binary oppositions such as believer/unbeliever, sacred/secular, and orthodox/heterodox. This perspective, rooted in the monotheistic traditions of Christianity, Islam, and Judaism, often fails to accommodate the complexity and diversity of religious and philosophical traditions outside this monotheistic framework. Let us delve into the implications of this monotheistic blindspot, specifically addressing its impact on understanding Hinduism and its non-theistic traditions.

Hinduism is an incredibly diverse religious tradition and cannot be easily categorised in monotheistic terms. It encompasses many beliefs and practices, with no creed or theological framework uniting all Hindus. This includes atheistic and agnostic schools of thought that do not believe in a personal God or are sceptical of religious claims.

While monotheistic religions typically have clearly defined boundaries between believers and non-believers, such boundaries are often fluid or non-existent in Hinduism. For instance, some people may identify as Hindu culturally or philosophically without necessarily adhering to theistic beliefs. This is different from the monotheistic understanding, where belief in God is central to religious identity, and those who stop believing in God often identify as 'ex-believers'.

The situation in Japan provides an interesting counterpoint to the monotheistic perspective where 'about two-thirds of people participate in Shinto practices, and about two-thirds of people participate in Buddhist practices. Most Japanese, it turns out, practice both religions'.[25]

Many Japanese people simultaneously identify with Shinto, a religion that reveres a multitude of spirits or *kami* and Buddhism, a tradition that does not posit a creator God. The ability to identify with more than one religious tradition challenges the monotheistic assumption of exclusive religious affiliation. This dual or even multiple religious affiliations can occur because the religious landscape in Japan, like many other Eastern cultures, doesn't demand exclusivity in the way that many monotheistic religions do.

Category Error in Philosophy

To fully appreciate the critique of the monotheistic blindspot, it's essential to understand the philosophical concept of a 'category error'. In his book *The Concept of Mind*, philosopher Gilbert Ryle defines a category error.[26] It occurs when things or events are represented as belonging to a particular category when they do not. For instance, if one were to enter a university and ask to see the 'university', misunderstanding that the university is not an entity separate from its buildings, students, and faculties but the collective sum of these parts, they would be making a category error.

A typical dictionary definition looks like this: 'The error of assigning to something a quality or action which can only properly be assigned to things of another category, for example treating abstract concepts as though they had a physical location.'[27]

A great way of understanding category errors is the pragmatic approach, where

> accounting for the infelicity of category mistakes is to maintain that they are syntactically well-formed, meaningful, and truth-valued but pragmatically inappropriate. The most natural way to develop a pragmatic account of category mistakes is to appeal to Grice's maxims of conversation. According to Grice's maxim of quality, one ought not to assert what one believes to be false. Since atomic category mistakes are arguably trivially false, it seems obvious to participants in the conversation that the speaker is uttering something that they do not believe, violating the maxim. Thus unless the speaker is interpreted as attempting to communicate something other than the literal content of the sentence (e.g., a metaphorical meaning), the utterance would be infelicitous.[28]

Category Error of 'Ex-Hindu'

Applying the concept of category error to religious identity, we can analyse the term 'ex-Hindu'. Within the monotheistic frame, it's common to encounter terms like 'ex-Christian' or 'ex-Muslim', which denote individuals who have disidentified with these religions. However, using the term 'ex-Hindu' is arguably a category error because it attempts to fit Hinduism, a complex and diverse tradition that encompasses a variety of beliefs, practices, and philosophies, into a monotheistic mould.

Unlike monotheistic religions, Hinduism does not have a single authoritative scripture, a single system of belief, or a single religious authority. It encompasses a wide range of philosophies, from theistic devotion to gods such as Vishnu or Shiva to non-theistic philosophical systems such as Sāṃkhya or the atheistic/materialistic Cārvākas.

As such, one can be an atheist and still be within the Hindu fold, even if they don't personally use the term 'Hindu' to describe themselves.

Therefore, the term 'ex-Hindu' falsely assumes that Hinduism is a monolithic belief system focused on a single deity or set of doctrines much like the Abrahamic religions. It implies that to be a Hindu, one must believe in specific doctrines or deities, and that departing from these beliefs constitutes leaving the faith. However, this perspective fails to account for the fact that many aspects of Hinduism, such as its philosophical systems, cultural practices, and social structures, can and do exist independently of theistic belief.

In essence, an individual can reject belief in a personal God and yet still identify with Hinduism's philosophical, cultural, or social aspects. The term 'ex-Hindu' does not capture this complexity and makes the category error of assuming Hinduism is a belief system akin to monotheistic religions, which it fundamentally is not.

We must move beyond the monotheistic framework and its associated language to understand Hinduism and similar religions better. The term 'ex-Hindu' can be seen as an example of the 'monotheistic blindspot'—the tendency to view and categorise all religions through the lens of monotheism. Recognising and addressing this blind spot is crucial to developing a more nuanced and accurate understanding of the world's diverse religious traditions.

The Abrahamic Privilege and Its Impact

The dominance of the monotheistic perspective in global discourse—a phenomenon that should be termed 'Abrahamic privilege'—has significant implications. It tends to marginalise or misinterpret non-monotheistic traditions, including those within the Hindu, Buddhist, Jain, Taoist, Shinto, and indigenous spiritualities.

For instance, atheists within the Hindu fold may feel suffocated or misunderstood because their philosophical positions are often misrepresented or undervalued due to the dominance of the monotheistic framework. The discourse, both academic and popular, often fails to recognise the profound philosophical traditions of atheism, agnosticism, and scepticism within Hinduism, such as those proposed by the Cārvākas or the Sāṃkhya philosophers.

This Abrahamic privilege also affects the understanding of the relationship between different religious traditions. Let us go back to the Japanese example we mentioned. From a monotheistic perspective, the Japanese who identify as Shinto and Buddhist may seem contradictory, but it's natural in the context of Japanese religious culture.

This dual identification reflects the complementarity of Shinto and Buddhism in Japanese culture. Shinto, with its focus on *kami* (spirits) and rituals for life events, and Buddhism, with its emphasis on philosophy and rituals for death and the afterlife, coexist harmoniously in the lives of many Japanese people. This underscores that the monotheistic lens, with its binary oppositions and exclusivity, often falls short of understanding the complexity and diversity of religious and philosophical traditions in different cultural contexts.

This privilege can manifest in various ways, from societal norms and legal structures to cultural representation and interpersonal interactions. Here are some additional aspects of Abrahamic privilege:

Legal and Institutional Privileges

Abrahamic religious values and beliefs significantly influence legal and institutional structures in many societies.

Consider the idea of resting on Sundays in Christian-majority countries or the observance of religious holidays such as Christmas or Eid. These structures may not consider or accommodate the needs and traditions of non-Abrahamic religions, effectively privileging the Abrahamic faiths.

A prime example of that in the Indian context is the essential religious practice argument. On 27 August 2018, a three-judge bench hearing a petition calling for the ban of female genital mutilation was told by the defence:

> On the one hand, the practice appears to violate the fundamental rights of women and, on the other, it appears to be protected under freedom of religion. The Dawoodi Bohras actively practice circumcision and describe it as a hygienic, non-invasive procedure that both women and men of their community undergo.[29]
>
> The lawyer Abhishek Manu Singhvi, arguing on behalf of the Dawoodi Bohra community, said, 'Female circumcision is protected under the freedom of religion guaranteed by Articles 25 and 26 of the Constitution.' Mr Singhvi urged the Court to show restraint in adjudicating on the essential customs of a religion. He asked the Court to avoid using external standards for understanding and judging an essential custom of the Dawoodi Bohras.
>
> Mr Singhvi reminded the Court of his previous submissions, where he had described female circumcision as an essential age-old practice going back 1,400 years. He argued that such practices should be considered religiously sovereign and immune from judicial interference.
>
> Mr Singhvi concurred and once again criticised the petitioners for using the phrase 'female genital mutilation' to describe circumcision. He disputed the claim that anything called FGM exists among the Dawoodi Bohra community. He went on to describe how female

circumcision is performed by the community, emphasising
that the clitoris is never touched during the procedure.
He exclaimed, 'it is neither cruel, barbaric, nor crude'.[30]

Some scholars criticised this doctrine for its potential bias
towards Abrahamic religions due to its focus on textual
sources as the primary determinant of what constitutes
an essential practice. In Abrahamic traditions, religious
doctrines and practices are usually explicitly outlined
in sacred texts, such as the Bible, Quran, or Torah, and
these texts are considered the ultimate authority for
determining religious practice. This fits neatly into the
ERP doctrine, which gives precedence to practices that
can be traced back to foundational religious texts.

However, many non-Abrahamic, particularly Indic,
faiths (like Hinduism, Jainism, Buddhism, or the variety of
tribal and folk traditions) often do not rely solely on textual
authority. Many practices are based on oral traditions, local
customs, or philosophical interpretations that may need to
be explicitly codified in a central religious text.

This discrepancy can lead to a situation where the ERP
doctrine, relying on textual evidence, inherently favours
religions with clearly defined texts and doctrines (like
Abrahamic religions) over those with a more diverse,
flexible, and orally transmitted set of practices (like many
Indian religions).

Another example of Abrahamic privilege is the
Sabarimala Case.[31] In this case, the Supreme Court
of India ruled that the ban on women of menstruating
age entering the Sabarimala temple was not an essential
religious practice under Hinduism. The dissenting
opinion, however, pointed out that the court was applying
an Abrahamic lens by looking for scriptural validation of
the practice, which is not always applicable in the context
of Hindu traditions.

Another was the Jallikattu Case.[32] In this case, the Supreme Court ruled that Jallikattu, a traditional bull-taming sport played in Tamil Nadu, was not an essential religious practice of the community, even though it had been part of the local tradition for centuries.

Cultural Representation

Abrahamic religions often enjoy greater representation in media, literature, and the arts. Stories, symbols, and references from these religions permeate Western literature and popular culture, often being treated as universal when they are, in fact, culture-specific. This can lead to a lack of visibility and understanding of non-Abrahamic religious traditions and philosophies.

There is a considerable presence of Abrahamic symbols and references in English-language literature and education in India, which often follow Western models due to the colonial history of English education in the country. Students reading English literature or studying in English-medium schools will likely encounter numerous biblical allusions and Christian metaphors, which can lead to a greater familiarity with Abrahamic religious symbolism than Indian traditions.[33]

The influence of Western (often American) popular culture, where Christianity is the dominant religion, on Indian media and entertainment can also lead to a certain degree of Abrahamic privilege. For example, a Christian holiday, Christmas, has become widely recognised and celebrated in urban India, often in its Western commercialised form of Christmas trees, Santa Claus, and gift exchanges. This is even though Christians make up a small minority of the Indian population.[34]

Indian media, like media globally, can sometimes fall into the trap of sensationalism and stereotyping when it comes to the portrayal of different religions. While this affects all religions, minority religions like Christianity and Islam can often receive disproportionate attention due to their minority status, leading to both positive and negative visibility.

However, it's crucial to note that the overall cultural representation in India leans heavily towards its majority religion, Hinduism, and other Indian religions like Buddhism, Jainism, and Sikhism. Festivals, myths, and symbols from these religions are deeply ingrained in Indian popular culture, arts, and media. Abrahamic religions, while having specific areas of privilege, especially in contexts where Western cultural influence is strong, are not the primary cultural influence in India.

Theological Debates and Interfaith Dialogues

Abrahamic privilege can also manifest in theological debates and interfaith dialogues, which often centre on monotheistic conceptions of God and related doctrines. This can marginalise or misrepresent non-Abrahamic perspectives that may not fit neatly into these frameworks.

Rajiv Malhotra, in his book *Being Different*, explains how

> Central to the Christian faith is the assertion that the prophetic revelations of the Bible are exclusive and God-given and that the person of Christ is uniquely divine. A feeling of superiority of 'us' over 'them' is bolstered by the importance given to the chronological narrative of prophetic revelations that have resulted in one saviour and one canonized book. These in turn have given rise to a normative set of practices and beliefs which are interpreted and enforced by a powerful Church. This, the Christian project, is seen as a God-sanctioned franchise to bring about religious homogeneity worldwide.[35]

Privilege in Academic Studies of Religion

Historically, the academic study of religion has often been Eurocentric and focused predominantly on Abrahamic religions. While this is changing, many non-Abrahamic religions still need to be represented or represented in religious studies curricula.

Here are some examples that highlight this issue:

Defining Religion

The definition of religion used in Western academia has often been based on characteristics of Abrahamic religions, such as a focus on belief, scripture, and monotheism. This can lead to misunderstandings or misrepresentations of religions that do not fit neatly into this framework. For example, in some forms of Buddhism, there is no belief in a creator god, and in many indigenous traditions, practice and community are more important than belief or doctrine.[36]

The Protestant Bias

Protestant Christianity, which emphasises individual belief and scriptural authority, has frequently influenced the academic study of religion. This can lead to a bias towards religions with similar characteristics and a misunderstanding of religions more focused on communal practices, rituals, or oral traditions.[37]

Eurocentric Perspectives

Non-Abrahamic religions have often been studied from a Eurocentric perspective, leading to misinterpretations or oversimplifications. For example, Hinduism has often been presented as a monotheistic religion with a central religious text (the Bhagavad Gita), which overlooks the diversity and complexity of Hindu traditions.[38]

Decolonising Religious Studies

There is a growing movement to decolonise religious studies and incorporate more diverse perspectives. This includes a greater focus on non-Abrahamic religions, indigenous traditions, and new religious movements, as well as an emphasis on understanding religions on their terms rather than through a Western or Abrahamic lens.[39]

Addressing Abrahamic privilege requires a conscious effort to understand and value religious diversity. This involves recognising the biases in our societal structures and cultural norms and actively seeking to learn about and represent a broader range of religious perspectives. It also involves creating space for non-Abrahamic voices in interfaith dialogues and the academic study of religion. This way, we can move towards more significant religious equity and inclusivity.

In conclusion, when interacting with various religious and philosophical traditions, the monotheistic blindspot that gives rise to this Abrahamic privilege, characterised by the propensity to view the world through monotheistic binaries, frequently causes misunderstandings and category errors. It's crucial to move beyond this monotheistic framework to appreciate the richness and diversity of human religious and philosophical thought, including traditions like Hinduism, Buddhism, and Shintoism.

Why Every Indian Is a Hindu

The concept of 'Every Indian is a Hindu' is a perspective that views 'Hindu' not strictly as a religious identity but as a civilisational or cultural identity, encompassing the diverse range of beliefs, traditions, and customs across

India. This perspective is rooted in understanding Hinduism as a socio-cultural sphere rather than a monolithic religion.

The Indian Experience: A Unique Experiment

India's experience is a unique sociocultural experiment. The nation is characterised by an incredible diversity of faiths, languages, customs, and traditions, yet it maintains a collective identity. This phenomenon can be linked to the concept of 'dharmic pluralism', a defining characteristic of the Hindu or Indian worldview.

In the Western context, cultural integration is often described using two analogies: the American 'melting pot', where different cultures are expected to assimilate into a dominant culture and the Canadian 'salad bowl', where cultures coexist side by side while retaining their unique characteristics. However, India's cultural integration pattern can be seen as a mix of both and yet entirely different, like an Indian dish called *khichdi*, reflecting the concept of 'unity in diversity'.

Dharmic Pluralism: A Unique Blend or a *Khichdi*

Dharmic pluralism, as observed in the Indian context, is a unique blend of the 'melting pot' and 'salad bowl' analogies. The dharmic traditions, including Hinduism, Buddhism, Jainism, and Sikhism, allow for a high degree of flexibility and diversity in beliefs and practices. This flexibility is rooted in the principle of '*Ekam sat, vipra bahuda vadanti*', a Sanskrit phrase from the Rig Veda, which translates to 'Truth is one; the wise call it by many names'.

This principle allows individuals and groups to stay within the fold of dharma while retaining their unique characteristics, leading to deep and broad integration. It's deeper than the American model of assimilation, where adherence to American exceptionalism often means giving up aspects of one's original culture. It's also broader than the Canadian model of multiculturalism, which, while allowing for cultural preservation, can lead to societal segmentation or 'ghettos'.

The Hindu Identity: Creating a Soul-Deep Diversity

The term 'Hindu' has evolved over time. Initially used as a geographical marker for people living beyond the Sindhu (Indus) River, it later came to represent a set of religious beliefs and practices. Today, some see it as a civilisational identity that transcends religious boundaries.

This understanding of the Hindu identity creates 'soul-deep' diversity. It acknowledges India's deep-rooted cultural, linguistic, and religious diversity as part of its inherent strength rather than a challenge to its unity. Unlike the skin-deep diversity of the Western world, where multiculturalism often focuses on external markers of diversity, the Hindu identity dives deeper to include diverse philosophies, thoughts, and paths to the divine.

The Critique and the Counter

However, this perspective is not without criticism. Critics argue that the idea of 'Every Indian is a Hindu' fails to acknowledge the unique identities of non-Hindu communities in India, including Muslims, Christians, Sikhs, Buddhists, Jains, Jews, Zoroastrians, Bahá'ís, and atheists, among others. They argue that labelling all Indians as 'Hindu' could potentially subsume the rich plurality of India under a single, majoritarian umbrella.

Countering this critique, proponents of the 'Every Indian is a Hindu' perspective argue that it's not about imposing a religious identity but acknowledging a shared cultural and civilisational heritage. They argue that the Hindu or dharmic sphere, with its inherent pluralism and inclusivity, provides a solid foundation for the unity and diversity of India.

Let's examine several ways the Hindu identity promotes unity and diversity in India:

Cultural Syncretism

One of the most visible manifestations of the Hindu identity's ability to promote unity and diversity is the phenomenon of cultural syncretism. Throughout history, Hinduism has shown a remarkable capacity to absorb and integrate elements from various cultures. For instance, Hindus and Muslims frequent many Sufi shrines in India, showcasing a shared cultural heritage. Similarly, the celebration of Puthandu (Tamil New Year) and Vishu (Kerala New Year) incorporates Hindu and regional traditions.

Festivals: People of all religions celebrate Indian festivals, many of which have a Hindu origin. Diwali, Holi, Pongal, and Raksha Bandhan are occasions for family gatherings and community bonding, regardless of religious affiliations. These festivals function as cultural rather than strictly religious events, creating a sense of unity through shared celebrations.

Regional Gods and Deities: The pantheon of Hindu deities is vast and varied, with numerous regional and village deities. This vast pantheon reflects the diversity of the Indian subcontinent and allows different communities to maintain their unique religious practices while still identifying as Hindu.

Yoga and Meditation: People from various religious and cultural backgrounds, both in India and worldwide, have adopted these Hindu tradition-based practices. These practices promote a sense of unity and shared cultural heritage, transcending religious boundaries.

Literature and Arts: Hindu epics like the Ramayana and Mahabharata have numerous regional versions across India, reflecting the diverse cultural interpretations of these shared narratives. Similarly, Hindu mythology and philosophy significantly influence India's classical dance forms like Bharatanatyam, Kathak, and Odissi, despite the fact that people of all religions perform and appreciate them.

While it would be inaccurate to say that every Indian visits churches and Sufi shrines, there is ample evidence of widespread participation in practices and celebrations outside one's religious tradition in India, often blurring the lines between religious identities. This intermingling of religious practices is a testament to India's pluralistic cultural fabric.

There are several instances where people from different religions, including Hindus, attend church services or participate in Christian festivals. For example, the feast of St Anthony in Siolim, Goa, attracts Christians, Hindus, and Muslims. The Velankanni Church in Tamil Nadu, often called the 'Lourdes of the East', hosts an annual feast attracting millions of pilgrims from different faiths.[40]

Sufi Shrines: Sufi shrines in India are renowned for attracting devotees from diverse religious backgrounds. One such example is the shrine of Khwaja Moinuddin Chishti in Ajmer, Rajasthan, known as the Ajmer Sharif Dargah. Devotees of all religions visit this shrine seeking blessings. Another famous Sufi shrine is the Nizamuddin Dargah in Delhi, known for its Qawwali music sessions that draw a diverse audience.[41]

Shared Festivals: There are numerous instances of Indians celebrating festivals across religious lines. For example, non-Christians who participate in festivities and exchange gifts all over India celebrate Christmas. Similarly, Jains, Sikhs, Buddhists, and Hindus celebrate the festival of lights, Diwali, for reasons unique to their respective religions.

Bollywood is an excellent example of India's diverse society and pluralistic culture. Many Muslim Bollywood stars celebrate Hindu festivals, reflecting India's syncretic traditions. Here are a few notable examples:

Shah Rukh Khan: Often referred to as the 'King of Bollywood', Shah Rukh Khan is known for celebrating Hindu festivals. He has been photographed celebrating Diwali and Holi with his family and friends. He has been quoted as saying, 'We have never discussed Hindu-Muslim. My wife is Hindu, I am a Muslim and our kids are Hindustan. When they went to school, they had to write their religion. My daughter came to me once and asked, "what is our religion?" I simply wrote in her form that we are Indian; we do not have a religion.'[42]

Salman Khan: Another big name in Bollywood, Salman Khan, is known for his secular approach to festivals. Every year, he is seen celebrating Ganesh Chaturthi with great enthusiasm. He has often been photographed immersing the Ganesha idol in a ritual performed at the end of the festival.[43]

Saif Ali Khan and Kareena Kapoor Khan: Saif Ali Khan and his wife, Kareena Kapoor Khan, are another Bollywood couple known for their dharmic approach to festivals. They celebrate various Hindu festivals, including Diwali, Holi, and Eid.[44]

Aamir Khan: Aamir Khan, one of the most respected actors in Bollywood, has spoken about celebrating both Hindu and Muslim festivals in his home. He has been photographed celebrating Diwali with his family.[45]

These examples show the pluralistic culture of India, where festivals are a shared cultural heritage rather than strictly religious events. In a nation as diverse as India, such cross-religious celebrations play a crucial role in promoting unity and harmony, where religious boundaries are often fluid and cultural practices and celebrations are shared across different religious communities.

With its rich tapestry of cultural, religious, and philosophical diversity, India has always encouraged a sense of 'unity in diversity'. It's a land where the devout Muslim can light diyas for Diwali, where the committed Hindu can revere a Sufi saint, and where an atheist, a Nirīśvaravādi, can find joy in the festivities of a religious holiday. This capacity for syncretism, for embracing a diversity of beliefs and practices, is indeed the Indian or Hindu way.

The Hindu way is not just a religious path but a complex philosophical system allowing a broad spectrum of beliefs. From *dvaita*, the dualistic understanding of the divine and the universe, to *advaita*, the non-dualistic belief in one ultimate reality, Hinduism accommodates an array of philosophical perspectives. This tradition welcomes the Nirīśvaravādi—those who do not believe in a personal god—while also making space for those who ardently worship their chosen deities.

In this context, it is unsurprising that a Nirīśvaravādi can celebrate Diwali. The festival of lights, commemorating the victory of light over darkness and knowledge over ignorance, can be interpreted in myriad ways. Diwali serves as a reminder of Lord Rama's return to Ayodhya, and even if a Nirīśvaravādi does not believe in Lord Rama as a divine being, they may still find meaning in the festival's symbolic representation of hope, renewal, and the victory of good over evil.

This is similar to how one can appreciate the poetry of Bulleh Shah or the bhakti of Meera without necessarily subscribing to their conception of the divine. The verses of Bulleh Shah, a Punjabi Sufi poet, express universal human experiences of love, longing, and self-realisation. Meera's devotional songs for Lord Krishna are not just expressions of religious devotion but are also metaphors for an individual's search for meaning and connection.

This ability to appreciate, participate in, and derive personal meaning from these diverse cultural and religious expressions is a characteristic feature of the Indian ethos. One may sing the devotional songs of Meera without considering Bhagwan Sri Krishna a literal god, or one may participate in the festivities of Diwali without believing in the divine aspects of the festival. These actions do not signify a contradiction but rather reflect the Indian spirit of pluralism and acceptance, which allows one to be a little bit of everything.

The Indian ethos does not shun materialistic understanding but relatively harmoniously blends it with spirituality. It is a tradition that sees divinity every day, finds spiritual significance in the material world, and allows one to be worldly and spiritual. It is a tradition that values experience over dogma and personal exploration over rigid adherence to doctrine.

In India, the devout and the doubter, the theist and the atheist, the materialist and the spiritualist, can all find a home. The Indian way is not about fitting into a singular, fixed identity but exploring the multiplicity of identities within oneself. It encourages one to embrace the contradictions, delve into the depths of diverse traditions, and carve out one's unique path.

To shy away from this would be to deny the very essence of what it means to be Indian or to follow the

Hindu way. Instead, one should take pride in this ability to encompass many beliefs and practices, find unity in diversity, and celebrate the pluralistic and inclusive spirit of Indian culture.

So, whether you are a devout Muslim celebrating Diwali, a Nirīśvaravādi finding joy in the festival of lights, or an admirer of Sufi poetry who does not subscribe to its conception of the divine, remember that this is the Indian way—a way of openness, acceptance, and celebration of diversity. And it is this way that makes India, in all its complexity and contradiction, a truly unique and vibrant cultural mosaic.

I was born a Hindu because of my parents. But I remain a Hindu by choice. Being born into a particular religious or cultural context is a matter of chance, but identifying with that context is a matter of personal conviction. In my case, I was born a Hindu owing to my parents, but I continue my association with Hinduism as a conscious choice.

The sights, sounds, and smells of my experiences have been my first exposure to Hinduism's vast and complex world. But as I grew older, my understanding of Hinduism evolved. I began to explore beyond the rituals and ceremonies, delving into the philosophy, ethics, and metaphysics that underlie the religion. I discovered that Hinduism is not merely a set of religious practices but a holistic worldview that can guide every aspect of your life.

I found wisdom and guidance in the verses of the Bhagavad Gita, the Upanishads, and the Ramayana. I was drawn to yoga and meditation practices, finding in them a path to inner peace and self-realisation.

I found profundity in the poetry of Bulleh Shah, who told me:

Munh aayi baat na rehndi ae
Munh aayi baat na rehndi ae

What's on the tongue must be said
What's on the tongue must be said

Jhoott aakhaan kuch bachda ae
I speak untrue and something remains
Sach aakhaan baambar machda ae
I speak the truth and the fire is lit
Donhaan galaan toun ji jachda ae
I am afraid of both outcomes
Jach jach ke jibhaan kehndi ae
Apprehensively my tongue quivers
Munh aayi baat na rehndi ae
Munh aayi baat na rehndi ae
What's on the tongue must be said

Jiss paya bheit qalandar da
Who puts on the garb of the dervish
Raah khojya apne andar da
Burrows the way into his self
O waasi hai sukh mandar da
Will inherit the temple of peace
Jithay charhdi ae na laindi ae
Where there is no rise or fall
Munh aayi baat na rehndi ae
Munh aayi baat na rehndi ae
What's on the tongue must be said

Ik laazim baat adab di ae
A point to be noted if I may
Saanu baat maloomi sab di ae
I know the secret of all
Har har vich soorat rabb di ae
Inside each is the face of the lord
Kitte zaahir kitte chhup behndi ae
Flowing apparent somewhere hidden
Munh aayi baat na rehndi ae

Munh aayi baat na rehndi ae
What's on the tongue must be said

Ae tilkan baazi vehrha ae
The world is a slippery place

Thamm thamm ke ttur anhera ae
Tread carefully for 'tis dark
Varh andar wekho kehrha ae
Go inside see who's there
Kyun khalkat baahar ddhunddindi ae
Why do the people search outside
Munh aayi baat na rehndi ae
Munh aayi baat na rehndi ae
What's on the tongue must be said

Bullah shou asaan toun vakh nahi
Bullah, the beloved is not separate from us
Bin shou te dujja kakh nahi
Besides the beloved there is naught
Parr vekhan vaali akh nahi
But the discerning eye is missing
Taain jaan judaiyaan sehndi ae
Therefore life endures separation
Munh aayi baat na rehndi ae
Munh aayi baat na rehndi ae
Munh aayi baat na rehndi ae
Munh aayi baat na rehndi ae
What's on the tongue must be said

Parh parh ilm kitaabaan da tu naam rakh leya qaazi
Learning through the rote of books you call yourself
a scholar
Hath vich parh ke talvaaraan tu naam rakh leya ghaazi
Grasping the sword in your hand you call yourself
a warrior

Makke Madinay ghoom aya tu naam rakh leya haaji
Having visited Mecca and Medina you call yourself
a pilgrim
Bullah tu ki haasil kita je yaar na rakhya raazi!

Bullah, what have you accomplished if you have not
remained true to your friend![46]

Hindu philosophy's inherent pluralism struck me as
I delved deeper into it. Hinduism does not enforce a
single dogma but instead embraces a diversity of beliefs
and practices. This openness appealed to me, allowing
me to interpret and understand Hinduism in a way that
resonates with my experiences and worldview.

The sense of belonging and shared identity that come
with belonging to a religious tradition also influenced
my decision to continue being a Hindu. Participating in
festivals, visiting temples, or engaging in philosophical
discussions with other Hindus strengthened my sense of
belonging and deepened my connection with the cultural
heritage.

Ultimately, the choice to remain a Hindu is a testament
to the value and relevance I find in its teachings. This
choice reflects my journey of exploration, understanding,
and self-discovery. It is a conscious decision to align
myself with a tradition that resonates with my beliefs,
values, and aspirations.

I'm actively participating in a living tradition by choosing
to be a Hindu, not just following the path my ancestors
set out for me. I am contributing to its continuity and
evolution, shaping it with my experiences and insights,
and ensuring its relevance for future generations.

My journey exemplifies the essence of Hinduism as a
flexible, adaptable, and deeply personal spiritual path.
It serves as a reminder that religion is not just about

heritage or tradition but is ultimately a personal choice, a conscious commitment to a set of values, and a path that brings meaning, purpose, and fulfilment. I do not know what happens to us once we die, and I do not care about it. But while I am alive, I live as a Hindu, and I am proud of that.

Notes

1 Nāstika, Nirīśvaravāda, and Atheism in the West

1 Stephen Le Drew. 2015. *The Evolution of Atheism: The Politics of a Modern Movement.* OUP Inc.

2 Michael J. Buckley. 1990 (rpt). *At the Origins of Modern Atheism.* Yale University Press.

3 Simon Glendinning. 2013. 'Three Cultures of Atheism: On Serious Doubts about the Existence of God'. *International Journal for Philosophy of Religion*, 73 (1) (February 2013): 39–55, Springer.

4 Richard Dawkins (Author, Narrator), Sam Harris (Author, Narrator), Daniel C. Dennett (Author, Narrator), Christopher Hitchens (Author, Narrator), Stephen Fry (Author, Narrator), and Random House Audiobooks. 2019. *The Four Horsemen: The Discussion that Sparked an Atheist Revolution.* Random House Audiobooks

5 Robyn E. Blumner. 2020/2021. 'Give the Four Horsemen (and Ayaan) Their Due. They Changed America'. *Free Inquiry*, 41(1). Available at: https://secularhumanism. org/2020/12/give-the-four-horsemen-and-ayaan-their-due-they-changed-america/?gclid=CjwKCAjwqZSlB hBwEiwAfoZUIAcwQ30AVPCM8QJzjcaRL4-WC_ EDLzGFv6PiSWN-i5wg_9cvM-X8WxoCnAAQAvD_ BwE

6 Claire Gecewicz. 2018. '"New Age" beliefs common among both religious and nonreligious Americans'. Available at: https://www.pewresearch.org/short-reads/2018/10/01/ new-age-beliefs-common-among-both-religious-and-nonreligious-americans/

7   The   Prābhākara   Mīmāṃsā   School.   Interview   by
    Richard   Marshall.   Available   at: https://www.3-16am.
    co.uk/articles/the-pr%C4%81bh%C4%81kara-
    m%C4%ABm%C4%81%E1%B9%83s%C4%81-school

8   BCC, Religions, God. 10 September 2009. Available at:
    https://www.bbc.co.uk/religion/religions/jainism/beliefs/
    god.shtml#:~:text=Jainism%20and%20God%20%2D%20
    the%20atheistic,support%2C%20where%20is%20he%20
    now%3F

9   BBC, Religions, Universe. 10 September 2009. Available
    at https://www.bbc.co.uk/religion/religions/jainism/beliefs/
    universe_1.shtml

10 Signe Cohen. 2019. 'The ancient connections between atheism,
    Buddhism and Hinduism'. *Quartz*, 3 April. Available at: https://
    qz.com/india/1585631/the-ancient-connections-between-
    atheism-buddhism-and-hinduism#:~:text=Atheism%20
    in%20Buddhism%2C%20Jainism,distraction%20for%20
    humans%20seeking%20enlightenment

11 BBC. Religions. Atheist Buddhism. 17 May 2006.
    Available   at: https://www.bbc.co.uk/religion/religions/
    atheism/types/buddhistatheism.shtml

12 E.B. Cowell and A.E. Gough. 2008. *The Sarva-Darsana-
    Sangraha of Madhava Acharya or Review of the Different Systems
    of Hindu.* Sri Satguru Publications.

13 Shoaib Daniyal. 2015. 'People without religion have risen
    in Census 2011, but atheists have nothing to cheer about',
    7 September. Available at: https://scroll.in/article/753475/
    people-without-religion-have-risen-in-census-2011-but-
    atheists-have-nothing-to-cheer-about

14 Kounteya   Sinha.   2013.   'More   Indians   have   stopped
    believing in God: Survey', 27 May. Available at:
    https://timesofindia.indiatimes.com/world/uk/More-
    Indians-have-stopped-believing-in-God-Survey/
    articleshow/20284261.cms

15 'Being Christian in Western Europe', 29 May 2018. Available at: https://www.pewresearch.org/religion/2018/05/29/being-christian-in-western-europe/

16 Ibid.

17 'About Three-in-Ten U.S. Adults Are Now Religiously Unaffiliated', 14 December 2021. Available at: https://www.pewresearch.org/religion/2021/12/14/about-three-in-ten-u-s-adults-are-now-religiously-unaffiliated/

18 Colin Mathers. 2021. 'Religiosity and atheism: revised estimates for 1980-2020'. Available at: https://colinmathers.com/2021/11/09/religiosity-and-atheism-revised-estimates-for-1980-2020/

19 Kushal Mehra. 2018. 'The kind of Indian Atheists and why they continue to be Hindus, unlike Abrahamics and Marxists'. Available at: https://www.opindia.com/2018/09/the-kind-of-indian-atheists-and-why-they-continue-to-be-hindus-unlike-abrahamics-and-marxists/

20 Available at: https://www.merriam-webster.com/dictionary/blasphemy

21 Available at: https://www.merriam-webster.com/dictionary/apostasy

22 Available at: https://www.wisdomlib.org/definition/devaninda#:~:text=Sanskrit%20dictionary-,%5B%C2%ABprevious%20(D)%20next%C2%BB%5D%20%E2%80%94%20Devaninda%20in,Devanind%C4%81%20(%E0%A4%A6%E0%A5%87%E0%A4%B5%E0%A4%A8%E0%A4%BF%E0%A4%A8%E0%A5%8D%E0%A4%A6%E0%A4%BE)

23 Available at: https://www.merriam-webster.com/dictionary/heresy

24 G. Buhler. 2012. The Laws of Manu, Kindle Edition. Available at: https://www.amazon.in/Laws-Manu-G-Buhler-ebook/dp/B00B0XL6TA/ref=sr_1_1?crid=

4CXZJW2DN556&keywords=manu+smriti+g+buhler &qid=1688586616&sprefix=manu+smriti+g+ buhler%2Caps%2C213&sr=8-1

25 Patrick Olivelle. nd. Manu's *Code of Law: A Critical Edition and Translation of the Manava-Dharmasastra.* Available at: https://www.amazon.in/gp/product/0195681487/ ref=dbs_a_def_rwt_hsch_vapi_taft_p1_i7

26 Available at: https://www.biblegateway.com/passage/? search=Leviticus%2024%3A10-23&version=ESV

27 'Military Expeditions Led by the Prophet (pbuh) (Al-Maghaazi)'. Volume 3, Book 45, Number 687. Available at: https://web.archive.org/web/20170610050937/http:/ cmje.usc.edu/religious-texts/hadith/bukhari/045-sbt. php#003.045.687

28 Ibid. Volume 5, Book 59, Number 369. Available at: https://web.archive.org/web/20170610043915/http:/ cmje.usc.edu/religious-texts/hadith/bukhari/059-sbt. php#005.059.369

29 Available at: https://end-blasphemy-laws.org/countries/

30 'The Freedom of Thought Report'. Available at: https:// fot.humanists.international/

31 Virginia Villa. 2022. 'Four-in-ten countries and territories worldwide had blasphemy laws in 2019'. Available at: https://www.pewresearch.org/short-reads/2022/01/25/ four-in-ten-countries-and-territories-worldwide-had-blasphemy-laws-in-2019-2/

32 Stephanie Kramer. 2021. 'Key findings about the religious composition of India'. Available at: https://www. pewresearch.org/short-reads/2021/09/21/key-findings-about-the-religious-composition-of-india/

33 Available at: https://indiankanoon.org/doc/1803184/

34 M.A. Chamupati. 1927. *Rangila Rasul.*

35 Cowell and Gough. *Sarva-Darsana-Sangraha of Madhava Acharya.*

36 'Exodus 20:5'. In The Bible. Available at: https://www.
    bible.com/bible/116/EXO.20.5.NLT
37 'Al-Baqarah'. In The Quran. Available at: https://quran.
    com/2
38 Ibid.
39 Ibid.
40 S. Radhakrishnan. 2006. *The Principal Upaniṣads*.
    HarperCollins.
41 Available at: https://www.wisdomlib.org/definition/neti-neti
42 Rajiv Malhotra. 2016. *Indra's Net*. HarperCollins.
43 'Nature of Ultimate Reality in Hinduism'. Available at:
    https://www.bbc.co.uk/bitesize/guides/zrf6pbk/revision/2
44 Swāmī Mādhavānanda. 1950. *The Bṛhadāraṇyaka
    Upaniṣad* (with the Commentary of Śaṅkarācārya).
    Available at: https://www.wisdomlib.org/hinduism/book/
    the-brihadaranyaka-upanishad/d/doc117939.html
45 Rajiv Malhotra, *Being Different*, 12.
46 Malhotra, *Being Different*, 30.
47 H.H. Wilson. 1866. *Rig Veda* (translation and commentary).
    Available at: https://www.wisdomlib.org/hinduism/book/
    rig-veda-english-translation/d/doc830789.html
48 '28 Biblical Passages Which Explicitly Teach There Is
    Only One God'. 22 August 2011. Available at: https://mit.
    irr.org/28-biblical-passages-which-explicitly-teach-there-
    only-one-god
49 'The Last Dialogue'. Available at: https://www.thelastdialogue.
    org/article/the-topic-one-god-mentioned-in-quran/
50 Mick O'Reilly. 2018. 'Pope Francis: A messenger of
    tolerance', Opinion, 21 December. Available at: https://
    gulfnews.com/opinion/op-eds/pope-francis-a-messenger-
    of-tolerance-1.61044119
51 'President Obama: Embrace Tolerance'. Available at:
    https://www.youtube.com/watch?v=Bua0tR0HlD0
52 Malhotra, *Being Different*, 20 and 21.

53   Malhotra, *Being Different*, 26.

54   Malhotra, *Being Different*, 141.

55   Sengupta, *Being Hindu*, 43.

56   'Giving Da`wah to Non-Muslims (1/2)'. Available at: https://www.dawahskills.com/abcs-of-dawah/giving-dawah-to-non-muslims-1/

57   Peter Boghossian. 2013. *Manual for Creating Atheists*. Pitchstone Publishing.

58   Brooke Kato. 2021. 'What is cancel culture? Everything to know about the toxic online trend'. New York Post, 31 August. Available at: https://nypost.com/article/what-is-cancel-culture-breaking-down-the-toxic-online-trend/

59   Malhotra, *Being Different*, 54.

2 Neo-atheism: Its Success and Failure

1   Sam Harris. 2015. 'Journey to Atheism Sparked by 9/11'. Available at: https://mindfulnessexercises.com/journey-atheism-sparked-911/

2   Richard Dawkins. 2016. *The God Delusion*. Available at: https://www.amazon.in/God-Delusion-Richard-Dawkins/dp/1784161926/ref=sr_1_3?crid=6BMBIGLMHWVO&keywords=the+god+delusion&qid=1689014883&sprefix=the+god+delusion%2Caps%2C269&sr=8-3

3   Gary Keogh. 2015. 'Theology after New Atheism'. *New Blackfriars*, 96 (1066) (November): 739–50. Available at: https://www.jstor.org/stable/24766379

4   Ibid.

5   Stephen LeDrew. 2013. 'Discovering Atheism: Heterogeneity in Trajectories to Atheist Identity and Activism'. *Sociology of Religion*, 74 (4): 431–53. Available at: JSTOR, http://www.jstor.org/stable/24580138. Accessed 10 July 2023.

6   Christopher Hitchens' quotable quote, Goodreads, https://www.goodreads.com/quotes/7611744-if-someone-tells-me-that-i-ve-hurt-their-feelings-i

7   Available at: https://www.youtube.com/watch?v=VxG
    MqKCcN6A
8   Available at: https://www.goodreads.com/work/quotes/
    3044365-the-god-delusion
9   Christopher Hitchens. 2011. *God Is Not Great*. Atlantic
    Books. Available at: https://www.amazon.in/God-Not-
    Great-Christopher-Hitchens-ebook/dp/B0064M9WHK/
    ref=sr_1_1?crid=27X9SPOYSV9VJ&keywords=god+is+
    not+great&qid=1689016413&s=digital-text&sprefix=god+
    is+not+great%2Cdigital-text%2C255&sr=1-1
10 Christopher Hitchens. 2012. *The Missionary Position: Mother
    Teresa in Theory and Practice*. Atlantic Books. Available
    at: https://www.amazon.in/gp/product/B007EPESOS/
    ref=dbs_a_def_rwt_hsch_vapi_tkin_p1_i0
11 Available at: https://www.goodreads.com/author/quotes/
    3956.Christopher_Hitchens
12 Hasan Salim Patel. 2011. 'Christopher Hitchens: A life in
    quotes'. *Aljazeera*, 16 December. Available at: https://www.
    aljazeera.com/features/2011/12/16/christopher-hitchens-
    a-life-in-quotes
13 Available   at: https://www.brainyquote.com/quotes/
    christopher_hitchens_168002
14 Larry Alex Taunton. 2016. The Faith of Christopher
    Hitchens: The Restless Soul of the World's Most
    Notorious Atheist. Thomas Nelson. Available at: https://
    www.amazon.in/Faith-Christopher-Hitchens-Restless-
    Notorious-ebook/dp/B010R1DZJO/ref=sr_1_1?keywor
    ds=The+Faith+of+Christopher+Hitchens%3A+The+Restl
    ess+Soul+of+the+World%E2%80%99s+Most+Notorious+
    Atheist&qid=1689018242&s=digital-text&sr=1-1
15 Nick Cohen. 2016. 'Deathbed conversion? Never.
    Christopher Hitchens was defiant to the last'. *The
    Gaurdian*, 5 June. Available at: https://www.theguardian.
    com/commentisfree/2016/jun/04/deathbed-conversion-
    christopher-hitchens-defiant-to-last

16   Daniel Dennett. 2007. 'Naturalism'. In *Stanford Encyclopedia of Philosophy*, 22 February. Available at: https://plato.stanford.edu/entries/naturalism/

17   Daniel Dennett. 2001. 'Physicalism'. In *Stanford Encyclopedia of Philosophy*, 13 February. Available at: https://plato.stanford.edu/entries/physicalism/

18   Sean Huang. 2023. 'Daniel Dennett on the Intentional Stance'. Available at: https://medium.com/@sean_tianxiang_huang/4-daniel-dennett-on-the-intentional-stance-ff9a5dc22924

19   Available at: https://www.samharris.org/podcasts

20   Ariane Sherine. 2009. *The Atheist's Guide to Christmas*. The Friday Project. Available at: https://www.amazon.in/dp/B002TU1Q5M?ref_=cm_sw_r_cp_ud_dp_4BTYG8TP6C713X43E29F

21   Robert Cohen. 2009. Freedom's Orator: Mario Savio and the Radical Legacy of the 1960s. OUP. Available at: https://www.amazon.in/dp/B003UV9160?ref_=cm_sw_r_cp_ud_dp_P45D3R7YM2TZPH574H49

22   Samuel Walker. 1990. *In Defence of American Liberties: History of the A.C.L.U.* OUP, Inc. Available at: https://www.amazon.in/dp/0195045394?ref_=cm_sw_r_cp_ud_dp_0GH7BHXQM7SAYA3XEGRJ

23   'New York Times Co. v. Sullivan, 376 U.S. 254 (1964)'. Available at: https://supreme.justia.com/cases/federal/us/376/254/

24   Tinker v. Des Moines Independent Community School District, 393 U.S. 503' (1969). Available at: https://supreme.justia.com/cases/federal/us/393/503/

25   Dawkins, *God Delusion*, 31.

26   Pew Research Center. 2019. 'In U.S., Decline of Christianity Continues at Rapid Pace'. https://www.pewresearch.org/religion/2019/10/17/in-u-s-decline-of-christianity-continues-at-rapid-pace/

27   Hitchens, *God Is Not Great*, 56.

28 José Casanova. 1994. *Public Religions in the Modern World*. University of Chicago Press.

29 Charles Taylor. 2018. *Secular Age: A Guide to Career Paths in Science*. Harvard University Press.

30 Pippa Norris and Ronald Inglehart. 2011. *Sacred and Secular: Religion and Politics Worldwide*. Cambridge University Press.

31 Diana L. Eck. 2001. *A New Religious America: How a "Christian Country" Has Become the World's Most Religiously Diverse Nation*. HarperOne.

32 Forrest Church. 2011. *The Separation of Church and State: Writings on a Fundamental Freedom by America's Founders*. Beacon Press.

33 Clayton Crockett. 2002. A *Theology of the Sublime*. Routledge.

34 A.C. Grayling. 2014. *The God Argument: The Case against Religion and for Humanism*. Bloomsbury, 6.

35 Phil Zuckerman. 2012. *The God Argument: The Case Against Religion and for Humanism*. OUP.

36 Jeffrey Gottfried and Elisa Shearer. 2016. 'News Use Across Social Media Platforms 2016'. Available at: https://www.pewresearch.org/journalism/2016/05/26/news-use-across-social-media-platforms-2016/

37 'Blasphemy Rights'. Available at: https://centerforinquiry.org/blog/category/blasphemy-rights/

38 Available at: https://www.atheistrepublic.com/

39 Win-Gallup International Global Index of Religiosity and Atheism-2012. Available at: https://www.scribd.com/document/136318147/Win-gallup-International-Global-Index-of-Religiosity-and-Atheism-2012#

40 Hannah Wallace. 2020. 'Men without God: The Rise of Atheism in Saudi Arabia'. *Free Enquiry*, 40 (2). Available at: https://secularhumanism.org/2020/01/men-without-god-the-rise-of-atheism-in-saudi-arabia/

41 'Arabic Translation of "The God Delusion" Downloaded 10 Million Times'. Atheist Republic. Available at: https://www.atheistrepublic.com/news/arabic-translation-god-delusion-downloaded-10-million-times

42 'Chapter 1: Beliefs About Sharia'. 30 April 2013. Available at: https://www.pewresearch.org/religion/2013/04/30/the-worlds-muslims-religion-politics-society-beliefs-about-sharia/

43 'FBI to help probe murder of US blogger Avijit Roy in Bangladesh'. *The Times of India*, 3 March 2015. Available at: https://timesofindia.indiatimes.com/world/south-asia/fbi-to-help-probe-murder-of-us-blogger-avijit-roy-in-bangladesh/articleshow/46444297.cms

44 Available at: https://www.arabbarometer.org/publications/?type=country-reports&survey=arab-barometer-wave-iv

45 Council of Ex-Muslims of Britain – CEMB. Available at: https://www.ex-muslim.org.uk/

46 'Atheism should be science and social justice, not science vs. social justice'. Available at: https://freethoughtblogs.com/pharyngula/2012/06/07/atheism-should-be-science-and-social-justice-not-science-vs-social-justice/

47 Greta Christina. 2012. 'Natural Allies: Humanism and Atheism'. 19 October 2012. Available at: https://thehumanist.com/magazine/november-december-2012/fierce-humanism/natural-allies-humanism-and-atheism

48 José van Dijck. 2013. *The Culture of Connectivity: A Critical History of Social Media*. OUP. 4

49 Patricia Hill Collins and Sirma Bilge. 2020. *Intersectionality*. Polity.

50 Michael Shermer. 2015. *The Moral Arc: How Science and Reason lead Humanity toward Truth, Justice and Freedom*. Pan Macmillan India.

51 Greg Lukianoff and Jonathan Haidt. 2018. *The Coddling of the American Mind: How Good Intentions and Bad Ideas Are Setting Up a Generation for Failure*. Penguin Press.

52 John McWhorter. 2022. *Woke Racism: How a New Religion has Betrayed Black America*. Swift Press.

53 Nina Totenberg. 'Supreme Court guts affirmative action, effectively ending race-conscious admissions'. 29 June 2023. Available at: https://www.npr.org/2023/06/29/1181138066/affirmative-action-supreme-court-decision

3 Why Religion Is Good and Bad but Inevitable

1 E. Durkheim. 1912. *The Elementary Forms of the Religious Life*. London: George Allen & Unwin

2 C. Geertz. 1973. *The Interpretation of Cultures: Selected Essays*. Basic Books.

3 S.N. Balagangadhara. 2015. *The Heathen in His Blindness: Asia, the West and the Dynamic of Religion*. Manohar Books.

4 Jakob De Roover and Sarika Rao, ed. 2022. *Cultures Differ Differently: Selected Essays of S.N. Balagangadhara*. Routledge.

5 Andrew Harvey. 1998. *The Essential Mystics: The Soul's Journey into Truth*. US: Castle Books.

6 Swami Achuthananda. 2013. *Many Many Many Gods of Hinduism: Turning Believers into Non-believers and Non-believers into Believers*. Createspace Independent Pub.

7 Carl Olson. 2007. *The Many Colors of Hinduism: A Thematic-historical Introduction*. Rutgers University Press.

8 Wayne Teasdale. 2001. *The Mystic Heart: Discovering a Universal Spirituality in the World's Religions*. New World Library

9 William James. 2017. *The Varieties of Religious Experience: A Study in Human Nature*. Createspace Independent Pub.

10 Charles Darwin. 2021. *Origin of Species*. Fingerprint! Publishing.

11 David Wilson. 2010. *Darwin's Cathedral: Evolution, Religion, and the Nature of Society*. University of Chicago Press.

12 Charles Darwin. *The Descent of Man and Selection in Relation to Sex*, Vol. 2, 1st Edition. Kindle Edition.

13 Richard Sosis and Candace Alcorta. 2003. 'Signaling, Solidarity, and the Sacred: The Evolution of Religious Behavior'. Wiley Online Library, 12(6): 264–274. Available at: https://onlinelibrary.wiley.com/doi/10.1002/evan.10120

14 Ara Norenzayan and Ian G. Hansen. 2006. 'Belief in supernatural agents in the face of death'. *Sage Journals*, 32(2). Available at: https://journals.sagepub.com/doi/10.1177/0146167205280251

15 Stewart Guthrie. *Faces in the Clouds: A New Theory of Religion*, 1st Edition. Kindle Edition. OUP.

16 Scott Atran and Ara Norenzayan. 2004. 'Religion's evolutionary landscape: counterintuition, commitment, compassion, communion'. Available at: https://pubmed.ncbi.nlm.nih.gov/16035401/

17 David Premack and Guy Woodruff. 1978. 'Does the chimpanzee have a theory of mind?' *Behavioral and Brain Sciences*, 1(4), 515–526. doi:10.1017/S0140525X00076512

18 J.L. Barrett. 2000. 'Exploring the natural foundations of religion'. *Trends in Cognitive Sciences*, 4(1): 29–34.

19 Pascal Boyer and Pierre Liénard. 2006. 'Why ritualized behavior? Precaution Systems and action parsing in developmental, pathological and cultural rituals'. *Behavioral and Brain Sciences*, 29(6): 595–613. Available at: https://www.researchgate.net/publication/5925738_Why_ritualized_behavior_Precaution_Systems_and_action_parsing_in_developmental_pathological_and_cultural_rituals

20 Richard Dawkins. 2016. *The Selfish Gene*. OUP.

21 Pascal Boyer. 2008. *Religion Explained: The Evolutionary Origins of Religious Thought*. Vintage Digital.

22 Limor Shifman. 2013. *Memes in Digital Culture*. MIT Press.

23 Scott Atran and Joseph Henrich. 2010. 'The evolution of religion: How cognitive by-products, adaptive learning

heuristics, ritual displays, and group competition generate deep commitments to prosocial religions'. *Springer Link*, 5: 18–30.

24 Steven Mithen. 2015. *The Prehistory of the Mind: The Cognitive Origins of Art, Religion and Science*. Thames and Hudson Ltd.

25 Robin Dunbar. 2003. 'The Social Brain: Mind, Language, and Society in Evolutionary Perspective'. *Annual Review of Anthropology*, 32: 163–181. Available at: https://www.jstor.org/stable/25064825

26 Armotz Zahavi. 1975. 'Mate selection—A selection for a handicap'. *Journal of Theoretical Biology*, 53 (1): 205–214.

27 Richard Sosis. 2004. 'The Adaptive Value of Religious Ritual'. *American Scientist*, 92 (2) (March–April): 166–172. Available at: https://www.jstor.org/stable/27858365

28 Joseph Henrich. 2009. 'The evolution of costly displays, cooperation and religion: credibility enhancing displays and their implications for cultural evolution'. *Evolution and Human Behavior*, 30: 244–260.

29 Sosis and Alcorta, 'Signaling, solidarity, and the sacred'.

30 Ara Norenzayan and Azim F. Shariff. 2008. 'The Origin and Evolution of Religious Prosociality'. *New Series*, 322 (5898): 58–62. Available at: https://www.jstor.org/stable/20144941

31 Peter J. Richerson and Robert Boyd. 2008. *Not by Genes Alone: How Culture Transformed Human Evolution*. University of Chicago Press.

32 Dawkins, *Selfish Gene*.

33 Susan Blackmore. 2000. *The Meme Machine*. OUP.

34 Scott Atran. 2001. 'The Trouble with Memes: Inference versus Imitation in Cultural Creation'. *Human Nature*, 12(4): 351–81. Available at: https://artisresearch.com/files/articles/atran_the_trouble_with_memes.pdf

35 David Wilson. 2010. *Darwin's Cathedral: Evolution, Religion, and the Nature of Society*. University of Chicago Press.

36   Pascal Boyer. 2008. *Religion Explained: The Human Instincts that Fashion Gods, Spirits and Ancestors*. Vintage Digital.

37   Daniel C. Dennett. 2007. *Breaking the Spell: Religion as a Natural Phenomenon*. Penguin.

38   Alex Mesoudi. 2011. *Cultural Evolution: How Darwinian Theory Can Explain Human Culture and Synthesize the Social Sciences*. University of Chicago Press.

39   Nicolas Claidière and Jean-Baptiste André. 2011. 'The Transmission of Genes and Culture: A Questionable Analogy'. *Evolutionary Biology*, 39(1): 12–24. Available at: https://www.researchgate.net/publication/225564633_The_Transmission_of_Genes_and_Culture_A_Questionable_Analogy

40   Jean Clottes. 2008. *Cave Art*. Phaidon Press.

41   Paul B Pettitt. 2002. 'The Neanderthal dead: exploring mortuary variability in Middle Palaeolithic Eurasia'. Available at: https://www.researchgate.net/publication/265379507_The_Neanderthal_dead_exploring_mortuary_variability_in_Middle_Palaeolithic_Eurasia

42   Klaus Schmidt. 2011. 'Göbekli Tepe - The Stone Age Sanctuaries. New results of ongoing excavations with a special focus on sculptures and high reliefs'. *Documenta Praehistorica*, 37: 239. Available at: https://www.researchgate.net/publication/270030960_Gobekli_Tepe_-_The_Stone_Age_Sanctuaries_New_results_of_ongoing_excavations_with_a_special_focus_on_sculptures_and_high_reliefs

43   Jean Bottero. 2004. *Religion in Ancient Mesopotamia*. University of Chicago Press.

44   Rosalie David. 2002. *Religion and Magic in Ancient Egypt*. Penguin.

45   Karl Jaspers and Christopher Thornhill. 2021. *The Origin and Goal of History*. Routledge.

46 Karen Armstrong. 2007. *The Great Transformation*. Anchor.
47 Peter Brown. 2013. *Through the Eye of a Needle: Wealth, the Fall of Rome, and the Making of Christianity in the West, 350-550 AD*. Princeton University Press.
48 Jonathan I. Israel. 2002. *Radical Enlightenment: Philosophy and the Making of Modernity 1650-1750*. OUP.
49 Durkheim, *Elementary Forms of Religious Life*.
50 Irvin D. Yalom. 1980. *Existential Psychotherapy*. Basic Books.
51 Norenzayan and Shariff, 'The Origin and Evolution of Religious Prosociality'.
52 Adam Cohen. 2009. 'Many Forms of Culture'. *American Psychologist*, 64(3): 194–204. Available at: https://www.researchgate.net/publication/24259597_Many_Forms_of_Culture
53 Richard Sosis and Candace Alcorta. 2003. 'Signaling, solidarity, and the sacred: The evolution of religious behavior'. *Evolutionary Anthropology*. Available at: https://onlinelibrary.wiley.com/doi/10.1002/evan.10120
54 Harold Koenig. 2012. 'Religion, Spirituality, and Health: The Research and Clinical Implications'. Available at: https://www.researchgate.net/publication/237200852_Religion_Spirituality_and_Health_The_Research_and_Clinical_Implications
55 Ed Diener, Louis Tay and David G. Myers. 2011. *'The religion paradox: If religion makes people happy, why are so many dropping out?'* Available at: https://psycnet.apa.org/record/2011-16524-001
56 Norenzayan and Shariff, 'The Origin and Evolution of Religious Prosociality'.
57 Cohen, 'Many Forms of Culture'.
58 Stephen T. Asma. 2018. *Why We Need Religion*. HighBridge Audio.
59 Ibid.
60 Ibid.

61 Ibid.

62 Available at: https://www.goodreads.com/author/quotes/ 1194.Richard_Dawkins

63 Ibid.

64 Ibid.

65 Available at: https://www.goodreads.com/author/quotes/ 3956.Christopher_Hitchens

66 Ibid.

67 Ibid.

68 Ibid.

69 Available at: https://www.bible.com/bible/114/LEV.18.22. NKJV

70 Available at: https://legacy.quran.com/7/81

71 Scott Siraj al-Haqq Kugle. 2010. *Homosexuality in Islam: Critical Reflection on Gay, Lesbian, and Transgender Muslims.* Oneworld Publications.

72 Caitlin Ryan, David Huebner, Rafael M. Diaz and J. Jorge Sanchez. 2007. 'Family Rejection as a Predictor of Negative Health Outcomes in White and Latino Lesbian, Gay, and Bisexual Young Adults'. *Pediatrics*, 123(1): 346–52.

73 Available at: https://ilga.org/state-sponsored-homophobia-report

74 Available at: https://database.ilga.org/criminalisation-consensual-same-sex-sexual-acts

75 Matthew Vines. 2014. *God and the Gay Christian: The Biblical Case in Support of Same-Sex Relationships.* Convergent Books.

76 Thomas Asbridge. 2012. *The First Crusade: A New History.* UK: Simon & Schuster.

77 Edward Peters. 1998. *The First Crusade: 'The Chronicle of Fulcher of Chartres' and Other Source Materials.* University of Pennsylvania Press.

78 Haim Beinart. 2002. 'The Expulsion of the Jews from Spain'. Translated by Jeffrey M. Green. Liverpool

University Press, Littman Library of Jewish Civilization. Available at: https://www.jstor.org/stable/j.ctv4rfr25.

79 Geoffrey Parker. 1997. *The Thirty Years' War*. Routledge.

80 Jr. Thackston, W.M. 2002. *The Baburnama: Memoirs of Babur, Prince and Emperor*. Modern Library Inc.

81 Aditya Kuvalekar and Kedar Phalke. 2021. 'The Truth About Aurangzeb: Was the Mughal Emperor a Fanatic?' 11 June, *Open*. Available at: https://openthemagazine.com/essay/the-truth-about-aurangzeb/

82 Venkat Dhulipala. 2016. *Creating a New Medina*. Cambridge English.

83 David McKittrick and David McVea. 2002. *Making Sense of the Troubles: The Story of the Conflict in Northern Ireland*. New Amsterdam Books.

84 Timothy Longman. 2011. *Christianity and Genocide in Rwanda: 112*. Cambridge University Press.

85 African Rights. 1994. *Rwanda: Death, Despair and Defiance*.

86 Harold J. Berman. 1985. *Law and Revolution: The Formation of the Western Legal Tradition*. Harvard University Press.

87 Israela Silberman. 2005. 'Religion as a Meaning System: Implications for the New Millennium'. *Journal of Social Issues*, 61(4): 641–63. Available at: https://www.researchgate.net/publication/229630284_Religion_as_a_Meaning_System_Implications_for_the_New_Millennium

88 Helen Pluckrose and James Lindsay. 2021. *Cynical Theories: How Activist Scholarship Made Everything about Race, Gender, and Identity – And Why This Harms Everybody*. Swift Press.

89 Justin L. Barrett. 2004. *Why Would Anyone Believe in God? (Cognitive Science of Religion)*. US: AltaMira Press.

90 Durkheim, *Elementary Forms of Religious Life*.

91 Martha C. Nussbaum. 2016. *Not for Profit: Why Democracy Needs the Humanities*. Princeton University Press.

92 Paul Bloom. 2018. *Against Empathy: The Case for Rational Compassion*. Vintage.

93 Jonathan Rauch. 2021. *Constitution of Knowledge*. Brookings Institution.

4 How to Live a Good Life Without a God

1 Mohammed Alassiri. 'Evolution is the disguised friend of Islam'. Available at: https://www.nature.com/articles/s41562-019-0771-7.epdf?sharing_token=0YCKU6nlKz

DtYwZnSlIPG9RgN0jAjWel9jnR3ZoTv0 P3xtM6sMcIhXCQtbHpjDaB5txl6u_VGAId Y3zAobMLkUIB63h_R8hi8YFz9H3Ffc3G8p6ww wMNtmzVcPu3dRpiwzpvskcQ5QMJaiWs9z_eJ Rn8slE4cOP_4idef7BAtuw%3D

2 Available at: https://science.thewire.in/the-sciences/novel-coronavirus-vaccines-drugs-evolution-charles-darwin/

3 https://timesofindia.indiatimes.com/india/study-reveals-majority-of-indians-accept-evolution/articleshow/65610007.cms

4 Felix Bast and Heena Tahilramani. 2018. 'Public Acceptance of Evolution in India'. *Journal of Scientific Temper*, 6(1–2), Jan–Jun: 24–38.

5 Shah Alam Khan. 2023. 'Why every Indian must learn about evolution'. *The Indian Express*, 14 June. Available at: https://indianexpress.com/article/opinion/columns/charles-darwin-theory-of-evolution-ncert-textbooks-periodic-table-8661377/

6 Ibid.

7 Janell Fetterolf and Sarah Austin. 2023. 'Many people in U.S., other advanced economies say it's not necessary to believe in God to be moral'. Available at: https://www.pewresearch.org/short-reads/2023/04/20/many-people-in-u-s-other-advanced-economies-say-its-not-necessary-to-believe-in-god-to-be-moral/#:~:text=Most%20Americans%20say%20it's%20not,34%25)

8   Christine Tamir, Aidan Connaughton and Ariana Monique Salazar. 2020. 'The Global God Divide'. Available at: https://www.pewresearch.org/global/2020/07/20/the-global-god-divide/

9   Ibid.

10 Frans de Waal. 2013. *The Bonobo and the Atheist: In Search of Humanism among the Primates*. W.W. Norton & Company.

11 Richard A. Shweder. 1991. *Thinking through Cultures: Expeditions in Cultural Psychology*. Harvard University Press.

12 Christopher Boehm. 2012. *Moral Origins: The Evolution of Virtue, Altruism, and Shame*. Basic Books.

13 Jonathan Haidt. 2001. 'The Emotional Dog and Its Rational Tail: A Social Intuitionist Approach to Moral Judgment'. *Psychological Review*, 108 (4): 814–34.

14 Steven Pinker. 2003. *The Blank Slate: The Modern Denial of Human Nature*. Penguin.

15 Michael Tomasello and Amrisha Vaish. 2013. 'Origins of Human Cooperation and Morality'. *Annual Review of Psychology*, 64: 231–55.

16 Boehm, *Moral Origins*.

17 Joshua Greene. 2014. *Moral Tribes: Emotion, Reason and the Gap between Us and Them*. Atlantic Books.

18 Michael Koenigs, Liane Young, Ralph Adolphs, Daniel Tranel, Fiery Cushman, Marc Hauser, and Antonio Damasio. 2007. 'Damage to the prefrontal cortex increases utilitarian moral judgements'. *Nature*, 446 (7138): 908–11. Available at: https://www.ncbi.nlm.nih.gov/pmc/articles/PMC2244801/

19 Frans B.M. de Waal. 2008. 'Putting the Altruism Back into Altruism: The Evolution of Empathy'. *Annu. Rev. Psychol.*, 59: 279–300. Available at: https://science.umd.edu/faculty/wilkinson/BIOL608W/deWaalAnnRevPsych2008.pdf

20 Tania Singer, Ben Seymour, John O'Doherty, Holger Kaube, Raymond J. Dolan and Chris D. Frith. 2004. 'Empathy for

Pain Involves the Affective but Not Sensory Components of Pain'. *New Series*, 303 (5661) (Feb. 20: 1157–62).

21 Ernst Fehr and Urs Fischbacher. 2004. 'Social norms and human cooperation'. *Trends in Cognitive Sciences*, 8 (4), April 2004: 185–90. Available at: https://www.sciencedirect.com/science/article/abs/pii/S1364661304000506

22 Colin Wringe. 2007. *Moral Education: Beyond the Teaching of Right and Wrong*. Springer-Verlag New York Inc.

23 Jonathan Haidt, 'The Emotional Dog and Its Rational Tail: A Social Intuitionist Approach to Moral Judgment. Available at: https://www.researchgate.net/publication/11655620_The_Emotional_Dog_and_Its_Rational_Tail_A_Social_Intuitionist_Approach_to_Moral_Judgment

24 Available at: https://www.joshua-greene.net/articles/book-chapters/the-secret-joke-of-kants-soul-pdf

25 B.J. Casey, Sarah Getz and Adriana Galvan. 2008. 'The adolescent brain'. *PubMed*, 28(1): 62–77. Available at: https://pubmed.ncbi.nlm.nih.gov/18688292/

26 T.E. Moffitt, L. Arseneault, D. Belsky, N. Dickson, R.J. Hancox, H. Harrington, R. Houts, R. Poulton, B.W. Roberts, S. Ross, M.R. Sears, W.M. Thomson, and A. Caspi. 2011. 'A gradient of childhood self-control predicts health, wealth, and public safety'. *PNAS Proceedings of the National Academy of Sciences of the United States of America*, 108(7): 2693–98. Available at: https://psycnet.apa.org/record/2011-06020-003

27 Roy E. Baumeister, Ellen Bratslavsky, Mark Muraven and Dianne M. Tice. 'Ego Depletion: Is the Active Self a Limited Resource?' Available at: https://faculty.washington.edu/jdb/345/345%20Articles/Baumeister%20et%20al.%20%281998%29.pdf

28 John M. Cooper and D.S. Hutchinson, eds. 1997. *Plato: Complete Works*. Hackett Publishing Company, Inc.

29 Julie Sickels, Alisa Huskey, Kathryn Scott, and Caleb W Lack. 2015. 'The relationship between intelligence and religiosity: A critical review of the literature'. *Journal of Scientific Psychology*. Available at: https://www.researchgate.net/publication/283062772_The_relationship_between_intelligence_and_religiosity_A_critical_review_of_the_literature

30 Donald E. Brown. 1991. *Human Universals*. Temple Univ Press.

31 'Relativism'. In *Stanford Encyclopedia of Philosophy*. Available at: https://plato.stanford.edu/entries/relativism/

32 Mitchell Silver. 2011. 'Our Morality: A Defense of Moral Objectivism'. *Philosophy Now*. Available at: https://philosophynow.org/issues/83/Our_Morality_A_Defense_of_Moral_Objectivism

33 Jonathan Haidt and Craig Joseph. 2011. 'Intuitive Ethics: How Innately Prepared Intuitions Generate Culturally Variable Virtues'. *Daedalus*, 133 (4): 55–66.

34 Jonathan Haidt. 2012. *The Righteous Mind: Why Good People Are Divided by Politics and Religion*. Penguin.

35 Jesse Graham, Jonathan Haidt and Brian A. Nosek. 2009. 'Liberals and Conservatives Rely on Different Sets of Moral Foundations'. *Journal of Personality and Social Psychology*, 96 (5): 1029–46.

36 Christopher L. Suhler and Patricia Churchland. 2011. 'Can Innate, Modular "Foundations" Explain Morality?: Challenges for Haidt's Moral Foundations Theory'. *Journal of Cognitive Neuroscience*, 23 (9): 2103–16.

37 Joseph Henrich, Steven J. Heine and Ara Norenzayan. 2010. 'The weirdest people in the world?' Available at: https://www2.psych.ubc.ca/~henrich/pdfs/WeirdPeople.pdf

38 Walter Sinnott-Armstrong. 2012. 'Does Morality Have an Essence?' Psychological Inquiry, 23 (2) (April–June): 194–97.

39 Daniel Kelly, Stephen Stich, Kevin J. Haley, Serena J. Eng and Daniel M.T. Fessler. 2007. 'Harm, Affect, and the Moral/Conventional Distinction'. Mind & Language, 22 (2) April: 117–31.

40 G. Kahane, J.A.C. Everett, B.D. Earp, L. Caviola, N.S. Faber, M.J. Crockett and J. Savulescu. 2018. 'Beyond sacrificial harm: A two-dimensional model of utilitarian psychology'. Psychol Rev., 125 (2) March: 131–64.

41 Sam Harris. 2011. The Moral Landscape. Transworld Digital.

42 Sam Harris, 2011. The Moral Landscape. Transworld Digital.

43 David Hume. A Treatise of Human Nature.

44 Russell Blackford. 2010. 'Book review: Sam Harris' The Moral Landscape'. Journal of Evolution and Technology, 21 (2) December: 53–62.

45 Available at: https://vedabase.io/en/library/bg/1/46/

46 Ibid.

47 Ibid.

48 Ibid.

49 John M. Koller. 2000. 'Syādvāda as the Epistemological Key to the Jaina Middle Way Metaphysics of Anekāntavāda'. Philosophy East and West, 50 (3) Jul., : 400–07.

50 Peter Beaumont. 2021. 'Afghan Women to Be Banned from Playing Sport, Taliban Say'. The Guardian, 8 September. Available at: https://www.theguardian.com/world/2021/sep/08/afghan-women-to-be-banned-from-playing-sport-taliban-say

51 Ibid.

52 Ashutosh Tripathi. 2021. 'Afghan Women Forced to Gather at Pro-Taliban Protest at University'. NDTV World,

14 September. Available at: https://www.ndtv.com/world-news/afghan-women-forced-to-gather-at-pro-taliban-protest-at-university-2539985

53 Ibid.

54 Ibid.

55 Robin Dunford. 'Toward a Decolonial Global Ethics'. *Journal of Global Ethics*. Available at: https://acrobat.adobe.com/link/review?uri=urn%3Aaaid%3Ascds%3AUS%3A901a6f85-9b3c-42f4-9cb1-64eb081db8e5#pageNum=1

56 Ibid.

57 Ibid.

58 Ibid.

59 Ibid.

60 Ibid.

61 Ibid.

62 Ibid.

63 Ibid.

64 Ibid.

65 RFE/RL's Radio Azadi. 2017. 'Afghanistan Marks 98 Years of Independence from Britain'. Available at: https://www.rferl.org/a/afghanistan-marks-98-years-independence/28685763.html

66 Robin Dunford. 'Toward a Decolonial Global Ethics'.

67 Ibid.

68 J. Sai Deepak. *India That Is Bharat*.

69 Available at: https://indiankanoon.org/doc/1803184/

70 J. Sai Deepak. 2021. *India That Is Bharat*. Bloomsbury India.

71 Ibid.

72 Ignacy Jan Paderewski. 2024. 'Intellectual isolation always follows commercial isolation'. Available at: https://www.azquotes.com/citation/quote/1262982

73 https://humanrights.brightblue.org.uk/blog-1/2017/8/18/bacha-bazi-afghanistans-darkest-secret

74 'Bachha bazi: Afghanistan's dark secret of keeping child sex slaves'. *Hindustan Times*, 19 Dec. 2016. Available at: https://www.hindustantimes.com/world-news/bacha-bazi-afghanistan-s-dark-secret-of-keeping-child-sex-slaves/story-h3wMXFVBaZGl3fOB79CJcI.html

75 Available at: https://www.refworld.org/reference/countryrep/aihrc/2014/en/108586

76 Ibid.

77 https://www.nytimes.com/2015/09/21/world/asia/us-soldiers-told-to-ignore-afghan-allies-abuse-of-boys.html

78 'Relativism'. *Stanford Encyclopedia of Philosophy*. Available at: https://plato.stanford.edu/entries/relativism/

79 Silver, 'Our Morality'.

80 Ibid.

81 Ibid.

82 Jonathan Haidt. 2012. *The Righteous Mind: Why Good People Are Divided by Politics and Religion*. Penguin.

83 Ibid.

84 Available at: https://www.goodreads.com/quotes/129606-never-let-your-sense-of-morals-prevent-you-from-doing

5 The Complexity of Indian Society

1 Diana L.Eck. 2012. *India: A Sacred Geography*. Harmony.

2 Wendy Doniger. 2013. *On Hinduism*. Aleph Book Company.

3 'The Changing Global Religious Landscape', 5 April 2017. Available at: https://www.pewresearch.org/religion/2017/04/05/the-changing-global-religious-landscape/

4 Pavan K. Verma. 2005. *Being Indian*. Penguin India.

5 Amartya Sen. 2006. *The Argumentative Indian: Writings on Indian History, Culture and Identity*. Penguin.

6 Sita Ram Goel. 2013. *Hindu Temples: What Happened to Them, Vol.1: A Preliminary Survey*. Voice of India.

7 Susan L. Huntington. 2016. *The Art Of Ancient India*. Motilal Banarsidass.

8   Aditi Narayani Paswan. 2023. 'How the G20 presidency brought India and Bharat together'. 12 September, *The Indian Express*. Available at: https://indianexpress. com/article/opinion/columns/how-the-g20-presidency-brought-india-and-bharat-together-8932198/

9   Eck, *India*.

10 Jared M. Diamond. 2013. *Guns, Germs and Steel*. Vintage Digital.

11 James Woodburn. 1982. 'Egalitarian Societies'. *Man*, New Series, 17, (3) (Sep.,): 431–51.

12 Marvin Harris and Orna Johnson. 1999. *Cultural Anthropology*. Pearson.

13 Cultural Anthropology. 1967. *The Evolution of Political Society: An Essay in Political Anthropology*. McGraw-Hill Education

14 Plato. Republic, Book 4. Available at: https://www.perseus. tufts.edu/hopper/text?doc=Perseus%3Atext% 3A1999.01.0168%3Abook%3D4%3Asection%3D419a

15 Ibid.

16 Available at: https://vedabase.io/en/library/bg/4/13/

17 David Grusky. 2019. *Social Stratification, Class, Race, and Gender in Sociological Perspective*. Routledge.

18 Dennis Gilbert. 1998. *The American Class Structure in an Age of Growing Inequality*. Wadsworth Publishing Co.

19 Marc Bloch. 2014. *Feudal Society*. Routledge.

20 Stephanie W. Jamison and Joel P. Brereton. 2014. *The Rigveda*. OUP.

21 D. Dennis Hudson. 2008. *The Body of God: An Emperor's Palace for Krishna in Eighth-Century Kanchipuram*. OUP.

22 Patrick Olivelle. *Manu's Code of Law: A Critical Edition and Translation of the Manava-Dharmasastra*.

23 Ibid.

24 Ibid.

25 Available at: https://www.wisdomlib.org/hinduism/book/
    gautama-dharmas%C5%ABtra/d/doc116304.html

26 Priya Moorjani, Kumarasamy Thangaraj, Nick Patterson,
    Mark Lipson, Po-Ru Loh, Periyasamy Govindaraj, Bonnie
    Berger, David Reich, and Lalji Singh. 2013. 'Genetic
    Evidence for Recent Population Mixture in India'. *Am J
    Hum Genet*, 93 (3): 422–38.

27 Available at: https://bmcgenomdata.biomedcentral.com/
    articles/10.1186/1471-2156-7-42

28 Y. Krishan. 1998. 'Buddhism and Caste System'. *East and
    West*, 48 (1/2) (June): 41–55.

29 Ibid.

30 Ibid.

31 Ibid.

32 Ibid.

33 Mukta Salve. 2015. 'Mang Maharachya Dukhvisayi
    (About the grief of the Mangs and the Mahars)'. *Savari*.
    Available at: https://www.dalitweb.org/?p=2947

34 Hemali Sanghavi. 2013. 'Jains and Caste System: Conceptual
    and Comparative Perspective'. *Global Research Analysis*, 2 (2).

35 Ibid.

36 Marcus J. Banks. 1986. 'Defining Division: An Historical
    Overview of Jain Social Organization'. *Modern Asian
    Studies*, 20 (3): 447–60.

37 Ibid.

38 Nandini Rathi. 2017. 'Why deras and sects find Punjab
    fertile for growth'. *The Indian Express*, 30 August. Available at:
    https://indianexpress.com/article/research/why-deras-and-
    sects-find-punjab-fertile-for-growth-gurmeet-ram-rahim-
    singh-rape-case-conviction-dera-sacha-sauda-4815609/

39 Express News Service, 'Rising casteism in Sikh society
    matter of concern', 24 November 2009. Available at:
    https://indianexpress.com/article/cities/chandigarh/rising-
    casteism-in-sikh-society-matter-of-concern/

40 Explained: Who are the Pasmanda Muslims, the group that BJP that the BJP is trying to woo?' *The Times of India*, 9 July 2022. Available at: https://timesofindia.indiatimes. com/india/explained-who-are-the-pasmanda-muslims-the-group-that-bjp-is-trying-to-woo/articleshow/92766145. cms

41 Vishu Gopinath. 2022. 'Who Are Pasmanda Muslims, Why Is BJP Wooing Them, and Will It Work?' *The Quint*, 19 October. Available at: https://www.thequint. com/explainers/explained-pasmanda-muslims-bjp-vote-meeting-atrocities-lynchings-why-what-who

42 Faiyaz Ahmad Fyzie. 2022. 'Ashraafs say Islam is casteless. Then what explains their views on kufu, khutbah, firqas?' *The Print*, 12 September. Available at: https://theprint. in/opinion/ashraafs-say-islam-is-casteless-then-what-explains-their-views-on-kufu-khutbah-firqas/1123584/

43 Ibid.

44 Ibid.

45 Ibid.

46 Faiyaz Ahmad Fyzie. 2022. 'Caste plays a role in selection of Caliph in Islam—"Only a Quraysh has the right"'. *The Print*, 30 August. Available at: https://theprint.in/opinion/caste-plays-a-role-in-selection-of-caliph-in-islam-only-a-quraysh-has-the-right/1106773/

47 S.M. Michael. 1999. *Untouchable: Dalits in Modern India*. Lynne Rienner Publishers Inc.

48 Swaminathan Natarajan. 2010. 'Indian Dalits find no refuge from caste in Christianity'. *BBC*, 14 September. Available at: https://www.bbc.com/news/world-south-asia-11229170

49 Sukhadeo Thorat and Katherine S. Newman. 2007. 'Caste and Economic Discrimination: Causes, Consequences and Remedies'. *Economic and Political Weekly*, 42 (41) (Oct. 13–19): 4121–24.

50 Available at: https://minorityrights.org/communities/dalits/

51 Availableat:https://www.thehindu.com/news/national/crime-against-scheduled-castes-scheduled-tribes-saw-a-rise-of-7-and-26-in-2019-ncrb/article32730990.ece#:~:text=A%20total%20of%2045%2C935%20cases,in%20Bihar%2C%20the%20report%20said. Site not allowing to cite.

52 Deeptiman Tiwary. 2020. 'NCRB data: Higher share of Dalits, tribals, Muslims in prison than numbers outside'. *The Indian Express*, 31 August. Available at: https://indianexpress.com/article/india/ncrb-data-higher-share-of-dalits-tribals-muslims-in-prison-than-numbers-outside-6575446/

53 Aatika Singh and Shubhkaramdeep Singh. 2020. 'Looking at mental health through Caste'. Available at: https://thelifeofscience.com/2020/12/17/psychiatry-caste/

54 Gail Omvedt. 1994. *Dalits and the Democratic Revolution: Dr Ambedkar and the Dalit Movement in Colonial India*. Sage India.

55 Mira Patel. 2023. 'The dark story of oil, the lubricant of the global economy'. *The Indian Express*, 4 September. Available at: https://indianexpress.com/article/research/the-dark-story-of-oil-the-lubricant-of-the-global-economy-8919029/

56 David N. Lorenzen. 1996. *Praises to a Formless God: Nirguṇī Texts from North India*. State University of New York Press.

57 Lala Lajpat Rai. 1991. *The Arya Samaj: An Account of Its Origin, Doctrines, and Activities*. Edited by S.K. Bhatia. Stosius Inc/Advent Books Division.

58 Eleanor Zelliot. 2012. *Ambedkar's World: The Making of Babasaheb and the Dalit Movement*. Navayana.

59 Dr B.R. Ambedkar. 2023. *Annihilation of Caste by Dr. B.R. Ambedkar: A Bold Critique of Social Hierarchies*. Namaskar Book.

60 Available at: https://savarkar.org/en/encyc/2017/5/22/Seven-shackles.html

61 Gail Omvedt. 2009. *Seeking Begumpura*. Navayana.

62 Available at: https://legislative.gov.in/constitution-of-india/
63 Available at: https://socialjustice.gov.in/writereaddata/
    UploadFile/The%20Scheduled%20Castes%20and%20
    Scheduled%20Tribes.pdf
64 Ashwini Deshpande. 2011. *The Grammar of Caste: Economic
    Discrimination in Contemporary India*. India: OUP.
65 A Twitter thread on Kapratri Maharaj that has all the
    primary sources of his ridiculous utterances. Available at:
    https://x.com/balajidbv/status/1421790535581278208?s=20
66 Available   at: https://www.youtube.com/watch?v=-
    K2yKPUIsqM
67 Klaus K. Klostermaier. 1994. *A Survey of Hinduism*. State
    University of New York Press.
68 A.H. Bittles and M.L. Black. 2010. 'Evolution in health
    and medicine Sackler colloquium: Consanguinity, human
    evolution, and complex diseases'. Proc. Natl. Acad. Sci. U
    S A., 107 Suppl 1(Jan 26;): 1779–86.
69 Available   at: https://threadreaderapp.com/thread/
    1421790535581278208.html
70 Jean Drèze and Amartya Sen. 2013. *An Uncertain Glory:
    India and Its Contradictions*. Penguin.
71 Swāmī Mādhavānanda. Trans. Swami Madhavananda. 2021.
    Brihadaranyaka Upanishad. Advaita Ashrama. Available at:
    https://www.wisdomlib.org/hinduism/
    book/the-brihadaranyaka-upanishad/d/
    doc118359.html#:~:text=Verse%20
    3.8.,-11%3A&text=%E0%A5%A7%E0%A5%A7%20
    %E0%A5%A5&text=11.,no%20other%20knower%20
    but%20This.
72 Ibid.
73 Ibid.
74 Ibid.
75 Olivelle, *Manu's Code of Law*.
76 Kautilya. 2000. *The Arthashastra*. Penguin Classics.

77 Archana Paudel and Qun Dong. 2017. 'The Discrimination of Women in Buddhism: An Ethical Analysis'. Open Access Library Journal, 4 (4). Available at: https://www.scirp.org/journal/paperinformation?paperid=75673.

78 Available at: https://zenstudiespodcast.com/buddhas-sexist-discourse-part-1/

79 Available at: https://zenstudiespodcast.com/gotami-sutta/

80 Devdutt Pattanaik. 2016. 'There's a misogynist aspect of Buddhism that nobody talks about'. Quartz, 6 January.

81 Manisha Sethi. 2009. 'Chastity and desire: representing women in Jainism'. South Asian History and Culture, 1 (1): 42–59.

82 Available at: https://www.jainfoundation.in/JAINLIBRARY/books/women_in_jainism_269551_hr6.pdf

83 Sri Guru Granth Sahib, Ang 473. Available at: https://www.searchgurbani.com/guru-granth-sahib/ang/473

84 Sri Guru Granth Sahib, Ang 787. Available at: https://www.searchgurbani.com/guru-granth-sahib/ang/787

85 Vishav Bharti, 'Centuries of killing girl child', 14 October 2018, The Tribune. Available at: https://www.tribuneindia.com/news/archive/features/centuries-of-killing-girl-child-667841

86 Harneet Kaur. 2011. 'Kurimaar: Custom and State in Contemporary Punjab'. Proceedings of the Indian History Congress, 72, Part 2: 1393–99.

87 Ravinder Vasudeva. 2021. 'Punjab's sex ratio at birth improves, but still below national average'. Hindustan Times, 25 November.

88 Ibid.

89 Nikky-Guninder Kaur Singh. 2004. 'Sacred Fabric and Sacred Stitches: The Underwear of the Khalsa'. History of Religions, 43 (4) (May): 284–302.

90 Sumati Thusoo and Shivangi Deshwal, 'Exploring the Formation of Jat Masculinity in Contemporary Punjabi Music', 17 April 2022, EPW Engage. Available at: https://www.epw.in/engage/article/exploring-formation-jat-masculinity-contemporary

91 Rajesh Gill, 'Masculinity continues to be the norm in Punjab', 20 February 2016, *The Tribune*. Available at: https://www.tribuneindia.com/news/archive/comment/masculinity-continues-to-be-the-norm-in-punjab-198550

92 Esha Roy. 2023. 'Nothing to be afraid of, says Lalpura on Law Commission's UCC call'. *The Indian Express*, 16 June.

93 Available at: https://www.census2011.co.in/religion.php

94 Available at: https://quran.com/4?startingVerse=3

95 Geeta Pandey. 2022. 'Polygamy: Muslim women in India fight 'abhorrent' practice'. *BBC*, 10 May. Available at: https://www.bbc.com/news/world-asia-india-61351784

96 Apurva Vishwanath. 2023. 'The law on polygamy among religious groups in India'. *The Indian Express*, 12 May.

97 Available at: https://supwr.org/struggles/bharatiya-muslim-mahila-andolan/

98 'BMMA survey contradicts census data on Muslim divorces'. *The Times of India*, 7 November 2016. Available at: http://timesofindia.indiatimes.com/articleshow/55280449.cms?utm_source=contentofinterest&utm_medium=text&utm_campaign=cppst

99 Available at: https://bmmaindia.wordpress.com/2015/08/11/summary-of-the-findings-seeking-justice-within-family/

100 Available at: https://www.bible.com/bible/111/EPH.5.22-24.NIV

101 Available at: https://www.biblegateway.com/passage/?search=1%20Timothy%202%3A11-12&version=NIV

102 Ibid.

103 Vibhuti Patel. 2017. 'All personal laws in India are discriminatory'. *Mint*, 22 August.

104 Haima Deshpande, 'A Cross to Bear', 5 February 2024, *Outlook*. Available at: https://www.outlookindia.com/national/a-cross-to-bear

105 Available at: https://www.mea.gov.in/Images/pdf1/Part4.pdf

106 Flavia Agnes. 1994. 'Women's Movement within a Secular Framework: Redefining the Agenda'. *Economic and Political Weekly*, 29 (19) (7 May): 1123–28.

107 Amana Begam. 2023. 'Indian govt has left Muslim women at the mercy of AIMPLB. Bring in UCC but consult us first'. *The Print*, 16 June.

108 Haima Deshpande, 'A Cross to Bear'.

109 '"UCC will be presented as biggest project of minority victimhood, Hindus will be pushed towards a compromise": Adv J Sai Deepak on Hijab row'. *OpIndia*, 13 February 2022.

110 G.R. Rajagopaul. 1975. 'The Story of the Hindu Code'. *Journal of the Indian Law Institute*, 17 (4) (October–December 1975): 537–58.

111 Shyamlal Yadav. 2023. ' Uniform Civil Code: How the BJP, RSS position has changed since Independence'. *The Indian Express*, 21 July.

112 Ibid.

113 Divyanshu Dutta Roy. 2019. 'Will Scrap "Triple Talaq" Law If We Come to Power, Says Congress Leader'. *NDTV*, 7 February.

114 Saubhadra Chatterji. 2023. 'Congress UCC meet: Party rejects uniformity in all laws'. *Hindustan Times*, 16 July.

115 Ibid.

116 Virendra Kumar. 2003. 'Uniform Civil Code Revisited: A Juridical Analysis of "John Vallamattom"'. *Journal of the*

Indian Law Institute, 45 (3/4), Family Law Special Issue (July-December): 315–34.

117 Esther Duflo. 2012. 'Women Empowerment and Economic Development'. Journal of Economic Literature, 50 (4) (December): 1051–79.

6 Why I Am a Hindu

1   Richard Dawkins. 2009. *The God Delusion*. Transworld Digital.
2   Wendy Doniger. 2015. *The Hindus: An Alternative History*. Speaking Tiger Books.
3   A.L. Basham. 2016. *The Origins & Development of Classical Hinduism*. Motilal Banarsidass.
4   Aravindan Neelakandan. 2022. *Hindutva: Origin Evolution and Future*. Kali.
5   Romila Thapar. 2015. *The Penguin History of Early India: From the Origins to AD 1300*. Penguin.
6   Available at: https://www.vichaarmanthan.org/profile/4f335514-99f7-4349-b6d5-d3e18a1305a1/profile
7   Brian K. Pennington. 2005. *Was Hinduism Invented?: Britons, Indians, and the Colonial Construction of Religion*. OUP.
8   J.E. Llewellyn. 2005. *Defining Hinduism: A Reader*. Equinox Publishing Ltd.
9   Martin E. Marty. 1994. *Fundamentalisms Observed: Volume 1*. University of Chicago Press.
10 Rajiv Malhotra. 2014. *Indra's Net*. HarperCollins.
11 Ibid.
12 Ibid.
13 Ibid.
14 Ibid.
15 Ibid.
16 Ibid.
17 Debiprasad Chattopadhyaya. *Lokayata: A Study in Ancient Indian Materialism*. People's Publishing House.
18 Wilhelm Halbfass. 1992. *Tradition and Reflection: Explorations in Indian Thought*. Sri Satguru Publications.

19   Available at: https://www.wisdomlib.org/hinduism/book/
     brahma-sutras/d/doc63666.html
20   Available at: https://sites.rutgers.edu/edwin-bryant/wp-
     content/uploads/sites/169/2020/06/2006HOY-Nyaya-
     Sutras-4.2.46-49.pdf
21   E.B. Cowell. 2017. *The Sarvadarshanasamgraha of
     Madhavacharya*. D.K. Printworld Pvt. Ltd.
22   Ramkrishna Bhattacharya. 2011. *Studies on the Carvaka/
     Lokayata: 2*. Wimbledon Publishing Company.
23   Debirasad Chattopadhyaya, ed. 2006. *Carvakalokayata:
     An Anthology of Source Materials and Some Recent Studies*.
     Munshiram Manoharlal Publishers.
24   Flood. 2004. *An Introduction to Hinduism*. Cambridge
     University Press.
25   Kushal Mehra. 2022. 'Imagine There's No Svarga:
     Rediscovering Cārvāka, India's 2,700-Year-Old Atheistic
     Tradition'. *Quillette*, 1 May. Available at: https://quillette.
     com/2022/05/01/rediscovering-the-indian-atheistic-tradition/
26   Gilbert Ryle. 2020. *The Concept of Mind*. Barakaldo Books.
27   Available at: https://plato.stanford.edu/entries/category-
     mistakes/#:~:text=A%20typical%20dictionary%20
     definition%20looks,location%E2%80%9D%20
     (Stevenson%202010).
28   Ibid.
29   Available at: https://www.scobserver.in/reports/day-5-
     arguments-2/
30   Ibid.
31   Available at: https://privacylibrary.ccgnlud.org/case/
     indian-young-lawyers-association-and-ors-vs-the-
     state-of-kerala-and-ors#:~:text=The%20Supreme%20
     Court%2C%20in%20a,women%20pilgrims%20
     entering%20the%20shrine.
32   Available at: https://www.scobserver.in/cases/challenge-
     to-the-practice-of-jallikattu/

33 Aijaz Ahmad. 1992. *In Theory: Classes, Nations, Literatures*. Verso.

34 Available at: http://www.languageinindia.com/may2003/annika.html

35 Rajiv Malhotra. *Being Different: An Indian Challenge to Western Universalism*.

36 Timothy Fitzgerald. 2004. *The Ideology of Religious Studies*. USA: OUP.

37 Max Weber. 2002. *The Protestant Ethic and the 'Spirit' of Capitalism: and Other Writings*. Edited and translated by Peter Baehr and Gordon C. Wells. Penguin Classics.

38 Edward Said. 2014. *Orientalism*. Vintage.

39 Linda Tuhiwai Smith. 2012. *Decolonizing Methodologies: Research and Indigenous Peoples*. Zed Books.

40 Available at: https://www.messengersaintanthony.com/content/lourdes-east

41 Richard M. Eaton. 2023. *The Rise of Islam and the Bengal Frontier, 1204-1760*. University of California Press.

42 'Shah Rukh Khan: 'I am a Muslim, my wife is a Hindu and my kids are Hindustan'. 24 September 2020, *Hindustan Times*.

43 'Ganesh Chaturthi 2022: Here's how actor Salman Khan celebrated the festival'. 1 September 2022. *The Economic Times*.

44 'Kareena Kapoor and Saif Ali Khan celebrate Diwali with Soha Ali Khan-Kunal Kemmu'. 24 October 2022, *The Indian Express*.

45 Shalvi Mangaokar. 2015. 'Here's how Aamir Khan celebrated Diwali'. 22 November, *Hindustan Times*.

46 Available at: https://nawaz.wordpress.com/2010/06/09/na-raindee-hai-a-kalaam-by-baba-bulleh-shah/

About the Author

Kushal Mehra is a former textile-entrepreneur-turned-podcaster based in Mumbai. He is a dharmic sceptic and believes that scepticism is elevating. His principal interest lies in articulating Indian scepticism using Indian epistemological frameworks. Kushal is the host of the hugely popular Cārvāka Podcast, where he discusses sports, philosophy, public policy, current affairs, history, economics, etc., with his guests. Kushal holds a master's degree in philosophy and draws heavily from it for his podcast, where he engages an eclectic list of guests on a wide range of topics. Today, when society is deeply polarised and discussions cantankerous, Kushal brings a breath of fresh air by conducting debates in a civilised manner. Through his podcast and writing, Kushal attempts to answer some of contemporary's most vexing topics.